Addendum

When serving as a detective at Biloela in the early 70's, I had a wonderful rapport with the Indigenous people of the Dawson River at Theodore. One day a local man named 'Teddy' said to me: "You know Mr Pointin, all my mob here on the Dawson, we all like you."
"Why is that, Teddy?" I asked.
"You always stop and say good-day," he said.

Teddy's words meant a lot to me, and have stayed with me ever since. They are more important than many more formal awards. This book sets out to acknowledge and give long overdue recognition to the vital role played by so many First Australians in policing and community safety. Perhaps we all need to say "good-day" just a bit more often.

KEEPING THE PEACE

VOLUME IV

YOU CAN RUN BUT YOU CAN'T HIDE

LAURIE POINTING A.M.

Published by:
Boolarong Press
38/1631 Wynnum Road
Tingalpa Qld 4173
Australia.
www.boolarongpress.com.au

First published 2021

A catalogue record for this book is available from the National Library of Australia

ISBN: 9781922643070 (paperback)

Front cover image: 1929 photograph of staff at Cloncurry depicting Acting Sergeant William James Hosier on extreme left and Constable Leslie Victor Hosier on far right

Back cover image: Tracker Sam Johnson and Grave of Tracker Sam Johnson (Dedication service — 29 September, 2015).

Cover design by Boolarong Press

Printed and bound by Watson Ferguson & Company, Tingalpa, Australia

Supported by

Contents

Dedication **ix**

Acknowledgements **xi**

Author's Note **xiii**

Foreword **xv**

Prologue **1**

Tracker Barry Port **5**

Vincent Augustine Walker **27**

Kenneth James Salmon **55**

Danny Murdoch **107**

Glenn Andrew Teske **145**

About The Author **221**

This book is dedicated to the late
Senior Technical Officer
(Fingerprint Officer)
Patrick Cornelius O'Brien
1928–2019

It was Patrick O'Brien's photographic memory that helped him become one of Australia's leading fingerprint experts. As Officer-in-Charge of the Brisbane Fingerprint Bureau, he frequently identified criminals from their fingerprints before he checked the records.

Pat was the first fingerprint expert in Queensland to give footprint evidence in a murder trial and was credited with being the first to use the super-glue technique in Australia. Pat joined the Queensland Police Force Depot at Petrie Terrace as a cadet in the year 1945 where he met fellow cadet Tom Pointing. They became firm friends which continued until Tom's untimely death in March, 1999.

In the year 1948, the Queensland Railway Department employees were on strike and the Queensland government instructed the Commissioner of Police to induct a number of police constables to help maintain law and order. Both Pat and Tom were sworn in.

Pat was transferred to the Commissioner's Office (Fingerprint Bureau) where he remained until he retired in the year 1983. He retired with the rank of senior technical officer and officer-in-charge of the Fingerprint Bureau. During his career Pat never wore a police uniform.

Pat was acknowledged as an expert on scenes of crime examination, subsequent identification and court presentation. He was a member of the International Association of Identification in the US, and regional vice-president for Queensland of that association. He held a certificate from the Australian National University, Canberra in relation to advanced chemical techniques in the development of latent fingerprints at crime scenes. During his career, Pat was awarded three favourable records and three commendations for outstanding police work.

A dedicated supporter of rugby union and league, he played for the police Rugby Union Football Club and A-grade for Eastern Suburbs.

A dedicated husband and father, Pat was a gentle man and was never heard to swear or use improper language. Following his retirement, he joined the Gold Coast Branch of the Queensland Retired Police Association and never missed a meeting for 33 years until ill health prevented him from participating. In his honour, the branch has dedicated the "Pat O'Brien table" to his memory.

Pat's grandfather. John Patrick O'Brien served as a member of the Queensland Police Force from 29 May, 1890 to the 27 April, 1924 and was allotted Registered Number 754. He served at Muttaburra during the Shearer's strike of 1891 and also at Winton during the Shearers strike of 1894. During his career, he was awarded three favourable records for good police work.

His father, Horace John O'Brien served with the Queensland Police Force from 4 January, 1918 until 11 September, 1948. His Registered Number was 2310 and he was promoted to Inspector of Police in the year 1943 and retired with the rank of Inspector. Prior to the year 1935, he was awarded a Favourable Record for good police work; however, I have been unable to obtain the necessary information pertaining to the award.

Pat is survived by his daughters, Christine, Michele, son-in-law Darryl, grandsons, Scott and Adam and great-grand children Ethan, Ayshia, Luella and Ashton. Ursula, his wife of fifty-eight years predeceased him. His grandson, Scott Collingwood is a forth-generation O'Brien Queensland Police Officer.

Acknowledgements

I acknowledge the contribution from the following people: Lindsay Cox, Manager, The Salvation Army Australia Museum, Retired Northern Territory Police Officer, Norm Breen, Retired Queensland Police Officer Chris Sang, Leisa Jones and Duncan Leask Queensland Police Museum, staff from the Maryborough War and Colonial Museum, retired Medical Practitioner Carmel Walker for allowing me to reproduce the Leslie Hosier story published by her late husband retired Senior Sergeant Vince Walker in his book, *Tales from the Bullymen*, retired Assistant Commissioner Lawrie Witham for his contribution regarding the late Senior Sergeant Leslie Hosier, Danny Murdoch, Ken Salmon and Glenn Teske for their police stories and contribution.

A special thank you also to Glenn Teske for his information pertaining to his working relationship with our last two Tracker's; the late George Musgrave and Barry Port and Senior Constable Adam Flew formerly of Laura Police Division and now Port Douglas and Cliff Parlett.

I also acknowledge the generous sponsorship I received from Q Bank, The Queensland Police Union of Employees, the Queensland Police Officers Union and the Queensland Retired Police Association.

Author's Note

On the front cover of *Keeping the Peace Volume I*, there appears a photograph of Indigenous Tracker Tommy Swan who assisted police in the 1965 murder investigation on Bulla Downs Station, Thargomindah. In Volume III, there is a photograph of then Constable First Class Lawrie Witham with Tracker Teddy Morris outside the Forsayth Police Station. In the same volume, the late Sergeant Brian Norris pays tribute to Tracker Noble Burns and his son Tracker Nardoo Burns when Brian was in charge of the Georgetown Police Division. Neville Travers-Jones then Sergeant in charge at Normanton had Nardoo Burns as his Tracker and a photograph of Nardoo appears in Neville's story (Volume I). Numerous Queensland Police Officers — Matt Moloney, Steve Kersley and Ben Sawden, to name a few — have worked with Tracker Barry Port and Tracker George Musgrave both at Coen and Laura in our Gulf country. Former Detective Sergeant Glenn Teske has contributed glowing accounts of these two men, outlining their dedication to duty, their ability, the strength of their character and their loyalty to the Queensland Police Force. Their contribution to keeping the peace was beyond question. Since the inauguration of the Queensland Police Service (Force) on the 21st January, 1864, there have been numerous Indigenous Trackers who served our state. However, it is impossible to gauge just how many as in years gone by their identity was not correctly recorded. The day of the Indigenous Tracker as a member of the Queensland Police Service has passed, and sadly I hasten to say will never return. I can understand the decision by Government and senior police administration to discontinue this service when we see how technology has so rapidly changed the face of our world. However, many have voiced their disapproval.

Foreword

Queensland police recruits from 1948 to 1980 had the followings words ingrained into their memory: "Come here that Man", delivered with a loud, heavy, Irish accent.

Initially it meant great fear, but its author Sergeant Tom Molloy was using his psychological skills to prepare new police recruits for the harsh reality of modern-day policing.

Over three generations of police recruits had the privilege of Sergeant Tom Molloy's wisdom, developed during his distinguished military career in the Royal Navy.

His experiences at sea during WW2 defined this great man who then devoted his life to his family and Queensland police recruit training.

The author could not have chosen a more interesting, respected and influential Queensland police officer for the Prologue and Valedictory of *Keeping the Peace Volume IV*.

Sergeant Tom Molloy's 32 years of service in the Queensland Police Department is part of our rich history, and its influence helped cornerstone our great culture which evolves during police training.

Fingerprints are the most irrebuttable evidence police can use in an investigation. While other advancements in forensic science have revolutionized policing in recent decades, fingerprints, discovered in the 1880s and first used in 1892, has been an investigator's sole forensic tool for many years.

Again, the Author's decision to Dedicate *Keeping The Peace Volume IV* to the late Technical Officer, Patrick Cornelius O'Brien, Queensland Police fingerprint expert from 1945 to 1983 (Australia's foremost fingerprint expert), acknowledges another historic cornerstone of forensic policing used daily in keeping the peace.

Aboriginal police trackers played a vital role in Queensland's operational policing from 1860 until they were sadly disbanded.

Many a person owe their life to Aboriginal police trackers, who were unique professionals often working in harsh environments with great bravery, dedication and skill.

Aboriginal police trackers were also responsible for the ultimate location and subsequent arrest of many criminals; their unique skills helped police solve crimes.

Their stories are inspirational and an especially important part of Queensland police history. A very worthwhile inclusion in *Keeping the Peace Volume IV*.

Volumes I-III of *Keeping The Peace* have captured the amazing policing lives and experiences of 35 men and women of the Queensland Police Department since 1860 in a collection of essays by them and the Author.

The *Tales of the Bullyman* by the late Senior Sergeant Vincent Augustine Walker in 2006, contains the story of a soldier and police officer, the late Senior Sergeant Leslie Victor Hoiser.

Again, the Author's decision to republish this story with permission is commendable because this story truly reflects the Australian digger's bravery at war (POW), interwoven with a dedicated policing career.

The Author also acknowledges Leslie's three brothers — one a Queensland Police officer, another brother a POW in WW2 who was also a Brigadier with the Salvation Army and another brother killed in action in WW1.

These stories are truly inspirational, a must read and an especially important part of the Queensland police history.

The Author finishes another amazing volume of *Keeping the Peace* with stories from three dedicated but different police officers, Kenneth John Salmon, Danny Murdoch and Glenn Andrew Teske. Together, they have decades of experience through metropolitan, rural and remote Queensland, creating more rich history for the Queensland Police Department.

The Author, Assistant Commissioner (retired) Laurie Pointing AM, had a great influence on my career after we first met in Proserpine in 1990, when he was appointed the first Assistant Commissioner, Central Police Region, after the Fitzgerald Inquiry. Laurie was the ideal change agent in this era, with all the old breed experience of policing, coupled with the vision to change into the new era.

It is pleasing to see that similar performance many years on still drives Laurie to record the wonderful history of the Queensland Police Department. Laurie, this will be available for generations to come, to read, learn and enjoy.

Thank you and I look forward to launching Volume IV in Townsville as I did for Volumes I-III.

Paul A Wilson APM
Assistant Commissioner
Queensland Police (Retired)
Director QBANK.

Prologue
Queensland Police Drill Instructor, Sergeant Thomas James (Tom) Molloy

Throughout the four volumes of Keeping the Peace, many retired police make mention of their association with the late Tom Molloy when they underwent their Probationary Training at the Police Depot, Petrie Terrace, Brisbane all those years ago. He was remembered as a rigorously tough man who did not suffer fools and quickly identified a weakness displayed by a probationary. Over the years some young men just could not accept Tom's discipline and walked out the Depot gates never to be seen or heard of again. However, some did return and completed their probationary training; they were sworn in and went on to carve a respectable career as a member of the Queensland Police Force serving with distinction. Tom frequently remarked, *"If they cannot handle my discipline here at the depot they will never succeed in the outside world as a police officer."* No matter what Tom threw at you, once you were inducted, he was your friend.

Thomas James Molloy was born on the 18 July, 1922 at Tullycaron, Artless, Country Down, Ireland. He joined the Royal British Navy in January, 1938 and served throughout the years of the Second World War and was discharged from the Navy in London in the year 1947.

Tom arrived in Sydney on the "Ormonde" on 39 June, 1948 and made his way to Brisbane where he lodged an application to join the Queensland Police Force. He was sworn in on the 1 November, 1948 and became the Assistant Drill Instructor at the Depot until 1950, when he took over the entire drill instruction duties. In the year 1949 Tom married Kathleen Rundles and over the years four children were born to the union.

Tom spent his entire police service as a *Drill Instructor* at the Petrie Terrace Police Depot and the Police Academy, Oxley. *On the 18 August, 1972 Sergeant Thomas James Molloy, Police Depot (Educational Section) was awarded a commendation for his continued devotion to duty particularly in regard to training of Probationaries and Cadets and organising police personnel at police ceremonial functions. Tom was also awarded the Queen's Police Medal in June, 1978.*

Tom retired from the Service on the 18 February, 1980 and when passed to eternal rest, his Cremation Service was held at Albany Creek Crematorium on 30 March, 1997.

VALEDICTORY

"Come here that Man!"

It was with much regret that the Queensland Police Service learnt of the passing of one of its favourite sons – Retired Sergeant Tom Molloy.

A service was held on Thursday, March 20, at the Albany Creek Crematorium and was attended by more that 300 people, including Commissioner Jim O'Sullivan and many other senior and retired officers.

Tom was piped to his last resting place by Brendan Hood of the Queensland Police Pipes & Drums.

Sergeant Molloy was noted for his positive attitude to discipline and found his place in the then Queensland Police Force as Drill Instructor at the police Depot and Oxley Academy. He is remembered as meticulous, hard-headed but soft-hearted, sometimes cruel to make a point, loyal with an Irish wit; but most agree he was a legend within the then Queensland Police Force.

Thomas James Molloy was born in Northern Ireland in July 1922. He left school to join the Royal Navy at the age of 16 years as an Abel Seaman in 1938 and served throughout the War on convey escorts in the Atlantic and the Mediterranean. His first ship, the *H.M.S Calypso* was sunk by a German U-boat in June 1940; his next ship, the *H.M.S Liverpool*, was torpedoed and suffered heavy losses.

He also served on the *H.M.S Londonderry*, which also suffered a torpedo attack, and the *H.M.S Hart,* which participated in the d-Day landings. Tom Molloy was aboard *H.M.S Hart* somewhere in the Atlantic when the War officially ended in Europe.

On his discharge from the Navy in London in1947, Tom migrated to Australia. In August 1948, he joined the Queensland Police Force and was sworn-in on November 1, 1948. He was posted to the training wing of the Police Depot, Brisbane, and followed recruit training when it moved to the new Oxley Academy in 1972.

Tom Molloy made it his personal mission to test whether recruits had the discipline for the job. His methods proved successful over 25 years and he had very few failures.

But his methods, while hard, were laced with Irish humour and most recruits often enjoyed trying to get the better of him.

Superintendent Fels recalls having to break down his pack (spare sheets and blankets) every night and painfully refold it to meet the meticulous standards set down by Sergeant Molloy. Some of the more artful recruits, who choose to pin their packs together so they would pass Tom's inspections, were ruthlessly summoned with the familiar: '*Come here that man*!' It was amazing how much volume he could achieve when he was riled."

These recruits would often be seen duck walking with a medicine ball held over their heads around Lang Park. Any shirkers of that punishment would be told very firmly from a distance of about three centimetres that they 'would duck-walk 'til they dropped, Superintendent Fels said.'

Retired Sergeant Dick Bromley said Sergeant Molloy seemed to be one step ahead of recruits. To cross him or to lie to him was not a good idea. Tom was certainly a hard man to fool. Many recruits tried and many regretted the attempt.

"He had the uncanny ability to judge a person's character instantly and was rarely wrong. Tom Molloy was always straight down-the-line, and if you were the same with him then you were fine," Sergeant Bromley said.

Love him or hate him, Tom Molloy had a heart of gold beneath his tough exterior and possessed a great talent and instinct for training. A plaque was dedicated to Sergeant Tom Molloy on his retirement in February 1980 and still stands at the Queensland Police Academy, Oxley.

Sergeant Molloy received a Commendation in 1972 and was awarded the Queen's Police Medal in 1976 for his devotion to duty.

In the words of Inspector Bob Good of the Southern Region, "Sergeant Tom Molloy was a man apart from other men … a real character, the like of whom we will not see again."

Tracker Barry Port

Former Coen police sergeant, Matt Moloney, is proud of their Coen Police motto, "You can run, but you really can't hide" attributed to the ability of Indigenous police trackers who have served our Gulf country and Western country districts with distinction for many years.

Tracker Barry Port's retirement in the year 2004 at the age of seventy-one years marked the end of an era for Queensland policing, with our State's last serving "Indigenous Police Tracker" retiring after a career of thirty-six years with the Queensland Police service. Barry was the last tracker to serve in that field after indigenous males had served with distinction for a period of over 150 years.

His services were invaluable before and after the introduction of technology; he assisted police officers in apprehending criminals for a variety of criminal offences, found lost children and travellers and located drug plantations in the vast wilderness areas of Cape York.

His base was the large Police division of Coen which covered an area of 32,000 square kilometres of coastal wetlands, dry eucalypt areas and savannah country.

Barry was a quiet man — a man of few words who always played down his achievements. "To be a good tracker," he said, "you have to use your brains and think."

Numerous country Queensland police officers who served at Coen and surrounding police divisions spoke of Barry in glowing terms, outlining his valuable service to the police department and local community to bring to justice those who had violated the statute law of this state.

About the year 1994, armed with a rations pack and radio, Barry Port was sent out by his superiors in search for a fourteen-year-old boy missing in the Kowanyama area. A search party couldn't find the boy. A helicopter also couldn't find him, but within a few hours Barry Port found the tracks of his horse. The boy had been mustering cattle which required him to cross water on several occasions, which resulted in him separating from the main mustering party.

Kowanyama Officer-in-Charge at the time, Senior Sergeant Steve Kersley said Mr Port's skills were amazing: "It was the wet season; it was muddy with brumby tracks everywhere. But he still managed to find the tracks from the kid's horse. He had amazing eyesight."

Barry Port has been playing a pivotal role for almost three decades in the Coen community, contributing his unique skills to aid the officers of the Far Northern Region. At the age of 67, you could be forgiven for believing he may be slowing down and perhaps even considering retirement, but retirement is not being considered by Barry. For 29 years, Barry Port had developed the skills nurtured by his father as they worked side-by-side on cattle stations.

Together they mustered and then walked overland with the 1500 herd of cattle from Coen to the Mareeba saleyards, three times each year. Barry and his father would track any beast that was lost or stolen, and hunt for food along the way. They noticed the small things, such as broken branches and wayward hoof prints. The signposts they saw were invisible to the eye of the white man.

"His skills were invaluable to the local police officers," said Senior Constable Ben Sawden. "Barry can get started on a search straight away." Helicopters and EPIRBs are often used to search these days, but what Barry has, which is unique, is his knowledge of the country. The Cape is savannah and anthill country, and Barry has grown up in this environment.

Barry was born at Lankelly Creek, some 576k north of Cairns in the year 1942 and has lived his whole life in Coen, marrying Yvonne in the year 1968. The couple have been married for forty-one years and have five children. Yvonne has been awarded with a clasp for 25 years service at the local school. That's the kind of family they are; they take great pride in their work.

Barry has worked for many different police officers at Coen. Police he worked for as constables back in the 1980s are now Inspectors. He is well regarded by many in the community and has been instrumental in fostering relationships between police and the community.

It is still talked about today how, in 1997, Barry Port helped locate two kiwi sisters and a Malaysian seaman who jumped overboard from a shipping vessel. Sarah and Joanne Ingram and Ja'afar Ban Mohamed Zan swam through crocodile-infested waters near Cairns, reached the shore and evaded authorities for weeks. They made their way to Coen before running into bushland where police spotted them.

Barry and tracker George Musgrave, from Laura, followed footprints from their sandals and the absconders were eventually located near the Coen River. Barry then said, 'They looked scared and unhappy, and the first thing they asked for was a smoke."

Commenting on Barry Port's retirement Sergeant Moloney said, "This is the end of an era. This is the day that the last tracker working in any law enforcement jurisdiction finished duty." Sergeant Moloney insists that Tracker Port's skills haven't been superseded by technology, saying, "His special observational powers" have come in handy at crime and vehicle crash scenes. Barry's entire police career has been spent at Coen, the town of his birth, where the Lama Lama elder is also a member of the local State Emergency Service and Fire Brigade.

Sergeant Moloney continued, "Barry learnt how to track from his father while working as a stockman, locating cattle and horses that had strayed from camp. It appears almost certain that Mr Port won't be replaced. But with the final tracker officially retired, the bush art seems inevitably lost and I feel very sad. For me it's not just because we're losing a man of character and incredible ability who I think very highly of; he's my friend and I'm not going to see him every day at work. So, it's not going to be the same."

In the month of November, 2001, the then Far Northern Regional Assistant Commissioner Allan Roberts presented Barry with the National Police Service Medal in recognition of his services with the Queensland Police Department.

Then in the year 2013, the Queensland Police Commissioner, Ian Stewart presented Barry with a meritorious service award for his distinguished services with the Queensland Police Department.

On receiving the award Tracker Port said, "We'd go out looking for drugs — people camping in the bush who had set up big plantations, and once we'd found it, we'd destroy it all. You could follow their footsteps through the scrub; they'd make a bit of a track to their camp. It was a pretty dangerous job — the dealers, they've got guns and knives and you'd have to be very careful."

Commissioner Stewart said, "Barry Port's tracking ability and bush skills caught the attention of police in the year 1980. He was signed up and would spend more than 30 years pursuing drug dealers, escaped prisoners and cattle rustlers."

Barry Port joins a long list of Indigenous Police trackers and other competent men from the gulf country; to name just a few who are spoken of with enthusiasm and respect — namely, Noble Burns at Georgetown in the 1970s and his son Nardoo Burns who followed his father when he retired.

Barry Port relaxing after a hard day's work

Deputy Commissioner Brett Pointing presenting Tracker Barry Port with a letter from the Minister for Police, Fire and Emergency Services Mr Jack Dempsey, congratulating him on his thirty-four years of service with the Queensland Police Service.

Barry aged 74 years passed to eternal rest at his home at Coen on Wednesday the 5 March, 2020 after suffering a heart attack.

Reference is made to both these gentlemen (Noble and Nardoo Burns) in Volume three of Keeping the Peace in the story as related by the late Sergeant Brian James Norris. A photograph of a Nardoo Burns accompanies the Brian Norris Story.

Tracker-Nardoo Burns was stationed at the Burketown Police Station in the 1980s when former Sergeant Neville Travers-Jones was the Officer-in-Charge of that police division. Neville cannot speak highly enough of Nardoo, both as an Indigenous Tracker and a human being. To Neville, "*Nardoo was a highly respected and competent gentleman.*"

Reference is also made to Nardoo Burns in Volume one of Keeping the peace in the story by former Sergeant Neville Travers-Jones and a photograph of Nardoo also accompanies that story.

Nardoo Burns has been immortalised in the pantheon of Australian music, called just that — 'Nardoo Burns' by the late and great Country Music Artist, Slim Dusty.

Courtesy Queensland Police Museum

George Musgrave . . . "Everyone leaves a track. Even a child must leave a track."

During his time as the Officer-In-Charge of the Laura Police Division and other areas of the Gulf country, Glenn Teske worked with both Tracker George Musgrave and Tracker Barry Port and has related his experiences working with these two remarkable men.

Taking up duty at Laura in the Gulf country in early 1983 on transfer from Landsborough, I was not told that I would be responsible for an aboriginal gentleman who I was later to know as George Musgrave. Nor was I informed that he was an official Queensland Police Tracker, one of the last trackers employed by the Police Force. On my arrival at the station, the relieving officer basically threw me the keys to the complex and vehicle and departed with the local carrier to return to Cairns, not even bothering to mention that I had staff in the form of one George Musgrave.

The following morning while unpacking, I heard a subdued knock on the door, and going out to see who it was, I saw an aboriginal gentleman, about 5'10" with a wiry build, dressed in a Police Uniform. I asked him his name and was informed that his name was George Musgrave. I asked him who supplied him with a Police uniform, and he advised it had been given to him by previous Police officers. The penny still not dropping, I asked him what he wanted from me.

He advised me that he normally reported for duty at this time each morning and asked what did I want him to do for the day.

On further questioning, he advised that he was in fact employed by the Police Force and that his official title was 'Tracker". Somewhat stunned, I told him to take the day off until I could get the residence and the station organised. Thus began a lifelong friendship with my esteemed partner.

Every weekday morning whilst I was at Laura George would turn up at the station to undertake whatever was requested of him. At this point I am sad to say, not releasing his unique abilities and steadfast faithfulness, the only work I had for him was mowing the station yard and some gardening. He would undertake perhaps three to four hours' work each weekday before I would give him the rest of the day off. My first indication that George was somewhat loyal came when I was confronted by three drunken "Cape Conquerors" who believed that as they were in the bush, they could do whatever they pleased.

These three gentlemen, and I use that term lightly, would not heed my warning to go down to the river and sleep it off. Seeing that the odds were heavily in their favour, they decided to take me on. During the ensuing fight I realised that a fifth person had joined the fray — none other than George (who I might add was twice these young ruffians age). The three were subdued and arrested, and George helped me walk them to the cells. I was to find out that George, a local, would report on the devious undertakings of his relatives, but would take a back seat when any arrests were made. I completely understood and respected his position on this — after all, he had to live amongst these relatives.

However, as our friendship and mutual respect grew, I did take him to disturbances in Hopevale and Cooktown Communities, where he would join me in helping resolve the situation. George, it would seem, had won my complete admiration and trust. I was soon to learn he had also won the respect of my neighboring Officer in Charge, Ken Salmon from Cooktown.

I took George everywhere it was possible, enjoying his stories of his life gone by and learning from his unique skills. As his salary was somewhat meager, I would take him hunting whenever possible to supplement his food stocks, thus saving him and his family money. My memory has lost count of the number of times I tried through the correct channels to have this man's salary increased, but on all occasions to no avail.

It was during these hunting trips that I found out that George's gift for tracking and knowledge of the bush knew no bounds. He was such an expert he could almost track a beetle over a rock, and I'm sure that if the beetle knew George was tracking him, George would follow the excrement droppings!

I found that George would be my early warning system, advising me when the men came in from the mustering camps flush with cash, enabling me to ensure that all their bills were paid and families fed before they wasted all the money on grog. The system worked and ensured that we had a relatively peaceful town. If any trouble from tourists erupted through excessive drinking, I would walk down to the hotel from the Police Station and always found that George, although not summonsed, would arrive soon after to assist in any way possible.

I have lost count of the number of arrests I made with the offender between George and myself, doing the walk of shame from the Hotel back to the cells. Sergeant Ken Samon from Cooktown requested my assistance in Cooktown for the forth coming festivities of the re-enactment of Captain Cook arriving in Cooktown. I mentioned to George that I had to travel to Cooktown for this event, whereon he told me that although he heard of the event he had never been. Say no more, and together we set out for Cooktown and all its glory.

It was a well-behaved and fantastic event, and any intoxicated troublemakers were soon dealt with, of course with George always by my side.

George's actions and steadfast loyalty earned him the respect of visiting Police Officers, both uniform and plain clothes officers, and I was extremely proud of him in the way he conducted himself. I should add that at this point, George was a complete teetotaller but would sit in on our reveilles after work quietly sipping a sarsaparilla or lemonade.

I recall an incident that necessitated George and I to travel during the "wet season" to a remote area to undertake an investigation. Travelling to our destination proved easy enough but whilst we were there for over a number of days, the heavens opened up and left our return journey a nightmare. You see, our vehicle was not equipped with a power winch, but a devil's device known as a Turfor — a hand operated winch. By attaching one end of the cable to a solid object and passing the cable through the device and then onto the vehicle, one could slowly remove the vehicle from the bog.

On the first occasion on becoming bogged, I set the device up and slowly pushed and pulled the lever, moving the vehicle forward. The strenuous exercise was fatiguing me, and on the power stroke I had neglected to wait for the locking click before letting the lever go. It then promptly flew back, hitting me in the head and rendering me unconscious. I came to with George crying, tears streaming down his face kneeling beside me, believing I was dead. George could not drive a motor vehicle or use the portable radio. He told me he was very concerned about our situation and was very much relieved when I regained consciousness. All was well and we eventually managed to return to our families in Laura.

Another similar incident occurred when we had to travel, this time in the dry, to a far-flung property to deliver legal documents. On arriving at the Station house, we found no one there. The entire family was out mustering, and no doubt would not return until late in the evening.

As it was a five-hour drive and not wanting to get home around midnight, I decided to leave. To this, there was one great problem: I had turned our Toyota off, and as is normal with these vehicles and the rough roads over which we were forced to travel, my battery had completely failed. I found a set of jumper leads in the workshop, but even this attempt at starting the vehicle failed.

There was another Toyota utility with its keys in the ignition parked in the workshop, so I made the decision to tow the police Toyota in an attempt to start the vehicle. This was not that simple as George could not drive a motor vehicle. I towed the Police Toyota to the airstrip runway, and after some rudimentary instructions on clutches and first gear and throttle, I left it to the now terrified George to tow start the Police vehicle.

On giving George the signal, we took off with George's foot firmly on throttle, hurtling down the airstrip. After starting my Toyota and having it running nicely, my memory fails me, but perhaps I didn't think to tell George how to stop. No amount of waving or blaring horn could slow George down. By planting my foot firmly on the brake, I somehow managed to stall George's vehicle. Now it was my turn to tow a mortified George back to the workshop to return the Station vehicle. I saw that on leaving, poor George was shaking and close to tears as I had frightened him so much.

Around my first Christmas at Laura, I was awakened one Christmas morning to the sound of children screaming in fun on my front lawn. Going downstairs, I saw that there was almost entire community of children holding buckets. Without further warning, they threw the contents of the buckets, which contained mud, all over me. Out the corner of my eye, I spied George and his wife who were also covered in mud — it was, I was soon to find out, a Christmas tradition. George and his wife and all the children thought it was hilarious and were laughing uncontrollably.

Seeking revenge, I turned the hose on the children which brought more squeals of laughter. What a morning! As a gift and a thank you, I had purchased some much needed cooking pots for George and his wife. On cleaning myself up and delivering his gift, I saw that most of the community was there — and yes, they too were covered in mud. With me being clean, at least the children waited until I gave George his gift before once again covering me in mud! Thoughtful don't you think?

Early one morning, I heard the Coen Police frantically calling me over the SSB wireless. Answering his call, I was advised that he was following two wanted men south. These men were wanted for the murder of a male person near Portland Roads, the victim having been shot in the head by a large calibre handgun. Grabbing my 12-gauge shot gun and the station .303 rifle, George and I travelled north, setting up a road block on the southern side of the single lane of Kennedy River Bridge.

My plan was that as the suspect vehicle was crossing the bridge, I would wait until they were almost across and then block the bridge and apprehend the two wanted persons. As my Police vehicle was not fitted with a radio and the Coen vehicle communications was non-existent, I had confirmed through VKR Cairns that the wanted men had passed through Musgrave Station about an hour or some previous and that the Coen vehicle was not following. This conjured up thoughts in my mind — had these two murderers stopped and shot the Coen Police Officer? My mind was running wild with all sorts of scenarios. Meanwhile, George sat calmly waiting, holding the shotgun.

After a while a Toyota motor vehicle with two ruffian males crossed the bridge. Putting our plan into action, we blocked the exit of the bridge, leaping from the Police vehicle yelling put "put your arms in the air" and other dramatic phrases. Pulling the two males from the vehicle at gun point, we placed them on the roadway face down. I saw that one had wet himself in fright! I soon learned on questioning that the two men were bull catchers from the nearby Olivevale Station. Releasing them, they went on their way and we resumed our hiding position near the bridge.

Eventually a clapped-out multicoloured Toyota shortie approached our position; re-enacting our plan, we stopped the vehicle. I could have sworn there were two males in this vehicle, had we stopped the wrong vehicle? Had I made another mistake? While getting the driver (who now appeared to be the single occupant) out of the vehicle and having him lay on the roadway with his hands behind his head, I suddenly heard George yell out: "Put that down!" Turning, I saw the other male holding a large handgun.

I saw that George had the shotgun pushed firmly into the second male's ear with the offender quickly losing the colour in his face. I could see that George was very animated, and I was worried that he would pull the trigger. I had to ask George twice before he lowered the shotgun, then telling the offender to hit the dirt. Although the offender was disarmed, George never stopped covering either offender with that shotgun. Both were searched and then handcuffed together as I only had one pair of cuffs.

After receiving numerous complaints about a white male stealing food from the station stores whilst the men were out mustering and the women of the stations being alarmed, George and I attempted on numerous occasions to track the offender through the bush on foot. Being unsuccessful, we borrowed horses and on one occasion while sleeping rough, George followed those tracks for three days. Try as we could, we could never catch up with our fugitive. We had to be slow and methodical to keep on his tracks whilst the offender was free to travel as fast as he wanted where he wanted. I later caught this offender, running him down with the Police vehicle.

Together with Sergeant Ken Salmon from Cooktown we utilized George's unique skills to track and locate offenders growing cannabis in both our Police Divisions. George was, to put it simply, incredible.

I recall a young toddler between three to four years of age missing from a remote station. Collecting George, we travelled to the scene. There on foot, George commenced tracking the toddler, halting only because of failing light.

I could see that George was as concerned as everybody and was keen to get started again at daylight. He tracked that toddler throughout most of the second day, before finding her wondering aimlessly through the bush. I saw a tear in George's eye when he located the toddler as such was his compassion, indeed, those present just might have shed a tear or two as well.

On another occasion we were called up to help find some missing pig hunters along the Normanby River who had been missing for 24 hours. On arriving at the pig hunter's vehicle, George immediately picked up their tracks, quietly but competently following those tracks upriver. George followed those tracks for three days, sleeping rough during this period. Never once did George lose those tracks, and indeed one of the gentlemen was wearing unique studded pattern joggers which George called "pussy cat tracks". We located the missing hunters late on the third day, after I had discharged my rifle to gather something to eat for the night. The hunters hearing the shot fired back and finally we were re-united. Sharing what food we had along with our meager ration of tea leaves, we again slept rough before returning to our vehicle the following day.

In yet another adventure, Sergeant Ken Salmon and I were called to investigate some matter near Cape Melville, at least a two-day drive from Cooktown. Believing we would need the skills of George, we squeezed him into the front seat of my short wheelbase Toyota. On the first night, Sergeant Ken opted to sleep in a small pup tent whilst George and I rolled our swags on the ground nearby. During the drive to our campsite, we had seen numerous clean skin bulls and taking the mickey for want of a better phrase, George and I related to Sergeant Ken just how dangerous these bulls were and how they would smell a human and attack with little to no warning.

We all retired for the night, and early the next morning George asked if he could mimic a bull's roar and see what sort of reaction we would get out of Ken. Having agreed, I sat back to watch the reaction. George started mimicking the roar of a scrub bull behind Ken's tent, he was really very good at it.

After a few short roars, Ken was out of his tent terrified, wearing only underpants. I thought George was going to wet himself he was laughing that hard! We finished the five-day patrol thoroughly enjoying ourselves, even though it was pretty tight within the confines of that Toyota.

George's wages were extremely meager and like I have related before, no amount of prompting from those higher up would get George an increase in pay. It greatly saddened me that this was the case, and so I devised a plan which would help George earn more money. As George was a really competent horseman, I borrowed some portable panels, erecting them in the Police compound and started taking unbroken horses from the nearby stations. The stations would pay me to break these horses in and I would give by far the majority of the money to George, keeping for myself "beer money". We charged $500 per horse and educated between 10/12 horses at a time.

As you can see, it amounted to a sizeable sum of money and we would undertake this work over the "wet season" when there was ample time available. Soon word got out, and we had more horses than we could handle. I would "vet" the horses and any ones I considered difficult I would take, leaving the quieter ones for George as he was by then in his 60's. George was patiently handling this gelding one day and had been riding this animal for some days when the brute began to buck and buck hard. I was fearful for the old fellow and was wondering if I had done the right by undertaking this task. I need not have worried; George rode that horse like the professional that he was.

He rode that horse to a standstill before giving it a breather and asking it to walk off which it did, clearly realising that George was the master. I was flabbergasted by his display of rough riding and here I was taking all the nasty ones! We would sometimes do three mobs depending on how long the "wet season" lasted. The money earned certainly gave George and his family a better standard of living. We trained these horses to "roll back" (spin on their hind quarters) and come to a sliding stop and overall, I think that the Stations appreciated the level of education given to these horses.

I do recall an incident which although solemn was somewhat humorous. An elder of the community, Molly Barney, had passed away after a short illness. With a Cause of Death Certificate forthcoming, it would normally be left up to the undertakers to perform the necessary tasks to bury the deceased. To my alarm there were no undertakers and to make things even more difficult, the local Fly-In-preacher was not available. The entire burial and service would be my responsibility — a ceremony I had had little to do with.

Getting some prominent sections from the Bible from the Preacher and getting a coffin delivered from Cairns, I set about conducting my first funeral. Having arrested two males the night before who were related to George, I marked out with a stick the length, width and depth of the grave and gave these men shovels, instructing George to supervise them to dig the grave. The funeral itself was scheduled for 1pm that day. The mourners gathered behind the utility carrying the coffin, and the funeral started with the mourners wailing and throwing flowers they had previously picked after the vehicle. On arrival at the gravesite, I recited the passages from the Bible I had been given.

Now it was time to lower the coffin into the grave. Lowering the coffin by using ropes, the coffin moved slowly into the grave before becoming wedged in the ever-narrowing hole. The grave had been dug correctly at the top, but my diggers were lazy and the lower they dug the narrower the hole became. Removing the coffin from the grave, I instructed our grave diggers to get into the grave and widen it. Both men looked like they would collapse, but on stern prompting both got in and finished the job.

Consenting, both men scrambled out with their legs becoming a blur as they shot out of that grave! I looked across at George who had a sheepish grin and shrugged his shoulders. Both these men were relatives of George. The grave widened, we continued with the ceremony to completion.

On being transferred from Laura, I was at pains to figure out just how I was going to say goodbye to such a revered friend and colleague.

I was not to worry, for on the day of my leaving, George and his entire family came over to the Police residence to bid me farewell. There were plenty of tears and hugs and promises to catch up again.

He was truly a great friend, workmate and mentor. As I drove out of Laura that one last time, I thought of George, his hilarious laugh and all the adventures we had undertaken, and I sincerely prayed that the next Police Officer at Laura would also appreciate the skills and the man I had grown so fond of. To this very day I can still hear George's loud fits of laughter and remember his generous and meritorious service.

George has since passed on and I truly believe that Heaven is a far better place.

George Musgrave commenced duty as a tracker with the Queensland Police Department at Laura Police Station on the 27 April, 1972. He was married and the father of four children. He was a good provider to his family and worked on almost every cattle property in the Laura Police Division which comprised 8,500 square miles. George was bred and born on the Peninsula and was a very competent horseman, with a sound knowledge of the terrain and movement of stock, using keen tracking skills passed down from his father.

He is famously remembered for locating a Normanton pig shooter in 1989 when he became lost in Cape York for a period of 10 day: "I walked all day and camped, I walked 35 miles, you have to keep walking. If you stop for lunch that boy keeps walking and you never catch up with him." In the year 2005 George Musgrave was recognised with an honorary doctorate from the James Cook University for his stewardship of Indigenous culture/culture burning. Dr George Musgrave passed to eternal rest at 85 years at Laura on 8 February, 2006.

Courtesy: Laura Cultural Centre.

My first contact with Tracker Barry Port was around 1984, when I was required to travel to Coen to pick up the Officer-in-Charge and then travel to Lockhart River community. As there were no police stationed at this community at this time, it fell into Coen Division and I was tasked to accompany the O/C to quell serious disturbances there. On arrival at the station, I recall seeing a slight built aboriginal gentleman dressed in a police shirt mowing the lawn. I engaged in a conversation with him and learned that his name was Barry Port and he was the Aboriginal tracker attached to Coen. I engaged in an in-depth conversation with Barry, and he informed me his father had run the butchers shop in town and that he had helped in the shop when he was young. He later became a stockman and was also a successful jockey before becoming the tracker at Coen.

We travelled to the distant Lockhart River Community in my short wheelbase Toyota loaded with all our clothes, spare fuel and food for 10 days, where our duties were satisfactorily completed.

Some months later I was again tasked to travel to Lockhart River to quell violent unrest. I was told that I would be taking Barry as my off sider. On my arrival at Coen to pick him up he was ready and waiting on the front lawn of the station. I was looking forward to again working with Barry and learning from his experience. I needn't have been concerned. Our trip, which comprised of about seven hours of driving over the most appalling roads you can imagine, was really enjoyable and I found that Barry had a great grasp of knowledge of the area and also an interesting past. I also formed the opinion that perhaps he was being underutilized.

On arriving at our destination, I found that the situation was actually worse than reported and certainly more violent since my last attendance. During the process of restoring Law and Order, I found that Barry never once left my side, and I could rely upon him totally, especially in facilitating any violent arrests. I was extremely impressed with his tact, professionalism, patience and utmost loyalty. Considering he was a successful jockey, the reader will understand that although small in stature, he had an enormous heart and unlimited courage.

Returning to Coen, despite the horrendous roads, it was one of the most enjoyable journeys I had undertaken. Later that afternoon back at Coen, Barry and I shared a few quiet beers at the local watering hole. There were a number of people in the bar at the time and I recall them being somewhat surprised to see a Police Officer drinking with the tracker, as this type of socialising was not normal.

Again, some months later, I was directed to the Edward River Community to investigate a number of criminal matters and general unrest caused by excessive drinking. I was advised that Barry would be transported to Musgrave Station/cafe where we would meet prior to travelling to Edward River.

On finalising our duties at Edward River, we returned through 'Strathleven Station'. Barry directed me to take a detour and showed me the formal burial ground of the traditional occupiers of the land. Each grave was marked with an upturned matchwood stump. Barry went on to relate that up until recently, this sacred site was guarded by the older youths of the tribe as the start of the initiation process.

I was to undertake a number of trips to both Lockhart River and Edward River communities with Barry and despite the violence encountered, I actually looked forward to his company. Knowing that Barry's wage was appalling and similar to my own tracker, George Musgrave, I suggested to the then O/C that Barry come down to Laura during the "wet" and supplement his income by breaking in horses, as both George and I were doing.

Both positions at Coen became vacant and Bill Gittoes became the relieving Officer-In-Charge. Bill and I experienced a professional working relationship.

Bill, not having been at Coen for that long, requested my assistance in locating an elderly gentleman who lived on the outskirts of Coen and was missing from his residence which was highly unusual. I travelled to Coen where I met Bill and Barry, and we travelled to the said gentleman's residence. Barry immediately saw that a vehicle had been loaded by two people, one of whom was our missing gentleman.

Barry told us that several trips had been made from the residence to the vehicle, indicating that our missing man was intending to be away for some considerable time. We also saw at least nine outboard motors and refrigerators and other white goods and furnishings that were brand new. There were also a large number of high-powered weapons lying about.

It didn't take much imagination to realise that our missing man was living way beyond his means. On asking Barry if he could follow the vehicle tracks, Barry indicated that he would do his best. We returned to Coen and got some food and fuel, squeezed into my Toyota shortie, and returned to the residence where Barry commenced tracking the vehicle.

Being just prior to the "wet", it was extremely hot and humid, and due to the vagueness of the vehicle tracks, poor Barry was forced to walk in front of the Police vehicle for nearly three days before he brought us to an occupied camp in an extremely isolated part of the Wenlock River. The camp was extremely well stocked with food and clothing and a footpath had even been formed between the creek and the camp for water.

The camp also contained quite a large number of heavy calibre firearms. There was no vehicle present and Barry indicating that such a vehicle had returned the way in which it had come. This was obviously a camp attached to a major drug growing operation. After a short discussion, it was agreed that I would climb and hide in a nearby tree and await the return of our missing man, while Bill and Barry would retire some distance away and await my signal of a gunshot to return to the scene. Some hours passed before I heard whistling, and then saw our missing man with a rifle slung over his shoulder, pushing a wheelbarrow back to the camp.

When he was well within range, I called on him to stop and drop the weapon, identifying myself as Police. Our missing man must have fancied his chances as he unshouldered his weapon and was trying to see where the voice came from, when I left him in no doubt as I fired a shot from my high-powered rifle at the wheel of his wheelbarrow. I then informed him that if he didn't drop his weapon, the next shot would be in his forehead, which had the desired effect.

On hearing my rifles report, both Barry and Bill came running up shouting Police, taking possession of the man's rifle and placing him into custody. Climbing down from my perch I saw that our "missing man" was in his early 70's.

On questioning, our now offender agreed to take us to the crop where we found approximately 10,000 marihuana plants growing healthily and from observations of the site, we determined that this certainly was not the first crop to be grown at the site. Having found that my SSB 25-watt portable radio was not serviceable, we were out of communication with Cairns, so I took numerous photos of the crop along with measurements and then commenced to pull out the plants and stack them prior to burning.

I retained a number of the healthiest plants for later analysis. As this was the start of the "wet season", we had no other options, as it could be up to five months before we might return. With the help of the offender, it took us at least a day and a half in the hot humid weather to pull the crop and eventually burn it. It was some two and a half days later before we moved out of this camp to turn home. Much to our offender's anger, we allowed Barry in the front with us whilst he had to return to Coen squeezed into the back.

On travelling towards Coen for some six or seven hours, it became too difficult and hazardous to continue on through the bush, so we were forced to make camp for the night. Barry quickly got a fire going, and we had a feed and a drink of tea before retiring for the night. I handcuffed the offender to my left wrist and soon fell into a deep sleep. I was awakened in the early hours of the morning by our offender who had somehow become entangled in a large amount of fishing line.

Barry, also awoken, told me that he had quietly tied some fishing line to our offender's leg and then onto his own ankle just in case the offender managed to get out of our handcuffs!

On returning to Coen, the Cairns CI.Branch was advised and soon arrived via air and took over our investigation. I have to give Barry credit for this, for without his skills and knowledge Bill and I would have wasted valuable time in searching for our missing man using conventional Police practices. Barry had made an indelible mark on Bill, and only enhanced Barry in my mind as a true professional and loyal friend. I believed Bill felt the same; he too became a lifelong friend and we often reminisced about this incident and Barry's skills.

As time marched on, I was transferred from Laura and had no further contact with either Barry or George for some years, until I was transferred to Mareeba Stock Squad. Our patrol area was huge and included not only all of the Gulf country but also Cape York Peninsula.

It was during this period that I was re-united with both George Musgrave and Barry Port. Between this, I had worked on Lakefield Station with a ringer known as Willy Fowler. It was during this intervening period that I found that Fowler had married Barry's very attractive daughter and had purchased the café in Coen. Whenever I was in Coen, I would often meet with Barry at the Café and catch up with Willy, and together would regale each other with tall and embellished stories.

During one return trip from Weipa and being alone, I called into Coen to refuel and later catch up with Barry and Willy. On fuelling up, I was approached by John and Mary Withers, publicans of the hotel. They informed me that a recent parolee who had served time for murdering his uncle with his bare hands was in town and was in essence destroying the town. They went on to say that both Police were absent from Coen and their whereabouts were not known. Cairns had been contacted about the situation but could offer no solutions.

Before our conversation could go any further, a huge aboriginal who I would later learn was Christopher J appeared. He was about 6'8" and about 150 kilograms, all of which was muscle. I saw that his right arm was heavily bandaged and bloodstained and was informed that he had injured himself by punching out the pubs windows when he was told to leave. Nonetheless, he refused and basically took over the bar.

On approaching this individual and identifying myself, it seemed like I had turned a switch on in his mind and he immediately rushed me, knocking me to the ground, where a struggle evolved in earnest. I was kept busy trying to stop his massive hands from grabbing my throat to squeeze the life out of me. It was during this extreme struggle that I found that my left leg was being forcibly twisted and at the same time being bent backwards.

Had this brute grown a second set of hands or had one of his mates come to his assistance? Barry immediately gripped the offender in a headlock, which although at the time was far from funny, looked like a dwarf grappling with Arnold S.

We eventually got the situation under control and holding our man, got the publican to get the handcuffs from my Police vehicle. Driving our prisoner to the cells, I asked of Barry where the Police Officers were. Barry informed me that they had left town and that he didn't know where they were. Calling Cairns VKR, they could not offer any explanations to their whereabouts. I found that although the cells were unlocked, the Station was locked up completely, forcing us to place the prisoner in the cells and lock the door using cob and co number eight wires. Every time we had to feed the prisoner, we had to cut the wire and then cob and co it again.

Barry, together with a lot of residents of the town, told me that in the absence of the two police officers, there was great unrest and violence in the town, mainly caused by our now prisoner. Using Willy's Café as a makeshift Police Station, I advised my inspector, Frank Wagner, of the situation in Coen and sought his advice. His advice was to stay in the town until it had settled down and relief had arrived. I then obtained an arrest warrant, handcuffing and returning our prisoner to Mareeba where it took four of us to get him in the cells.

Our prisoner caused so much trouble in the Mareeba cells that it was decided to transfer him to Cairns Watch-house, which had better facilities. I was asked to assist in getting him into the panel van, and after a very violent struggle, we were able to get him loaded with a forewarning to Cairns to be ready. He was later mistakenly released on bail; and on being free for only a couple of hours, attacked a marked Police vehicle in Sheridan Street whilst it was stopped at the lights, to the utter surprise of the occupants.

During a violent confrontation with a number of Police and a Police dog, he was again arrested and placed in the Watch-house. This incident alone would allow the reader to see not only Barry's dedication to help a fellow officer, but his courage to unhesitatingly enter into a fray when the odds were well and truly against him.

My last job with Barry involved the theft of a number of cattle from the Edward River Community. The details of this theft were sketchy at best but after picking Barry up at Musgrave Station/Café, we travelled on the unmade road towards Edward River. The offender was well known to both of us, and knowing the "wet season" was fast approaching, we commenced our search on the unfenced boundary of our suspect.

After several hours of searching, Barry located the tracks of a mob of cattle being driven by about six horsemen into the neighbouring Edward River country. Following these tracks, we found where the bulls had been tied to trees and driven back into the mob, which as each day progressed, was getting larger in number. Barry followed those tracks for three days, finding a black akubra hat during the process.

Barry was able to get me close enough to be able to climb a tree and film the mustering in progress. By this time, we were between 40-45 kilometers inside the Edward River boundary. Around midday, I seized all the cattle, and having organised men from the Edward River Community to meet us, they took possession of all the cattle.

Barry was carrying the hat he had found when one of the offender's men claimed the hat and thanked Barry for returning it! After a number of days of walking the cattle back to Edward River yards, Barry organised the men there to process and brand some 300 head of cattle, while I documented each beast and photographed some. On interviewing the offender's men, I found that this muster was an annual event and that all evidence was removed by the oncoming "wet season".

Not realising that this would be the last time I would work with Barry, I returned him back to Coen, enjoying every minute of the journey. I shouted him to a few beers at the pub, and just prior to leaving, Barry heartily shook my hand and then expectantly embraced me. I was quite taken aback but touched by his gesture nonetheless.

Having left Cape York for several years, I would sometimes come across articles about Barry, and this would bring a tear to my eye and revive the fondest of memories.

To this very day, I cannot understand the mentality of the Commissioner of Police in disbanding the trackers as they were in my opinion a most valuable resource, and a source of company and security to the Police Officers tasked with policing the remoteness of Queensland.

I have learned that Barry has since passed away and somehow, together with his colleague, George Musgrave who has also crossed that Great Divide, I feel that if there is any skullduggery afoot in heaven, both these men will be on top of it.

Glenn Teske

Vincent Augustine Walker
Retired Senior Sergeant of Police
1931–2009

The following story outlining the life and career of the late Senior Sergeant of police, Leslie Victor Hosier, belongs to the late Senior Sergeant Vincent Augustine Walker and is situated between pages 214 and 221 of — *Tales of the Bullyman,* the second book of police stories published by Vince Walker in the year 2006. It is a fascinating story that I believe needs to be resurrected and given the publicity it rightly deserves. I have received permission from retired medical Practitioner, Carmel Walker, (nee Coogan) to use the Hosier story. Carmel is the widow of Vince Walker.

I classed Vince as a friend; however, we were never stationed together at any policing establishment, but we both did attend two live-in educational courses at Chelmer College, Brisbane back in the 1980s.

Vince entered the Police Depot as a probationary constable on the 4 July, 1960, aged 29 years and was sworn in as a Constable of police on the 19 October of that same year. He commenced his career at Roma Street Police District and within a short period of time was transferred to Mt Isa Police District. Over the next twenty-six years, he served at a total of 16

Queensland Police establishments and completed his service to this State back where it all began, this time; Brisbane Mobile Patrols. He retired on the 23 July, 1986 with the rank of Senior Sergeant. Prior to joining the police service, Vince served with the Queensland Railway Department.

He served twice at Mt Isa; on the second occasion with the State Emergency Service (S.E.S.).

In addition to his Queensland police service, Vince was selected along with other Queensland police officers to be part of the Australian Police Contingent to act as a *'Peace Keeping Force'* for the U.N in Cyprus and served from 18 May, 1969 to 24 August, 1970. (UNCIVPOL)

On 9 April 1964, Vince was commended for good police work relative to the apprehension and arrest of two offenders on two charges of unlawfully using motor vehicles, one charge of breaking and entering, and four charges of stealing.

In retirement, he researched and published four books pertaining to policing in this State: *Riding the Plains in Poddy-Dodger Country, The Long Long Long Queensland Cattle Guard — 27/4/62 — 31/7/63, Tales of the Bullymen* (a collection of over 330 Queensland Police Stories) and *Packhorse Policemen.*

No doubt Vince used the basis of his extensive Queensland country service for the stories referred to in these valuable publications. A highly respected police officer, dedicated to his every day duties, Vince Walker is a household name in many Queensland outback towns.

Some years ago, I learnt that Vince and Carmel had retired to Brandon, North Queensland and on my way south from Cairns I stopped for a break at Brandon and decided it was an opportunity to visit Vince and renew our acquaintances. My efforts in locating him proved fruitless until I spoke to a` resident who said to me, "Which direction are you travelling?" "South," I replied. The lady then said, "Well, if you take the third street to the left and travel a couple of hundred yards up that street you will see a new house where the yard landscaping has not been completed. If you ask there the occupants may be able to help."

I walked to the front door and there was Vince, sitting at a table typing a document on his old typewriter. He was home by himself on that day. He looked at me and said, "How did you find me? I haven't been here that long, and no one knows me. The lady at the Post Office would not divulge that information and I haven't been to the pub so no one from there knows me either. How did you find me?"

I replied, "Vince, like you, I am a retired police officer, and down through the years have gained some knowledge on how to find people one is looking for."

With that Vince replied, "I never thought of it like that. Come in and take a seat." We then spent some considerable time talking about old times.

As Vince Walker said, "The name Les Hosier will continue to live on and be mentioned from time to time, for many years to come."

In the following story, I will endeavour to do justice to Vince Walker, Les Hosier and other members of the Hosier family. Les and his brother William were both Queensland Police Officers; their brother Ernest was killed in the First World War, aged 21 years. Les was a Prisoner of War in the Second World War and Brother Harold Hosier, a Brigadier with the Salvation Army Corps, was also a Prisoner of War in the Second World War.

Leslie Victor Hosier

Patriotic soldier and dedicated police officer from 1900 to 1967

Story by retired Senior Sergeant Vincent Augustine Walker

On 9 May, 1960, just eight weeks before I entered the police depot, Brisbane, a Senior Sergeant of police retired at Charleville after almost 32 and a half years of service for his state and country.

Part of his time in uniform included four years and seven months as a member of the A.I.F. (Australian Imperial Forces). His name was Les Hosier, who from all accounts was a colourful police officer, about whom many stories have been told over the years, some true and some untrue, so it is for both reasons that I am including this story, especially to dispel the myths that have been allowed to surround the late former Sergeant over a long period of time.

Leslie Victor Hosier was born at Booie, Nanango, Queensland, on the 9 May, 1900, being one of eight children of William and Sarah Hosier, who were graziers in the Booie district. His brother, William James Hosier, was also a member of the Queensland Police Force, attaining the rank of Sub-Inspector of Police. Prior to entering the police depot as a probationer on the 26 September, 1927, aged 27 years, Les Hosier was employed as a linesman by the then Post-Master General's Department (P.M.G.)

On being sworn in on the 22 December, 1927, Les Hosier was, as usual, transferred to Roma Street Station, after which he was transferred to Cloncurry on 6 July, 1928. Then followed a succession of transfers, all in the western and northern areas of the state, these being: Townsville (13/3/1930); Winton (20/4/1932); Tully 10/7/1933); Cairns 6/10/1934; Dimbulah (Temporary-19/10/1937); Cairns (24/2/1938.)

From Cairns, he was transferred on 29 June 1939 to Iron Range, where a gold mine was located, and a new police station recently constructed, which was opened by Constable Hosier. The present police station in that area is now called Lockhart River.

The Iron Range gold field, located approximately 150 miles (240km) north of Coen, was discovered by a prospector named Jack Gordon in 1933 and the main mine was named the Claudie River gold mine. Iron Range is located north of the present Lockhart River Community Settlement. In 1934, a 300 foot jetty was built in Portland Roads, being the sea port for the Iron Range gold field.

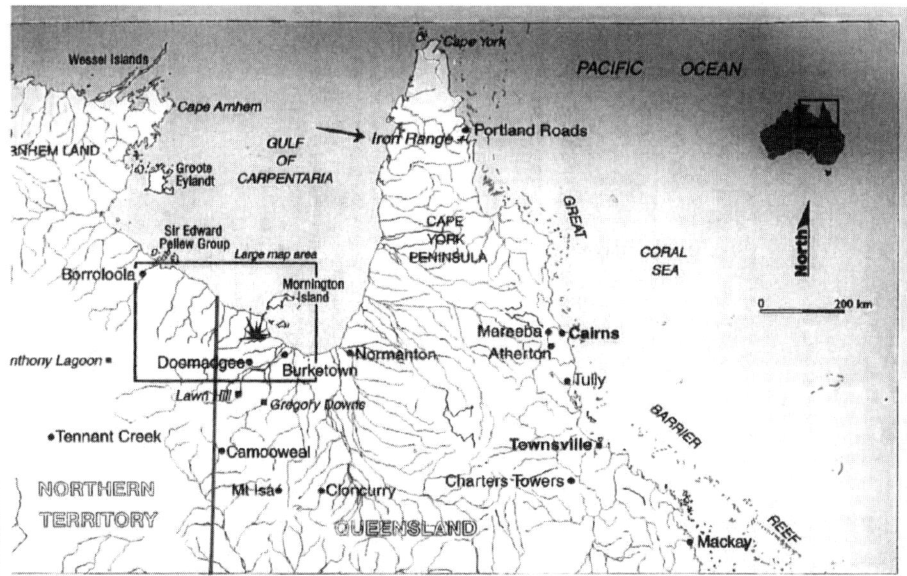

Iron Range has had a very colourful history, beginning with the visit by Captain Bligh in his long boat. Some features bear the names of his crew members. In 1848, the explorer Edmund Kennedy was in the area and members of his expedition were rescued from Weymouth Bay. During World War II, the area was taken over by the Australian and American Military and a very large aerodrome was built and connected to the port, Portland Road, by a sealed road. Extensive fortifications were constructed, and the areas were connected to the Australian telephone system via a line 60 miles (96km) long to the Peninsula Overland Telegraph Line.

Les Hosier's penchant for temporarily leaving the Queensland Police Force and joining the A.I.F first surfaced in June, 1941. It would appear that his brother Harold, who later became a Brigadier in the Salvation Army, had joined the A.I.F sometime after the outbreak of W.W.II in 1939. However, while serving with the Australian troops in Greece, he was taken Prisoner of War.

In a police report from Iron Range dated 17 June, 1940, when making his application for permission to join the Australian Imperial Forces for service abroad, he stated that he was a returned soldier, which is believed to have been towards the end of W.W.I, with the Armistice being signed on 11 November, 1918.

It is said that at 17 years of age he took part in the historic "March for Freedom," which started at Stanthorpe, passed through part of the Darling Downs, then on to Boonah, before finishing in Brisbane. This march was held to seek recruits for the first A.I.F.

As Les Hosier was born in May, 1900 and was 17 at the time of the famous march, it would seem that the march was held in 1917, which I was always under the impression that it was held in 1915. Irrespective of when the march was conducted, it would appear that Les Hosier put up his age to join the Australian Army and be part of his country's military force in W.W.I.

As well as his application to enlist in the A.I.F, a separate application was furnished on the same date, requesting that he be granted leave without pay for the duration of the War, if his first application was successful.

His application for leave of absence without pay for the duration of the War, was refused by Commissioner Carroll vide in his memorandum to Inspector B. Honan, of Cairns, dated 21 June, 1940.

On having his initial application for leave without pay rejected, Constable Hosier remained at Iron Range for over 12 months, until July,1941, when he tendered his resignation from the Queensland Police Force, giving the customary three months' notice required by the relevant police regulation, but requesting that this requirement be waived. The resignation was accepted by Commissioner Carroll and he was discharged from the police force at Cairns on 31 August, 1941. The Iron Range Station was officially closed on 24 August, 1941, having operated for only a little over two years.

On 25 August, 1941, the first and last Officer-in-Charge of Police at Iron Range, Constable Leslie Victor Hosier, left for Cairns from Portland Roads on the steamship S.S. Wandana, taking with him all government property that had been on issue at Iron Range Station. Constable Hosier arrived at Cairns on 27 August 1941.

During the five days that he was at Cairns prior to his resignation date, the Constable performed his duty at that station, handing over all government property that he had brought with him from Iron Range, as well as attending to business on behalf of other Departments that he had previously represented. He also furnished a report to the effect that prior to departing from Iron Range, he had securely locked the building, and arranged with a Mr. A.G.Thompson of Iron Range, to give the premises attention and prevent any unauthorised person from interfering with it.

Well, it is not known what Mr. Thompson was doing the following year, 1942. Perhaps he was out fishing at Portland's Road on the night in question when the former Iron Range Police Station disappeared overnight, without a trace to be seen the following morning.

As is well known, after the bombing of Pearl Harbour by the Japanese on 7 December, 1941, the American Army and Air Force arrived in Australian *en masse* and soon afterwards centred on Iron Range to build airstrips for their Liberator long range bombers to operate in the Coral Sea area. It is believed that they had their eyes on the unoccupied police station.

However, the Australian troops who were also camped in the area were aware of this, and one night quietly removed it to Portland Roads and shipped it out to a base in New Guinea. The Americans were furious when they arrived the next day with removal equipment to find the police station missing. Not even a stump was left.

On resigning from the Police Force, Les Hosier had 69 days of recreation leave due to him, as from the 1/9/1941 to 8/11/1941, inclusive; however, having a much-earned holiday after being in an isolated area for quite some time was the last thing that was on his mind. Records show that on 10 September, 1941, only ten days after leaving the Queensland Police Force, Les Hosier finally reached his goal when he was accepted into the A.I.F., aged forty-one years.

After a period of training, his regiment was moved to Singapore, which was where he was stationed when Singapore fell to the Japanese in February 1942. He spent the remainder of the War in a Japanese Prisoner of War Camp in Malaya, including time on the infamous Burma Railway Line. He went into the Army weighing a solid 15 stone (95.5kg) and on release his weight was eight stone (51kg). He was discharged from the Army on 5 February 1946.

On 1 April 1946, less than two months after his discharge, Leslie Victor Hosier was re-sworn in as a Constable in the Queensland Police Force and was stationed at Roma Street. At that time, his previous 13 years and eight months service was credited to him, with respect to pay, seniority and superannuation. On 30 June 1946, while at Roma Street Station, he was promoted to the rank of Sergeant Second Class.

However, shortly afterwards on 7 August 1946, he was transferred to Longreach, where he stayed for eleven years and nine months, being promoted to Sergeant First Class at that station on 10 August 1953. On 6 May 1958, he was transferred to Charleville where he was promoted to the rank of Senior Sergeant on 16 June 1958. As mentioned at the beginning of this story, Senior Sergeant Les Hosier retired from Charleville aged 60 years, on 9 May 1960.

I hate to be a spoil sport, but now for the task of dispelling one of the myths that have surrounded the name Les Hosier for years. In my case it was while I was a probationer at the Police Depot, where I purposely mentioned at the beginning that I first heard of the exploits of Les Hosier, and over the years the story of his going to the Second World War without permission has continued to grow. It is a good story, but simply is NOT TRUE.

The true facts of him going through the correct procedure to finally achieve his apparent burning desire to enlist in the A.I.F. during Second World War have been clearly documented in this story, with all details being transcribed from relevant police reports furnished by me. To confirm the authenticity of the facts contained herein, a copy of a report by Inspector B. Horan, District Officer at Cairns at the time to the Commissioner of Police, is being included for the information of readers, along with other relevant reports.

On his retirement, Les Hosier and his wife, Mary moved to Scarborough; however, in mid March 1967, Les Hosier, aged 67 years passed away, and a few days later he was buried at the Pinnaroo Lawn Cemetery, Bridgeman Downs. On the following Sunday, 19 March 1967 an article appeared in the then *Sunday Truth* weekly concerning the late Leslie Victor Hosier, written by The Truth's police reporter, Brian Bolton, in which there were many inaccuracies.

The most glaring of these mentioned was the reference to Les Hosier going off to War without permission, which in my opinion, although the article may not have started the rumour, more likely fuelled it to a great extent over the years, to the point until now it has been accepted as "*The Gospel.*"

After reading the true account of what happened at Iron Range and Cairns back in 1940 and 1941, now read part of the Sunday Truth's version, published in March 1967, and I quote — "He asked permission of the then Police Commissioner, Mr Cec Carroll to enlist. Permission denied. The Commissioner thought Sgt Hosier could serve his country better by remaining where he was. So, Les Hosier locked up the Iron Range Police Station — which he had been sent to open two years earlier — took all the keys and correspondence and dumped them on the desk of the Police Inspector at Townsville." End of quote.

The first small error is that at the time Les Hosier held the rank of Constable and not Sergeant. However, the obvious falsehood in the story is where it is stated that all items taken from Iron Range Station, apparently without permission, were left on the Inspector's desk at Townsville and not at Cairns, which was the District Headquarters for Iron Range station and still is for the area.

It is 600 kilometres from Iron Range to Cairns and a further approximant 350 kilometres from Cairns to Townsville. Travelling to Cairns would have been far enough, without having to go to Townsville with Government property.

It is surprising the number of police and former police officers who have heard of the Les Hosier story. They may not know his name, but when the subject is aired, they immediately say something like this, "Is that the bloke who locked up the police station up north, took everything into his Inspector and went off to War?" They add, "And they let him rejoin the job when he came back."

The latest edition to this fantasy was told to me about 18 months ago here at Bamaga, of all places, by a former Queensland Police Officer. When talking about the O/C at Iron Range during the War (he didn't know his name), he said that he had heard that when the O/C locked up his station during the War and went away to join the Army without permission, he first typed his monthly returns in advance.

He then gave them to the Postmaster to forward to the District Officer each month. I trust they would have all been "Nil Returns," which would have become a 'little suspicious' to the Inspector, after a while. Takes a bit of beating, don't you think?

Although I did not ever meet Les Hosier, I do know two former police officers, Tom Powell and Geoff Leeson, now in Townsville, who both worked with him at Longreach during the 1940s and 1950s respectively; both Tom and Geoff spoke highly of him.

As a young Constable, Tom Powell was very impressed with Sergeant Les Hosier during his time at Longreach after the War. At that time there was quite a number of larrikins (these days they would be called louts or hoons) roaming the streets of Longreach and Les Hosier, although he wasn't a well man after his ordeal as a Prisoner of War, soon put an end to their shenanigans with a little summary justice meted out in a diplomatic manner.

While at Longreach, Sergeant Hosier used to recall his time at Iron Range, and Tom Powell remembers well two stories that Les related to him.

It appears that two or three miners from the gold mine had an altercation with Constable Hosier, during which they threatened to throw him off a cliff and into the blue waters of the Pacific far below. On another occasion, Les had a feeling that his water tank had been tampered with, but he wasn't sure. Shortly afterwards, his dog drank some water from the tank and died. It was believed that the water had been poisoned. Apparently, they didn't muck around at Iron Range in those days.

From all accounts, Leslie Victor Hosier was a good bloke, as well as being a colourful police officer, who was well known for looking after the underdog, and for handing the down-and-out a quid or two.

There is a book, that is, or was, in circulation called "Battlers of the Bush. The Batavia Goldfields of Cape York" by William Joseph (Joe) Fisher, in which there is a reference to one Leslie Victor Hosier. If you are interested, a check of our bookshop, if you are lucky, or your local library, might be successful.

On reflection, as well as looking forward after a glance into my mystical "Crystal ball," I am sure that even though, hopefully, some of the false mystique has been removed from the "Les Hosier Stories," his name will continue to live on and be mentioned from time to time, for many years to come.

Vince Walker

Cairns District
Iron Range Station
17th. June 1940

Application by Constable L.V.Hosier Reg.No. 2985 for leave of absence without pay for the duration of the present War.

Sir/ I have to request that I be granted leave without pay for the duration of the present War.

I am at present in charge of Iron Range Police Station, and feel that it is my duty to enlist in the A.I.F. for service aboard, and desire leave for the period I anticipate being absent on such duty.

In the event of this application receiving your favourable consideration, I respectfully request that I be granted leave from the 1.9.1940, which will provide ample time for the necessary arrangements to be made regarding my relief, and the finalisation of my Police duties generally at Iron Range.

L.V. Hosier
Constable 2985
The Inspector of Police
Cairns

Cairns District
Iron Range Station
17th. June 1940

Application by Constable L.V.Hosier Reg.No.2985 of Iron Range Station for permission to enlist in the A.I.F. for services abroad.

Sir/

I beg to request that I be granted permission to enlist in the A.I.F for services abroad.

I am a returned soldier, and would again like to offer my services to the country in the present world crisis.

I am at present in charge of Iron Range Station, and am the complainant in three Police Court summonses set down for hearing at Iron Range on 4.8.40, and on completion of such cases I desire to enlist in the A.I.F.

In a separate report I am making application for leave without pay for the duration of the present War, and in the event of such application being not approved, I respectfully request that my resignation as a member of the Queensland Police Force be accepted from 1.9.40.

I am loathe tendering my resignation as a member of the Queensland Police Force but feeling that it is my duty to offer my services to my country by enlisting in the A.I.F. for service abroad, and would appreciate your consideration in permitting me to re-join the Police Force on my return from active service.

L.V. Hosier
Constable 2985

21st. June, 1943
MEMORANDUM
Inspector of Police,
Cairns

With reference to your B/C of the 17th instant, forwarding an application by Constable L.V.Hosier, No 2985, for leave of absence, without pay, or the duration of the War, you are advised that I am not prepared to grant leave of absence at present.

C.J. Carroll
Commissioner
The Inspector of Police
Cairns

H.H
QUEENSLAND POLICE
RESIGNATION
Police Station
Iron Range

Constable L.V.Hosier Reg.No.2895
Begs to give three months' Notice to Resign his Office
As a Constable in the Queensland Police Force.

The Constable, however applies that his resignation be accepted before the expiration of three months notice, if satisfactory arrangements can be made regarding relief, as I am desirous of offering my services to the Country to serve with the A.I.F. abroad, with the least possible delay.

REPORT ATTACHED

Signature L.V.Hosier
Constable No 2895

29th. July,1941
Memorandum

Inspector of Police
CAIRNS

In confirmation of my telegram of the 28th instant, you are advised that Iron Range Police Station is to be closed. Constable Hosier should return to the Station, and arrange for the removal of all Government property from there to Cairns Police Station.

On his return to Cairns his resignation is accepted, as desired.

Report the date on which he is discharged on resignation and pay up to and including that date, less any proper deductions. He would appear to be due for 83 days leave.

C J Carroll
Commissioner

Commissioner of Police
BRISBANE
10th. September, 1941

Sir,

With reference to your memorandum dated 29th. July, 1941, Ref. No.2985 F 61, respecting the closing of Iron Range Station, and the resignation of Constable L.V.Hosier, No 2985, who was in charge of that Station, I have the honour to report that Constable Hosier arrived at Cairns on the 27/8/41, per the S.S.Wandana, and brought with him all Government property from his Station.

From the 27th to the 31/8/41 he performed duty at Cairns in connection with the handing over of property and business on behalf of other Government Departments. His resignation was accepted as from the 31/8/41 and he commenced on (69) days Recreation leave on the 1st. instant. This leave extends to the 8/11/41 and represents the whole of the Recreation leave due to him. Salary and Allowances were paid to him from this office up to and including the 8/11/41, and the voucher covering the payment was forwarded to the Accountant, Police Department on the 8th. Instant.

Constable Hosier has furnished a report to the effect that prior to departing from Iron Range he securely locked the building and arranged with a Mr.A.C.Thompson of Iron Range, to give the premises attention and prevent any unauthorised person from interfering with same.

The Constable's Record of Conduct and Service Sheet will be forwarded you in the course of a few days

I have the honour to be,

Sir,

Your obedient Servant
B.Horan
Inspector

For many years, it was the responsibility of the police department to escort people suffering from mental illness from outback Queensland to places such as Rockhampton and Townsville, to name just two locations. The method of travel was by rail and, I might add, in a second-class railway carriage. Should the patient be a female, the senior sergeant or the senior office in charge of the particular establishment had the responsibility of securing the services of a female escort to accompany the escorting male constable. (There were no female police officers stationed outside Brisbane in those days.)

Both the constable and the escorting female wore plain clothes so that they could not be identified by the other rail passengers as people in authority. If possible, the services of an off-duty nurse or a female with nursing experience was the preferred option.

In Volume Three of Keeping the Peace, the late Kevin Robert Guthridge in his story tells of being stationed at Cloncurry in the year 1954. It was at Cloncurry where Kevin met his wife and mother of their six children, Cynthia. Cynthia, a native of Victoria, was nursing at the Cloncurry District hospital and, being off duty for several days, agreed to be the escorting female.

Les Hosier's first posting as a newly sworn-in constable was Cloncurry on the 6 July 1928, and on 27 March 1929 he married Ailsa Doris Batterbee.

In August 1929, Ailsa Hosier was the female escort who accompanied Constable Hosier in escorting a female patient suffering from mental illness from Cloncurry to Townsville. In all probabilities Alisa, at the time of her marriage to Les, was nursing at the Cloncurry hospital and was the ideal female escort to undertake this arduous task.

The author in 1961/62, as a junior constable at Blackall, performed the duty of escorting a male mental patient from Blackall to Rockhampton on more than one occasion, and has some understanding of the discomfort and responsibility associated with such escorts. The rail journey from Cloncurry to Townsville is certainly much further than Blackall to Rockhampton.

In the years 1928/29, Cloncurry was the far western northern Police District; no doubt Burketown formed part of that district, so there is the possibility that both brothers at some stage performed duty together at Cloncurry.

October, 1934 saw Les Hosier stationed at Cairns. On the 23 June, 1935 Ailsa, accompanied by a female friend, was cycling along Freshwater Road when she collapsed. Conveyed to the Cairns District Hospital, she passed to eternal rest that same day.

Apparently Les Hosier was a staunch member of the Queensland Police Union of Employees, and there is a 1939 Queensland Police Union photograph of all branch members. Les Hosier's photograph appears in that photograph. The location of his photograph is unknown to me.

Several police officers dressed in their navy-blue uniforms formed a 'Guard of Honour' at Ailsa's funeral on Monday the 27 June, 1935. There were no children to the union.

After the death of Ailsa, Les remained single for many years, and on 7 June 1958 married Mary Jane Mahoney at St Stephens Cathedral, Brisbane. Mary is believed to have been the Licensee of an hotel at Barcaldine in western Queensland. At the time of their marriage, Les Hosier was 58 years of age. Mary outlived her husband and died in Brisbane on the 29 September, 1975. There were no children to the union.

On the 6 August, 1929, Les was accorded a favourable record while stationed at Cloncurry for good police work, in connection with the conviction of R.A.G.Tooloey and T.C.Graham for having in their possession beef reasonably suspected of having been stolen.

On the 26 November, 1929, Leslie Victor Hosier, police constable of Cloncurry, was fined one pound ($2.00) for assaulting William Little. Due to the interest in the particular matter, the courtroom was packed with spectators.

In the month of August, 1928, he was granted a` reward of FIVE POUNDS ($10-00) by Aerolax Blinds Ltd for good work in conjunction with Constable Voigt in the arrest of three men for stealing Road advertising signs.

In August 1928, Constable Leslie Hosier was stationed at Cloncurry; the good police work performed in conjunction with Constable Voigt in all probability occurred while Hosier was stationed at Roma Street Police Station in 1927. The Constable Voigt mentioned would no doubt be the late Superintendent Jim Voigt who had a distinguished career with the Queensland Police Force.

In the year 1931, he is mentioned as having arrested an Italian cane cutter for assaulting a woman with a pocketknife. At the time Constable Hosier was stationed at Townsville, so no doubt the offence and arrest occurred within the Townville police district.

In 1933 at Tully, North Queensland, Constable Hosier is mentioned when he carried out smart detective work to establish that a man cut off his own finger and lodged a compensation claim.

On the 16 August, 1935, Les was accorded a favourable record for good police work, in conjunction with other police officers, in connection with the search for and arrest of five aboriginals on a charge of murdering another aboriginal in the Mt Garnet district.

I did as Vince Walker suggested, and through my local Gympie Library obtained a copy of the book *"Battlers in the Bush" — The Batavia Goldfield of Cape York — Author Joe Fisher.*

Joe Fisher spent many years with the Mining Industry, and on page sixty-eight of that book has this to say:

"On one trip to Portland's Road with Eleanor, baby Jef and Mabs, we were running late and it was raining heavily. The prospect of a wet camp late at night was not appealing. A modern police station had recently been built at Iron Range at the junction of the road with the Lockhart River Mission road in verdant rain forest.

We called on the police officer, Les Hosier, to say hello and he invited us to stay and occupy the cells overnight. They were clean and dry and hadn't yet been occupied, and we could use his kitchen facilities. The offer was too good to refuse so we accepted, and this was the start of a good, but short-term friendship. Les later enlisted and his unit was stationed at Singapore and he was captured. Apparently he was feared by the Japanese and they treated him badly, destroying his manhood during captivity."

Apparently a Mr. W.S.Patterson, C.O.P. of the C.Club, H.M.A.S. Penguin, Sydney, New South Wales, was enquiring as to the whereabouts of Les Hosier shortly after the War had ended. In a report furnished by his brother, Sub-Inspector William Hosier, on the 4 January, 1946 when he (William) was the Officer-In-Charge of the Bundaberg Sub-District, he stated that his brother (Leslie Victor) at that time was a patient at Greenslopes Military Hospital, Brisbane, and was occupying bed 25 in Ward number 18. At this stage I have not unearthed any further information regarding the hospitalisation period for Les Hosier. No doubt after being a Prisoner of War for many years, hospitalisation was a necessary requirement when former prisoners returned to Australian soil.

When Les Hosier arrived on transfer at Longreach, he found himself serving in possibly one of the largest police divisions in the State of Queensland and being a single man, he spent a considerable period of his service as a relieving officer for that district. Over the next eleven years he performed relieving duty at locations such as Winton, Muttaburra, Ilfracombe, Barcaldine, and Blackall.

Former Cooloola Regional Council Mayor, Mick Venardos O.A.M., grew up in Blackall where his family operated a café and an hotel. Mick remembers

Les performing duty in that town in the late 1940s. Mick was aged in the 13/14 year age group, and Sergeant Hosier made a huge impression on the young future Queensland police officer. "Les frequented the café almost on a daily basis, where he would stand in the same spot every time and order a vanilla milk shake with two scoops of ice cream," said Mick.

Mick remembers that Les Hosier was well known and highly respected in the Blackall district, where it was a known fact that he was as former Prisoner of War. He had almost a hero status and stories from his past life abounded.

Two stories in particular impressed the young Mick Venardos about Les Hosier. One was about the sale of the Iron Range police station building. "It was rumoured," said Mick, "that when Commissioner Carroll refused him permission for leave of absence to join the A.I.F., Hosier sold the police station building, typed out his resignation, collected all Government property and travelled by train to Brisbane where he entered the Police Commissioner's office and placed his possessions on the Commissioner's desk."

Another story that abounded about this colourful police officer had him joining the American Army and sailing off to War. When peace was declared, it was rumoured that Hosier returned to Brisbane on an American war ship only to be met by a senior Queensland police office with a warrant for his arrest. Upon the intervention of the Ship's American Captain, the warrant was not executed.

After reading the research undertaken by the late Senior Sergeant Vince Walker into the life of Leslie Victor Hosier, it is apparent that folk law of this nature regarding Hosier is not true.

Retired Assistant Commissioner of Police, Lawrence Noel Witham, has fond memories of working with Les Hosier at Longreach, who at that time was the young Constable's superior officer.

This is Lawrie's memory of those long-ago days at Longreach Police District from more than 60 years ago:

One April day in 1957, I stepped off the Midlander train at Longreach Railway Station, where I was greeted by Constable Brian Webb, who then drove me to the Police Station. On arrival I reported to the Officer in Charge, Senior Sergeant George Pflugradt, then recently promoted to Sub-Inspector rank, and whose departure on transfer was imminent. In the scheme of things, Sergeant 1/c Les Hosier was the appointee to the acting Officer in Charge.

I soon became acquainted with Sergeant Hosier, an experienced and competent N.C.O and a seasoned bush policeman then nudging retirement. I had come face to face with a legendary figure whose police and military history is so well documented as to require but little future reference by this writer. For my part, I was a green and inexperienced first year Constable, of the full age of nineteen years, and then the most junior staff member attached to the Longreach Police District. As time passed, a correct, although friendly, working relationship developed between us, but to no greater level than that enjoyed by my peer group.

In my initial settling in period, I learned that among junior staff Les was affectionately known as "Dad," but I do not recollect anyone addressing him by that name. "Dad" was a well-deserved nickname as both on and off duty he was a fatherly figure — helpful and supportive, passing on the distilled wisdom of his years; but that is not to say he was always placid, far from it. If in his opinion a junior man had committed an act or omission deserving of censure, Les was capable of delivering an oral admonition commensurate with his perception of the misdeed; but very sharp "needles" were rare, and once delivered, forgotten and not resurrected. (I pause at this stage to avoid self-incrimination.)

Les, a widower, resided in barracks. He occupied a single room, situated within hearing distance of the room I shared with Brian Webb (retired as a Superintendent; sadly now deceased). Les always slept with the electric light turned on. It was noticeable that he suffered a disturbed and irregular sheep pattern, tossing round in bed, often mumbling. At times he experienced a nightmare accompanied by thrashing arm movements. On occasions, it was necessary for the sole Constable working the 10 pm to 6 am shift to wake Les to report a major incident or to seek advice. Staff knew to call Les from the bedroom doorway and not to approach his bed, as he would throw wild punches when his sleep was interrupted.

I have no recollection of Les ever discussing the mental demons which tormented him; or of the horrors he experienced as a Prisoner of War, although he often spontaneously recounted past events associated with his police service.

Staff assumed — reasonably I would say — that his bedroom behaviour was an unfortunate legacy of years of mistreatment while a Prisoner of War.

The descriptors, post-traumatic stress disorder, together with the abbreviated form, PTSD, had not yet come into vogue.

A feature which distinguishes Longreach town today, from that of yesteryear, is the absence of the wandering goat herd that roamed unsupervised through the streets. These were domesticated animals kept for the purpose of supplying milk and meat for the benefit of respective family owners. As a general practice, the animals were released each morning — having been penned overnight, free to wander the town by day, and ever foraging for greenery to satisfy a voracious appetite. Some residents considered them a pest, especially when house gardens were raided.

However, the Longreach Shire Council of the time took a lenient view; but not so Les, who was far from unforgiving, as I was soon to discover. It was not unusual for the roaming goats to enter the police yard and camp under the low-set station building to find shade during the heat of the day. This caused annoyance to the human occupants above. The repetitive noise of horns scraping against floorboards, coupled with the sound of bleating animals, was irritating and distracting. One memory transcends all others.

A much vexed Les vacated the O/C's office and entered the barrack accommodation. In retrospect, I don't believe he singled me out; perhaps I was the first off-duty Constable he sighted. Even to this day I vividly recall his asking me if I owned a .22 rifle. Upon my answering in the affirmative, Les then instructed me to dispatch two intruding animals. In just a few words, Les's short discourse combined elements of goat anatomy, marksmanship and firearm safety, respect for higher rank and a short dissertation on Queensland legislation.

In essence, I was advised to aim an angled shot at the butt of the ear — not the bony forehead; to be careful and exercise safety; not to shoot Les through the floorboards and further, the proposed cull was lawful under the provisions of the Animals Protection Act. Soon afterwards, with mission accomplished, two lifeless wether goats were dragged out from under the building, to be later removed by Council workmen — Les had been quick to make a telephone call.

In another memory of Les, I recall the practical side of his nature, perhaps best illustrated by the innovative way he cleaned the accumulated dust and crud from his old Remington typewriter. After dispensing with the ribbon,

Les would carry his typewriter into the police station yard, whereupon he liberally doused the inner mechanism with petrol!

One negative feature of our barrack accommodation was the lack of cooking facilities — a rusted hulk of a wood fuel stove, far beyond redemption, adorned the kitchen. I recall Les making determined, but unsuccessful, efforts to obtain a replacement electric stove. His endeavours through official channels and the Police Union failed to untie the tight purse strings of an unsympathetic Public Works Department. All but one barrack resident purchased their meals at either the Lyceum or Royal Hotel. The late Gavin Bishop cooked his breakfast and evening meal in the open yard adjacent to the barracks and out of public view. One remaining memory is of Gavin grilling a steak on an upturned camp oven lid on top of an improvised firebox fashioned from a four-gallon kerosene tin.

During his tenure within the Longreach Police District, Les accumulated considerable relieving experience as Officer in Charge of N.C.O. stations, first as Sergeant 2/c and later, as Sergeant 1/c level, following his promotion to that rank. He made many friends over time and was widely known and respected. It was not uncommon for an out-of-town person to call at Longreach Station to visit Les. The same level of respect existed in Longreach, especially by returned veterans of World War I I.

My retrospective of Les would be incomplete without mention of some snippets associated with his private life. He was a generous person who was not backward in assisting genuine people who had fallen on hard times. He was sociable and sought company off duty.

He was partial to sharing a cold drink with his mates at the Welcome Home Hotel and he often travelled to Barcaldine on his rest days to enjoy the company of other friends. Les was a keen supporter of the Longreach volunteer fire brigade. He owned a Holden utility and always visible on the tray floor would be an axe, a shovel and a well stocked tucker box. He was fond of imported tinned salmon. Les had an abiding interest in pony breeding, keeping brood mares at a nearby property. Hopefully, these short snapshots of Les provide the reader with a brief insight into the private life of a man for whom I had the greatest respect.

As our respective police careers continued to unfold, both Les and I departed Longreach on transfer at about the same time — our paths never crossed again. Les moved on promotion to Charleville as Senior Sergeant and I was transferred to Muttaburra, then a two-man station.

The late Neal Murphy was a life-long friend of Les Hosier, who was his mentor during Murphy's early police career. He spoke of him with admiration, referring to him as either 'dad' or 'pop.' Murphy was stationed at Barcaldine for many years when Hosier was stationed at Longreach, and no doubt they performed duty together on many occasions.

On the 25 October, 1950- Sergeant 2/c L.V.Hosier. Longreach, Senior Constable W.A.Stewart, Blackall, Constable N Murphy, Barcaldine and Constable N.W.H. Richard-Preston and Constable A.C.Ross, Blackall were commended for good police work regarding the arrest and committal for trial of Gordon Douglas and Frederick Charles Goodman, on a charge of stealing 64 wethers.

This is conclusive proof that Hosier and Murphy did perform duty on occasions within the Longreach Police District.

This is what Neal Murphy related in regards to Les Hosier.

After enlisting in the A.I.F., Les Hosier was shipped off to Singapore. Shortly afterwards, the British surrendered to the Japanese, with the result that Hosier and others were taken as Prisoners of War and incarcerated at the notorious Changi Prison Camp where he remained until Peace was declared. Prior to departing Australia, it was rumoured that Hosier sold the Iron Range police station building to the "Yanks."

It was also rumoured that when the Japanese surrendered, Hosier and other prisoners were on parade when he (Hosier) gained possession of a weapon (type unknown) and was alleged to have killed or injured a number of Japanese guards.

On returning to Australian soil, it was rumoured that people in authority wanted to take action against Hosier over the alleged sale of the Iron Range police building to the Americans; however, he had cemented strong relationships with senior Military Personnel during his time at Changi and no such action was forthcoming.

Neal Murphy was of the view that his wartime record was taken into account when he rejoined the Queensland Police Force, and he was immediately promoted to Sergeant Second Class. This is not true as Hosier had qualified for the rank of sergeant prior to resigning to join the A.I.F. and, on rejoining, his previous service was taken into account when he was promoted to sergeant and transferred to Longreach.

Upon retirement, Leslie Victor Hosier and his wife Mary retired to Scarborough in close proximity to Redcliffe. Sergeant Neal Murphy was stationed at Redcliffe from 1970 to 1973 and there they renewed their friendship and kept in constant touch with each other. Murphy said that Hosier had taken a part time job at one of the hotels on the peninsula, where he was engaged in operating the bottle shop. His duties were attending to customers and wrapping beer bottles in newspaper, it being then customary for hotels to wrap cold bottles of beer in newspaper prior to placing them in the cool room.

Redcliffe generally being a windy location, a palm sized stone was placed on top of the newspaper to prevent it from blowing away. One day Les was confronted by an armed male endeavouring to rob the bottle shop of their daily takings. Hosier immediately took hold of the large stone and clouted the offender on the side of head, rendering him unconscious on the driveway.

It is not known if any action was taken against the offender or Hosier.

William James, the eldest male in the Hosier family, was born on the 3 October, 1887 and joined the Queensland Police Force as a recruit on the 21 July, 1909 at age 21 years and eleven months. Sworn in on the 1 October, 1909, he served extensively throughout Queensland, both city and country,

Leslie Victor Hosier passed to eternal rest on the 15 March, 1967 and his body was interred at the Pinnaroo Lawn Cemetery, Bridgeman Downs, and Brisbane.

and retired at age limit on 3 October 1947. At the time of his retirement, he held the rank of Sub-Inspector and was in charge of the Bundaberg Police Sub-District. In the year 1947, Maryborough was the main Police District and Bundaberg came under the control of that District.

During his police career, William Hosier received some 14 transfers as far north as Burketown in the Gulf country.

Commissioner Whitrod, shortly after his appointment in the 1960s, abolished the rank of Sub-Inspector of police and those who held that rank automatically became Inspectors.

Ernest, the second youngest Hosier male, was born on the 27 May 1896 and enlisted in the 42nd Battalion, D Company on 30 September 1915, aged 19 years. His unit embarked from Sydney, New South Wales, on board HMATS A30 Borda on 5 June 1916. Ernest was killed in action On the 4 October 1917 at Passchendaele, Ypres, Belgium. He has no known grave.

Ernest Hosier's name was projected onto the exterior of the Hall of Memory, Australian War Memorial, Canberra, A.C.T. in 2020.

As mentioned by the late Vince Walker, the Hosier family originated from the Booie district near Nanango, Queensland. Additional material shows that their father William was a fencer by occupation, working for a Mr Youngman in the district of Nanango and actually fenced the property called 'Kingaroy' before the township of Kingaroy was established.

The fourth child in the family of eight, Harold Hosier, was born at Kingaroy on 7 June, 1892 and left school at age 14 years to become a '*carpenter*' on the same property where his father worked.

In July 1907 Harold made his commitment to God at the Kingaroy Salvation Army Corps and gave service to the Corps until entering the Melbourne Training College on 30 May, 1914.

His first appointment back in Queensland (Eastern Territory) was to the Prison Gate Brigade, the forerunner of the now Corrective Service Department, then administered through the Men's Social Department. Throughout his distinguished career, Harold had a long association with the Riverview Boys Training Home, Eventide Homes, Industrial Homes, Boys Homes and the People's Palace, where he always displayed a caring spirit, endearing himself to both staff and clientele. His longest serving appointments were with the Red Shield War Service and the Stanley Street Men's home in Brisbane.

Harold was appointed as the Red Shield representative to the 16th Australian Infantry Brigade on 30 December, 1939. He sailed with the originals of the 2/2nd Battalion which was part of the 16th Australian Brigade, which in turn was part of the 6th Division, on 9 January, 1940 for the Middle East.

He served in Palestine from February 1940 until 14 September, 1940, and then on 15 September 1940 was transferred with his Brigade to Egypt and Libya for six months service.

In March of 1941, the Brigade was located in Greece where it came under heavy attack, and together with other survivors, Harold was taken Prisoner of War on 28 April 1941. On the day in question Harold Hosier was offered a seat on the last aeroplane out of the country by Major Cedric Edgar, but the plane had insufficient room for the 30 or so soldiers with him.

Harold refused the invitation and stated his intentions of remaining with his men, knowing full well it meant being captured by the Germans and becoming a Prisoner of War. A communiqué received at the Territorial Headquarters read "... Major Harold Hosier remained a prisoner in German hands. He was last seen by a Captain of the Unit — down on his knees helping a wounded digger."

Kr.-Gef. Offizierlager IX A Ausgestellt: Spangenberg

Hauptlager

~~Zweiglager~~ , am 8.7 194

Kennkarte für Kriegsgefangene

Nur gültig für den Lagerbetrieb und in Verbindung mit der

Erk.-Marke Nr. 119 Oflag V B

Dienstgrad: Geistlicher (Hauptm.)

Name: Hosier

Vorname: Harold

Lichtbild

119

Zur Beachtung!

Die Kennkarte dient als Ausweis der Krf. gegenüber den Organen der deutschen Lagerkommandantur. Sie ist wie die Erk.-Marke stets mitzuführen u. mit dieser auf Verlangen bei namentlichen Appells und beim Verlassen des Lagers vorzuweisen.

Verlust ist sofort zu melden.

Der Kommandant

Red Shield Representative Harold Hosier's German Prisoner of War identity card

After his release from the German Prisoner of War Camp and returning to civilian life in Australia, Harold's Representative, John McCabe, who was transferred to the 16th Brigade to take over Harold Hosier's responsibilities, recalled being told of Harold's plight:

Harold Hosier had gathered a number of fellows together and was looking after them. Major Cedric Edgar caught up with him near where they had to rendezvous. The 21/C said, "Look Harold, if you'd like to come with me, I can get you out." Harold says, "What about these other fellows?" The 21/C answers, "No. I can't take any more. I can only take you with me." So old Harold says, "If these fellows can't go, I can't go; because my responsibility is to look after these fellows!"

From the book — Cuppa Tea, Digger- Salvos serving in World War Two-Author- Lindsay Cox

Back on Australian soil, Harold Hosier resumed his Salvation Army career and retired with the rank of Major. In the period of the late 1950s and early 1960s, Major Hosier would be seen at the Brisbane number one Magistrates Court (Court of Petty Sessions) and provide assistance to those homeless people who had been charged mainly with drunkenness and Street offences and other individuals less fortunate than himself.

The four male members of the Hosier family had a remarkable life and gave service not only to their home State, but to our Nation.

William James Hosier, a Queensland Police Officer, served with distinction for almost 37 years; Ernest Hosier killed in the First World War, aged 21 years; Leslie Victor Hosier, served briefly in the First World War and then as a Queensland Police Officer, a Private with the A.I.F. in the second World War and Prisoner of War and once Peace was declared again a member of the Queensland Police Force where he served until retirement at age 60 years; and finally Major Harold Hosier, a career member of the Salvation Army Corps and also a Prisoner of War in the Second World War.

Kenneth James Salmon

I arrived at Cairns as the District Superintendent some eight months after Ken Salmon was promoted and transferred to Maryborough. During my 12 months in that northern part of our State, I visited Cooktown and the local police officers on a number of occasions and can relate to the difficulties that law enforcement officers are confronted with in the far northern parts of Queensland. During my years as a serving officer, I never had the privilege of working with Ken and we never met until we became associated through the Retired Police Association at both the Sunshine Coast and Gympie.

Ken had a wealth of experience and served this State with distinction, both as a city and country police officer. As a leader of staff, he commanded the respect of his subordinates and did the Service proud in the role of community policing. Ken is an excellent communicator and commanded the respect of both his superiors and subordinates. He chose not to seek promotion to 'Commissioned Rank', and retired with the rank of Senior Sergeant of police.

Laurie Pointing

Kenneth John Salmon Story
(AKA Sockeye)

"You tell your dear lovely mother that square cuts are not allowed here."

I was born in Brisbane on the 7th July 1949. My parents owned a 10-acre small crops hobby farm at Gumdale, Brisbane and when I was eight years old, moved to a five-acre hobby farm at Kallangur, north of Brisbane. My father worked for Massey Ferguson tractors. I attended Kallangur State School and later Redcliffe High School where I completed grade 10 in 1964. After completing my schooling, I worked on a sheep station at Durong, west of Brisbane, as a general roustabout for nine months before gaining employment as an apprentice boilermaker for Transteel in Brisbane.

Upon reaching 19 years of age, I applied to join the Queensland Police Force. I was accepted and entered the old Petrie Terrace Police Depot in November, 1968. I must admit, it was a bit of a culture shock for me as I was a bit of a larrakin at that time. My sports were surfboard riding and rugby league football. There has been a lot said about the legendary Sergeant

Tom Molloy by previous retired officers in other editions of these books, so I will only comment on a few incidents that related to me personally.

The first time was during an inspection parade. I had a crew-cut hairdo on going into the depot but had the back of my neck shaved square. Tom immediately noticed, and told me that only bodgies had square cuts and bodgies were not allowed to join the police force. He asked me who had cut my hair, so I thought quickly and said: "My mother, Sergeant." Tom said, "You tell your dear lovely mother that square cuts are not allowed here." He then sent me to the barber to have it rectified.

On another occasion, we were at Ithaca Pool for swimming and were instructed by Tom to make three lines lengthways by the pool. He then instructed the first rank of three persons into the pool. I was second on the left in the front line. When I surfaced Tom said, "Where do you think you are going, Salmon?" I replied, "In the pool, Sergeant." He said, "That meant the first three men in line. That would be typical of you son, Salmon by name, Salmon by nature."

I was sworn into the Police Force on the 20th February 1969 as a Constable and allocated Reg No 7835. I was transferred to Petrie (my home area) on training. My first late shift was with Constable Richard (Dick) Matttingley. Dick and I became close friends over time and still are to this day. Unknown to me at the time, Dick was given my original handwritten application to join the police force to investigate if I was a suitable applicant for admission to the Queensland Police Force. Upon my retirement, I received back my original handwritten application along with a copy of Dick's report.

We often joke about that as he claims I owe him big time because he lied to get me in to the job. A funny thing happened soon after my arrival at Petrie on training; the previous Officer In Charge (O.I.C.) of Petrie Station, Sergeant Dick Pascoe, called in to the Station as he still lived nearby. He was talking to the then O.I.C., Sergt. Ray Egan, when I walked into the office. I said, "Hello Mr Pascoe." He looked at me and said, "I know you from somewhere. What is your name?" I then told him. He looked at me in surprise and said "You, how the heck did you get in the job? I kicked your arse heaps of times. You were one of the Kallangur hoons." I replied, "That is probably why I changed for the better, Mr Pascoe." I think I made his day that afternoon knowing that he had helped someone to better their life.

One late shift at Petrie, on training and working alone, I attended both a house fire and a dead body. Thank God for the Policeman's Manual. I carried both in a bag in the car and they helped me get through that shift. After one month training at Petrie, I was transferred to Fortitude Valley training. My duties at the Valley comprised of beat duty, traffic duty, driving a patrol car, counter duties and inquiries. My preference was traffic control and for the majority of shifts over the next three years, I was performing traffic control mainly at the intersection of Brunswick and Ann Streets. I also relieved often at Petrie Station and once at Redcliffe over the Christmas period.

I went through several pith helmets when directing traffic at Brunswick and Ann streets. A friend of mine since state school days was driving trucks for Finney Brothers at the time and often travelled on Ann Street. If I was on point duty when he came past and I had not noticed him, I would feel this wack to the back of my head; my pith helmet would go flying onto the road and more often than not, be flattened by a vehicle going the other way. All I would notice was a hand come out the window of a truck and give me thumbs up.

Another time, I was directing traffic at the intersection of Gipps and Wickham Streets at peak hour in the afternoon when I waved through a truck containing a load of gas bottles travelling towards the Story Bridge. The truck was travelling up a steep incline on Gipps Street when the chain holding the bottles snapped, and all the gas bottles fell of the back of the truck and bounced down the hill towards me. I was in the middle of the intersection, ducking and dancing around, endeavouring to miss the flying gas bottles. After it was over, all the pedestrians at the intersection gave me a round of applause.

I was directing traffic on the 'Valley corner" intersection of Wickham and Brunswick Streets in July 1969 when man first walked upon the moon. The traffic had become light prior to the direct television broadcast which, from memory, was sometime around lunchtime. I walked off the point and into Myers store and watched the broadcast on one of their showroom televisions along with hundreds of other people. This was a huge event at the time. The nation stopped to watch this event.

On my 20th birthday, the 7th July 1969, I won the biggest thing I have ever won in my life: the ballot for national service. As I had only completed training to be a police officer some five months prior, I opted to do five years of compulsory Army Reserve or Citizens Military Forces (CMF) as it was known then. Due to having been a boilermaker, I could have joined the Naval Reserves and obtained the rank of Petty Officer or — as I was now a Police Officer the Military Police — as a Corporal, but I opted for the Medical Corp as a Private for two reasons.

One, they paraded in Water Street, Fortitude Valley and two, in my present career as a police officer, I may be in a position to save a life should the need arrive. I stayed in the Army Reserve for in excess of ten years and for the majority of that time as a sergeant rations clerk for a reserve field hospital.

I relieved at Redcliffe for six weeks over Christmas in 1969. I was involved in an incident which occurred one Saturday night in February 1970, about 8.45 pm on Redcliffe Parade. I was driving a patrol vehicle, accompanied by Detective Senior Constable Frank O'Gorman and Senior Constable Graham Burgemeister, when we became involved in a melee with a large group of youths. During the melee, Det. O'Gorman received abrasions to the head, face and body along with two broken bones to his foot and Sen. Const Burgemeister, a broken nose.

I received two dislocated shoulders. At the time, we only managed to arrest one offender. As quick as we placed them into the police car, they got back out and into the assault on police; one was even handcuffed with his arms behind his back. After taking the one arrested to the station, we then went in search of the offenders. During the altercation, Frank practically had his shirt torn off and it was hanging around his waist. One shoulder strap of his singlet was torn and was hanging down his chest. He was half bare chested but still had the tie on. That is how he looked when we recommenced our patrol in search of the others.

We went to a house where it was suspected that one or more of the offenders may have been. I was told to go around the back in the event that they tried to get out the back. I heard Frank talking to a lady at the front of the house, and then a noise came from the back near where I was. Suddenly a male person jumped out a window, practically into my arms. I apprehended this person and took him back to the front of the house and called the others.

This person was not in the melee, but a juvenile court absconder wanted on numerous breaking and entering offences. He was arrested by Frank and I recall his mother saying to Frank, "You won't hurt my son, will you?" Frank replied, "Madam – Do I look like the violent type to you." I never forgot that moment and had trouble not to laugh. Throughout the night, we caught and arrested the other offenders involved.

Whilst at the valley, I was working night work with another constable on beat duty in the middle of winter on a very cold night. The manager of Brendan's car sales opposite the Wickham Hotel would trade old cars and store them at the rear of the car yard unlocked. He told me that if we wished to get out of the cold on night work that we could use one of these cars.

This particular night, we both fell asleep in one of these cars. I was awoken to a clanging noise and looked out the windscreen to see two male persons attempting to push a car out of the yard through a cut chain at the entrance. I woke my offsider, we got out quietly and apprehended both offenders. They could not get over where we had appeared from so quickly and we did not tell them

In July 1972, I was transferred to Petrie. Petrie was an extremely busy station at the time as the Bruce highway ran through Strathpine, Lawnton and Kallangur. We received numerous accidents on this Highway, particularly on weekends. Nundah CI.Branch handled all serious Criminal matters until late 1974, when Petrie received two detectives. In addition, we received a very large volume of files each per week. In those years we dealt with correspondence from numerous other government departments. I worked with Wayne Bennett at Petrie. Wayne was training for the State and International Rugby League sides at the time and on most shifts worked the front counter on day shifts.

On one day shift, he accompanied me to a job in Samsonvale Road, Strathpine, where there was supposedly an armed male person sitting in a car outside a residence waiting for his estranged wife and children to return home from school. A mobile patrol unit was sent to assist us. The only firearm that Wayne and I had was a station issue WW2 Smith and Weston, six shot, 38cl revolver which I carried in my trouser pocket. Prior to reaching the address, we stopped and pulled over approaching traffic to ascertain if any person had noticed the suspect vehicle.

One person had, and noticed that a male person was seated in the vehicle. We established a plan that the mobile patrol vehicle would proceed first at the speed limit, pass the suspect vehicle then suddenly apply the brakes and pull in at angle and stop. Our vehicle would then pull in in front of the suspect vehicle, thereby placing the driver in a crossfire if the need arose. On doing this, the driver alighted from his vehicle carrying a rifle, ran into the front yard and tried to take cover behind a tree, but there were none large enough for him to do so.

Both mobile patrol officers alighted and squatted on the roadway with firearms drawn. I alighted and leaned over the bonnet with our one and only pistol whilst Wayne and I had a domestic over how he was going to get out and what he was going to do. I think, from memory, I told him to crawl out over the seat and get beside me behind the engine and if I should get shot, he could pick up the pistol and continue on. Thinking back, it was quite comical at the time. I called on the offender to drop the weapon otherwise I would shoot him and to my surprise, he did.

I told him to walk to the roadside which he did. He was handcuffed, and then collapsed unconscious. Unknown to us, he had taken an overdose prior to our arrival. His weapon had been purchased that morning and was a 16 shot, semi-automatic, .22cl rifle and he had modified it to be fully automatic. The ambulance was contacted, and he was removed and later charged by me for this offence.

I was working at Petrie during the 1974 floods and the only way to and from work at the peak of the floods was by means of a motorised railway maintenance cart. As I only lived a couple of kilometres south of the Pine River which was in flood, I was picked up and dropped off on a couple of occasions near my house by a railway employee on the cart.

I also recall going into Chelmer Police College to do the Detectives Crime Course just as the flood waters were subsiding in the Brisbane River at Chelmer. The houses below the college went partially under water and we could see the poor occupants sweeping mud out of their houses.

I recall after successfully completing the course, I was interviewed by two Detective Inspectors who displayed an interest in me applying to join the CI.Branch in the near future. I advised them that I desired to apply for the CI.Branch but not for some time; I had only been at Petrie for 18 months, and had mainly applied to do the course to increase my knowledge in interviewing and processing criminal offenders as the nearest CIB was at Nundah.

They were not impressed with my answer and both gave me a good old serve. A short time later, I was transferred to Brisbane Mobile Patrols or Siberia, as it was referred to at that time. I was not impressed and lost any interest in applying for the CI.Branch. I worked for the best part of three years at Mobile Patrols, mainly patrolling the Fortitude Valley Divisions. I had a permanent male partner for that time, Const. J.A.Mair, who I reckon I got to know better than my wife over that time.

One incident that I was despatched to was to guard a murder scene in Stafford, where the manager of the National Hotel, Brisbane was shot dead on his way home from work in the very early hours of the morning. We were to guard the scene until the arrival of the CI.Branch. As daylight broke, the deceased's vehicle was in eyesight of his family home and we had trouble keeping the family away from the immediate murder scene.

On one early shift at mobiles, we were travelling east on Wickham Terrace and approaching traffic lights at the intersection with Gregory Terrace. It was a dual lane carriageway and the traffic in the middle lane was not moving when the lights turned green. As we got closer, I could see that there appeared to be no one in the vehicle. I got out of the police car and walked up to this car to discover an unconscious young female driver slumped over onto the passenger seat with blood oozing from her mouth. There was a large amount of blood on the passenger floor well.

My army training as a medic kicked in and I felt for a pulse. She had a very faint pulse and due to the amount of blood lost, I considered there was no time for an ambulance and notified VKR of the circumstances, requesting that they urgently contact the Royal Brisbane Hospital and that we would be conveying the seriously ill woman to the emergency section. With lights and siren activated, we conveyed her to the RBH. The young lady was found to have a burst ulcer and survived and, according to a doctor present, only due to our quick action.

About a month later, we were despatched to a boarding house in Spring Hill where lodgers were concerned for the welfare of a resident in one of the apartments. On entering, we found an elderly, naked man crawling around the kitchen, floor on his hands and knees mopping up blood on the floor with newspaper. He told us that he had been spewing and pooing blood. We requested the ambulance, and upon their arrival and examination of the patient, I put in my now expert opinion that he must have a burst ulcer. Out of the patient's earshot, the ambulance officer informed me that more than likely, he had a burst cancer as the blood was coming from both ends and that he would probably die as a result of that.

Some things always stick in your mind. Just over 10 years ago, I awoke one morning in the middle of the night feeling very weak and nauseous. I was unable to walk to the toilet and had to crawl. I vomited pure blood into the toilet and then had to go the other end where again I passed pure blood. I immediately thought of that ambulance bearers remarks all those years ago and did not believe that I would be returning home. I was conveyed by ambulance to the Wesley Hospital at my request after having been examined at Gympie Hospital. After examination, I was found to have a ruptured left gastric artery which was repaired by an angiogram by crimping off that artery. I was home a couple of days later. Things are not always what they may seem to be.

Whilst at Brisbane Mobile Patrols, I undertook four subjects of the Police Arts and Science Degree to obtain the rank of Senior Constable after seven years of service. After nearly three years at mobiles, I was transferred to Chermside Station at the rank of Senior Constable. The officer in charge was the legendary Sergeant First Class Tom Dwyer. Tom could be very abrupt at times. I hit it off on the wrong foot with him right from the start. There were three things that Tom didn't like: Senior Constables appointed after seven years under the Police Arts and Science Course, Police officers serving in the CMF, and police officers from Brisbane Mobile Patrols.

I fit all three categories when I started at Chermside. It was probably after two years at Chermside when I resigned from the CMF that things then changed for the better. He was a hard boss, but he certainly supported his staff. The worst duties at Chermside were attending children's deaths under anaesthetics at the Prince Charles Hospital. As it was a heart/lung hospital, there were a lot of children born with severe heart deformities and the parents were groomed from birth that they would not live to teenage years. As we had to frequently attend the deaths on the operating table, we were not groomed like the parents and had children similar ages; we were at times brought to tears attending these deaths.

Another job that consumed a lot of time at Chermside were shoplifters as the police station adjoined Myers Shopping Centre. Due to the location of the Police station at the intersection of two very busy roads, Hamilton and Gympie Road, we had a constant dangerous situation where we had new and second-hand dealers of numerous caravans, boats, trailers and motor vehicles on Gympie Road who were required to bring the respective vehicles and trailers to the police station for registration purposes. As there was insufficient parking space in the police station yard for them to park, they had to try and park in Hamilton Road.

I spoke with the Sergeant and the various dealers to rectify this problem. Other Constables assisted in this process. As a result, a decision was made that the officer or officers working a 2-10 pm inquiry shift on weekdays would telephone the dealers, obtain a list of what was to be inspected and visit each dealership before their close of business. This system worked very well and was a win-win situation for all concerned.

Another incident that I will never forget whilst stationed at Chermside was at a demonstration in the city. I think that I attended every demonstration that occurred in the City whilst at Chermside. We had a constable at Chermside at the time who was a university student and had made it known to me and his colleagues that he was mainly in the police to help him through university. He had a girlfriend who was also a university student and was involved in the protest movements at university. This particular day, a number of us from Chermside were on standby under a building in Ann Street when the demonstration commenced.

This particular officer, who I will only name as Mike, was worried that if our group was despatched to the demonstration, he may be confronted by his girlfriend who would possibly be leading a group of demonstrators. We asked him if he would like us to speak with a commissioned officer to have him made a driver of a paddy wagon. He decided that the chances of running in to her were slim so he would remain with the group. Not long after, the demonstrators marched down Queen Street near the city hall.

Our group was dispatched to stop their movements. Low and behold, our constable's girlfriend was at the front of the demonstration. A police officer who was known to me but not from our station arrested her and she began struggling with him. Mike lost control and ran to assist his girlfriend and tried to pull her away from the arresting officer. All the media present became aware of this, and rushed to the scene. I thought to myself, this is going to be bigger than "Ben Hur". Several high-ranking officers converged on the scene, placed Mike in a police car and drove off.

After the demonstration ceased, we returned to our station. I told our OIC, Tom, what had happened, and he appeared lost for words. Very shortly after this, police cars arrived at the station carrying high ranking officers and Mike. They asked Tom for the key to Mike's locker and upon opening it, one said words to the effect: "Ours, yours, ours, yours etc there's the door." I was standing at the bottom of the stairs outside and said to Mike as he walked past, "I suppose a send-off is out of the question Mate." I have never seen an officer dismissed from the service so fast in my entire career.

Also, whilst stationed at Chermside we were experiencing a lot of problems with youths congregating in Corrie Street, Chermside, outside the business precinct. The newsagent proprietor was often expressing his concern to the Chermside police over the various problems experienced. One Sunday, myself and another officer from Chermside, Sen. Const. Les Lawrence, were working when we got wind that the Chermside and Zillmere youths were having a game of cricket on an oval near Corrie Street. We attended the game and called all the young guys over and had a talk to them about the concerns of the Corrie Street business people.

After the talk, we asked them if we could join them in the game for an hour or so. They agreed and we played cricket with them. As a result, they got to know us and gained our trust and understand what was expected of them by the local police. After this, all problems and complaints stopped in Corrie Street.

One Friday afternoon around five pm, in August, 1981, whilst stationed at Chermside and off duty, I was with a group of friends in the private bar of the Kallangur hotel, when my attention was drawn to the fact that the bottle shop at the front of the hotel, in view of the private bar, had just been held up. I looked out the window and saw a male person wearing a balaclava and clutching a handful of money run past the front of the private bar towards a car park. I then gave chase, followed by several of my civilian friends.

I caught the offender in the car park and conveyed him back to the manager's office. As I had to remain with the offender, I took charge of the situation and had the civilians do a check of the grounds, as it was believed that there were three to four males involved. I emphasised to them not to place themselves in harm's way. The police by then had been contacted. My friends located a vehicle with two males in it in one of the car parks. They kept it under surveillance whilst one reported back to me. I told them to keep it under observation until police arrived.

A short time later, police arrived, took details from me and took the offender to the police vehicle. This person looked vague to me as if he had been taking drugs. They placed him in the police vehicle and then followed my friend's directions to the car containing the other possible offenders. On searching the car, the officers located a knife used in the holdup and more cash, proceed of the robbery. Shortly afterwards, Detectives from Redcliffe arrived and took over the investigation. I briefed them and then returned to the bar to finish my first beer of the afternoon.

Shortly after the police had left, a reasonably well-dressed young fellow came into the bar and asked the attendant for a box of matches and directions to Redcliffe which I thought was odd enough, but what was really odd was that he was sweating, and it was the middle of winter. He left and walked out to the roadway and began hitchhiking. I made up my mind that he too was possibly involved in the robbery, so I had a friend drive me in his old Holden utility to this person.

I informed him that I was an off-duty police officer and that there had been a holdup at the Kallangur hotel. I requested that he return to the hotel with us, which he did without question. I thought that this was odd. I kept my eyes on him at all times and upon arrival back at the hotel, I searched him and located more money stuffed down the front of his underpants. The detectives returned and took this person into custody. I later supplied a statement. In all, five offenders were located and charged over this hold-up.

A list of five target premises was located on one of the offenders, the Kallangur hotel being the first on the list. As a result, two of my civilian friends received

APPENDIX C

PLACE ON PERSONAL FILE OF SENIOR CONSTABLE K.J. SALMON, CHERMSIDE 1773F115

QUEENSLAND POLICE DEPARTMENT

Our Ref. 31.C.1640

Your Ref.

COMMISSIONER'S OFFICE
30 MAKERSTON STREET
BRISBANE

BOX 1440,
G.P.O., BRISBANE 4001
TELEGRAPHIC ADDRESS:
VEDETTE, BRISBANE
TELEX: 40337
TEL.: 226 6001

5 August 1982

Regional Superintendent
NORTH BRISBANE REGION

istant Commissioner
IE AND SERVICES

your information.
. Branch file No.
59.C.62-1 refers.

J.M.L.

. LEWIS
MISSIONER OF POLICE
.82

I refer to the attached correspondence concerning the arrest and subsequent conviction of Gregory Allan Creevey, Francis John Hudd, Allan Charles Edwards, Stephen Albert Creevey and Raymond Paul Kavney for robbery at the Kallangur Hotel on 14 August 1981.

The good police work by Senior Constable K.J. Salmon, Chermside, Senior Constable J.H. Klibbe and Constable G.R. Conroy, Petrie, has been noted.

Please convey my compliments to the members concerned.

A copy of this memorandum has been placed on these members' personal files.

Certificates of Appreciation will be forwarded as soon as possible for presentation to Daniel Walter Alexander, Douglas John Bell and Brian Thomas Feeney.

T. M. LEWIS

T.M. LEWIS
COMMISSIONER OF POLICE

Letter of appreciation from the Commissioner

letters of appreciation from Commissioner T.M.Lewis and for my part, good police work noted on my record by the Commissioner.

As that was the only recognition I received, I could only surmise that the powers that be must have thought that I was on the grog at the time of my involvement. Little did they know that I had not even consumed my first beer. Furthermore, we did not even receive any thanks from management of the hotel.

In 1982, I was seconded to work at the Brisbane International Airport for the duration of the Commonwealth Games, from memory, for approximately four weeks. Our role was mainly security which involved a lot of public relations with the competitors. There were two detectives also in the airport contingent, one being our officer in charge, Det. Sen Sergt Frank Swindells and the other Det Sergt First Class Jim O'Sullivan. Outside the arrival times of competitors and dignitaries, there was little to do.

As we had a key to security gates that led to swamplands and Serpentine Creek at the rear of the airport, we had crab pots set in Serpentine Creek. As the airport was planning a further runway, the airport authority had acquired all of the area known as Cribb Island and Serpentine Creek. All houses had been removed from Cribb Island, and Serpentine Creek had been closed off to boating traffic some 12 months prior and was about to be filled in, so the crabs were thick.

As we worked three shifts, a crew on each shift was to check the pots, remove the crabs and rebait the pots; that way, everyone could have a share in the crabs. Frank had also got a key from us and put his own pots in the creek. On one particular day shift that I was working, the Queen was due to arrive late afternoon. We decided to do the pots early, well prior to her arrival. We were halfway through doing this when we received a radio call from Frank asking where we were. On telling him our location, he instructed that we return immediately as her plane was early and about to touchdown.

We made a mad dash back to the terminal and only had enough time to clean our uniform and boots before her arrival. Frank claimed one massive crab which we had in our possession for the stress we had caused him on this occasion. Whilst performing duty at the airport, the police gazette came

Ken – second left – with Federal Police at Brisbane International airport

out listing both Jim O'Sullivan's and my promotion – Jim to Det. Sen. Sergt. and mine to Sergeant Seconds Class, Officer in Charge of Cooktown.

Also, whilst at Chermside in 1982 and having the rank of Senior Constable, Sergeant Dwyer had applied for recreation leave; and as there was no one available from the Valley Station to relieve him, he had recommended that I relieve him at the rank of Sergt 1/c for a period of one month. The station strength at that time was the OIC, 10 constables and two civilian AO's. A senior Constable relieving two ranks higher was practically unheard of and Tom's recommendation went through the chain of command, practically to the top before being approved. I think this work experience helped greatly on my promotion to OIC of Cooktown when only having 13 years' service.

Cooktown Police Division

I commenced work at Cooktown on the 1/1/1983. I had applied for that position due to the diversity of work involved in that it was a remote area. The division consisted of 14,500 square kilometres of mainly tropical coastline. There were two aboriginal communities in the division to police, one being Hopevale with approx. 780 residents, and the other Wujal Wujal with approx. 450 residents. There were approx. another 100 aboriginals living in the town area. The industry was mainly farming (cattle, grain and peanuts), commercial fishing, tourism and mining. There were also a great number of alternate life stylers (commonly referred to as feral hippies by the locals) living and squatting throughout the division, particularly in the remote coastal rain forest areas.

This was shortly after the well-publicised Cedar Bay incident. I had two constables and one administration officer under my control, and we were responsible for policing both aboriginal communities. I was also responsible for training community police officers, although most could not read or write, which made it very difficult. What also made it difficult was the fact that I had no say in the hiring and firing of those officers. This was done by the respective aboriginal councils.

As quite often was the case, no local aboriginals would accept those positions due to retaliation from other aboriginals. At times, the only persons that would accept the position were persons with serious criminal convictions, even for murder. This was particularly the case at Wujal Wujal Community.

Cooktown police station was a small demountable construction and was not air-conditioned, although it was large enough to house us all at that time. For the entire time that I was at Cooktown, we only had one police vehicle. Initially, this was a short wheelbase Toyota Land cruiser, which was not suitable for the corrugated roads in the division and on many occasions when travelling around a corner on a corrugated section of road, would bounce around and end up facing the direction you had come from. Unlike most western dirt roads, the roads in the Cooktown division consisted mainly of shale, rock and bulldust and caused a large amount of damage to the battery, the body and the chassis.

From memory, this vehicle cost more in repairs than what it was purchased for and this was not due to the manner in which it was driven. After several reports, it was replaced with a Toyota Landcruiser troop carrier with a built-in cage. This vehicle was a great improvement and did not require as many repairs. A lot of our time was spent travelling south to Wujal Wujal aboriginal community; although only 85 kilometres from Cooktown, it was three hours travelling time one way due to the road conditions and mountain ranges which worsened in the wet season.

Hopevale community was approximately a one hour drive north of Cooktown and had a far better dirt road. The main road from Cairns, the Cooktown Development Road, consisted of bitumen to Mount Carbine just north of Mareeba, and then dirt for approximately 250 kilometres to Cooktown. There were small sections of bitumen in between. It would take between five to six hours to travel to Cairns. The roads were only graded once or twice a year.

There was a large farming community, Lakeland Downs, off the main road about 85 km south of Cooktown at the junction of the Cape York Peninsula Development Road. Corn and peanuts were grown on a large scale and trucked to Mareeba. When my family and I travelled to Cooktown on transfer, I drove a HZ Holden premier station wagon, and on the journey, because of the road conditions, the exhaust system disintegrated. I swore and declared that the next time that vehicle travelled on that road to Cairns, it would be traded in for a four-wheel drive.

This did happen six months later when I purchased a Toyota Troop carrier for the family vehicle. I had this vehicle for 25 years. Right from the start of my duty in Cooktown, I found it to be a very busy division with a large volume of disturbances, both domestic and public, around the three licensed premises. There were numerous complaints of assaults, both in the town area and at both aboriginal communities. In addition, drugs were a major concern; in particular, the cultivation of marijuana throughout the tropical rainforest areas of the division.

Unlicensed driving and unregistered vehicles were also of great concern as tourism throughout the area was growing. As many of the aboriginals on the communities were unable to read and write, it was not possible for them to either learn the traffic code or pass a written examination to obtain a driver's license. Most were capable drivers, and were doing so on a regular basis unlicensed and most were driving unregistered motor vehicles.

In the first year of my arrival, I met with both community managers to devise a plan to address these issues. It was established that the Caucasian mechanics and the managers would teach them the traffic code by painting roads and intersections with traffic lines onto a bond wood door. Homemade traffic lights and signs would be attached, and different coloured matchbox cars would be used. The board was placed on trestles in a room for training purposes at both communities. Those wishing to get a driver's license took part in these lessons.

This method of teaching worked very well and when we visited either community, we would test the applicants by use of the door for their written test and should they pass that, give them a manual driving test either while on the community at the time, or in Cooktown at a later date. Another initiative I implemented was a bi-monthly meeting to both communities on alternate months by both me and the Clerk of The Court/Acting Magistrate.

A notice would be placed on their community notice board, advising the date that we would be attending and the issues we would be addressing. The Clerk of the Court would discuss court procedures and motor vehicle registrations and I would discuss any policing issues or driver's license requirements. These public addresses would be conducted in the respective community halls followed by individual consultations in separate offices.

I can recall a rather amusing occurrence on one of these visits to Wujal Wujal. I discussed the new photographic driver's license that was replacing the old 10-year paper license. After the public address, I went to an office for individual discussion. A young community police officer was the first person in line to speak with me and he wanted to know how he could get the new picture license. I explained to him that he had to attend the police station between office hours, sit for his photo to be taken and pay for the driver's license. This conversation was in hearing range of others waiting on the veranda. Another person who had been waiting to see me then had his turn.

He told me that he had heard me speaking with Andrew about the new picture license, and that he was not able to get to Cooktown during weekdays as he drove a tractor for a living on the Community. He asked if Andrew could get a picture license for him as Andrew was going to the police station to get one. I explained to him several times that he had to be there to have his photo taken, but I could not get that through to him. I eventually told him that he would have to take time off work and come in personally to get the new license.

In my first year at Cooktown, there were a number of murders at Wujal Wujal, and several serious assaults and unlawful wounding at both communities as well as in the town area. I adopted a zero-tolerance policy regarding assaults. All assaults apart from minor, common assaults were to be investigated and action taken should there be sufficient evidence. This did occur, and the murders over the following 12 months dropped to zero and other serious assaults and unlawfully wounding offences dropped dramatically. When we received information regarding drug related matters, this information was entered in a book that was kept in the safe.

This was for jobs that could not be carried out alone by our staff — for example, large crops that would require additional police to affectively conduct a raid or for smaller jobs, when the three of us could afford the time to do the job ourselves. There was normally only one officer rostered for duty on a Sunday. This was the only shift where we had time to do fatigues. Clean the cells, station, police vehicle and mow the lawn. Should there be drug raids to perform, the two off-duty officers would come in and either two or three of us would conduct the raids.

I told my staff to make sure the information was right, as I had a motto when doing these raids, "no body, no overtime". We had a very unrealistic overtime budget as it was. I think budgets were first implemented in the first or second year that I was at Cooktown, and my annual overtime budget allocation was 120 hours. In fact, whilst at Cooktown, I performed approximately 60 hours per week, 20 of which were in my own time. On most shifts apart from Friday and Saturday late shifts, we worked alone.

When I first arrived, one constable and I had a departmental residence, and my residence had the only telephone. The other was on an extension to my line from memory. The other constable was in a rental house for a time, until another departmental residence was built next to mine on the police reserve. As we had three officers at Cooktown, I did not receive an on-call allowance or an O.I.C allowance but would have to answer all telephone calls. I conducted a survey at one time on after-hours telephone calls and found that I received, on average, 22 calls per day, outside of rostered hours.

At night time, the adrenalin would kick in when the telephone rang. As on many occasions, the call would be to attend a serious disturbance, at other times, only to find that some tourist was planning a trip to Cooktown in the coming months and wanted to know what the road conditions would be. It was very hard to be civil, when awoken at all hours of the night to answer inquiries of this nature. Over the six years that I was the OIC of Cooktown, I submitted several applications for a diverter to Cairns police station and a second telephone to be installed at my residence.

I submitted that I was even prepared to pay for the installation and cost for the second telephone myself. All applications were rejected. After several applications, I would then send a copy to the Queensland Police Union. I still had no success, and at one time a senior commissioned officer from Cairns was in Brisbane for a command conference when he heard my name mentioned by a very high-ranking officer who referred to me as, 'That militant sergeant from Cooktown'. This was over the numerous applications to rectify the telephone issue. The matter was not addressed whilst I was at Cooktown.

Further to the drug raids that we conducted on a Sunday, we may hit several targets on that day. If we located a crop near a residence and the offender was present, we would photograph the crop with the offender, take possession of the exhibits (if possible), interview the offender and if he/she was known to me, have them remain at their home until we returned that day. We would then continue to the next target and so on for the remainder of the day. We would then return, pick up the offenders and proceed to the station to process them. Not once did one abscond from their house.

After processing them at the station, they would be released on bail (on most occasions) and I would return them to their homes. I never had one plead not guilty. During my time at Cooktown, the Drugs Misuse Act was enacted, and I think we were the first in the state to make an arrest under that act. Acting on information received, me and a constable conducted a dawn raid on a property at an area known as Rossville. The offender was caught watering a large number of plants at the rear of his house. The tallest plant was no more than 40cms in height. In all, there were approximately 500 plants and seedlings that would have weighed no more than three kgs. The offender was so surprised when we stepped out from behind trees and called out "police" that when he looked and saw us, he then collapsed to the ground. As it turned out, I knew the offender, having had a beer with him at the Lions' Den Hotel on several occasions.

I knew him to be a tin miner in the area. He was a reasonable guy for one living in that area and claimed that this was his first attempt at growing marijuana, as he had been told that he could make $1,000 a plant for a good healthy plant. The area of Rossville, a tin mining area, was a community where people acquired 99yr miners homestead, perpetual leases, and built shacks and dwellings.

There were a lot of shady persons living in this area and very few worked for a living. Drugs were rife in the area. Anyway, he was charged with having over 500 plants which under that act, when first enacted, could have meant life imprisonment as there was no weight stipulation, just the number of plants, which I think was over 100 plants, to warrant the maximum penalty. This was later amended. The only way that bail could be granted was through the Supreme Court, from memory.

He later applied for and was granted bail but did not appear on the day and a warrant was issued. In the meantime, he and his family had left the area. Some months later, I received a telephone call from him. He apologised for not fronting court, would not disclose his whereabouts but informed me that he was not going to be one of the first under the act to be sentenced and would watch what penalties were handed out for similar offences down the track.

When satisfied that he would not get a lengthy sentence, he would return and hand himself in. He was true to his word and handed himself in to us about six months later, after having returned from Tasmania. During his time on the run, the act had been amended and I think from memory, he did not receive a custodial sentence.

Ken, not happy on a drug raid, Walker Bay

On patrol, rough track, Palmer River NQ

My duties in Cooktown also involved minor prosecutions. I frequently performed these duties. As mentioned, the Clerk of The Court was also Acting Magistrate. In my time at Cooktown, firstly Mr Dean Wilkinson, and later Mr Lawrence Mellors, became Magistrates and both became good friends of mine. I recall a comical incident one day when I was off duty and mowing the police station yard.

Court was in session next door for a committal proceeding. A magistrate and a female depositions clerk had been flown in from Cairns and were conducting proceedings, when they held an adjournment to hear a local matter against a regular offending aboriginal person from Wujal Wujal, Charlie Sykes, whose nickname was 'killer'. "Killer" was about five-foot tall, thin build and always wore a handkerchief with knots tied in the corners on his head.

He was a very placid and polite person until intoxicated, and then his personality changed. He had been arrested for disorderly conduct and obscene language. Whilst having the charges heard, he became agitated, stripped off naked in the courtroom, apart from the handkerchief, and was prancing around the courtroom with his fists raised

My attention was raised when I noticed both the sergeant police prosecutor and the legal aid solicitor standing on the veranda and one of them was calling out, "Help Police!" I left the mower and ran to the Court-house, was told what was happening, went into the courtroom and noticed that the magistrate had left the courtroom along with most others.

The female clerk was standing on something, horrified, and 'killer' was still as I described earlier. I told killer to behave himself and put his clothes on. He replied, "Yes boss" and immediately got dressed. I then removed him from the courtroom and returned him to the Watch-house. As I was leaving and passing the prosecutor, I said, "In case you have forgotten, you are the police. This guy is no bigger that a pygmy."

After a time of prosecuting minor matters where aboriginals were involved, I got to know their Cairns based, legal aid solicitor, Mr Mark Stower quite well. On all serious charges, such as assaults, wilful damage or stealing matters, Mark would attend the initial court hearing. Over time, Mark realised that I dealt with aboriginal offenders fairly and asked me one day if I would notify him by telephone of any criminal matters coming before the court involving local aboriginal offenders.

I did this, and we discussed if there was a requirement for him to attend court in Cooktown, should there be any reasonable defence to the charge. If not, and a guilty plea was forthcoming, he would only waste time and expenditure in attending. He would request that I deal with the matter and make a submission for the defendant on his behalf. So, in essence, I not only prosecuted the matter but spoke on behalf of the defendant as well. I was also requested to do this for many of the other defendants, particularly those on drug related matters. I dealt with each one fairly, based on the circumstances.

I made several submissions for an additional vehicle and staff. Regarding staff, I was informed that the only way I would get an increase was to increase arrests. There are only so many hours in a day, so to do this we had to work smarter. Mainly, the constables would conduct investigations and arrest offenders. I would take most of the witness's statements to put the brief together. If the matter went to the District Court in Cairns, which many did, then the A.O. would organise witnesses travel and accommodation in Cairns, thereby saving the constables these time-consuming duties. This system worked well, and the arrest rate increased.

Eventually, after about five years at Cooktown, I received one additional permanent constable and one detective on trial but still, no additional vehicle. Getting the additional constable meant that I would not get relief for either leave or courses for constables. So, in actual fact, I received an additional constable for approximately six weeks of the year.

The one police vehicle was a major concern. Any time that it was away either on a lengthy job throughout the division or in Cairns for Court, escort duties or other reasons, the division had no police vehicle. This occurred often. Cooktown had one taxi, which was mostly engaged conveying aboriginal people to and from the communities and was rarely available for police use and, at most times, not practical. On most occasions, I had to use my private vehicle or walk the offenders to the police station.

After consultation with the shire clerk, it was agreed that we could borrow one of the shire vehicles, if one was available. This worked well for some time until threats were made to council workers that their vehicles were being used by the police for drug surveillance. This of course, was not true. The shire clerk then had to stop us using council vehicles. Around that time, I was instrumental in recommencing the State Emergency Service (SES). Cooktown had a group prior to my arrival, but it was no longer operating when I arrived.

All the equipment was rotten and had to be dumped. There was no building or vehicle and all members had lost Interest. I had meetings with council and in a short time, advertised for volunteers. We got many volunteers, built a shed on council property, appointed a group leader and obtained a large amount of new equipment. Training then recommenced. I joined the S.E.S. even though, in my police capacity, it was not required.

After a short time, a vehicle was acquired for the S.E.S. This vehicle was then utilised for police work when ours was not available. This was still the case when I left Cooktown. Talk about no resources! It was often said in the north, the service consisted of two sections – Brisbane, and the rest. If you were in the rest, you got nothing. I once had a commissioned officer say to me when I had applied for another police vehicle, "What? Do you want one each?" I honestly do not think that they could understand the severity of the problem.

Once or twice a year, time permitting, I would do a joint patrol of both Laura and Cooktown police divisions with the constable from Laura, Glen Teske. My constables were either not available or had no desire to camp out, so I would go and we would use the Laura police vehicle and conduct patrols for about seven days. We would visit property owners, mining camps and professional fisherman and look for any criminal activities being conducted in the divisions.

On some patrols, Glen would bring his aboriginal tracker, George Musgrave. George was excellent at his job. He could spot anything from a long distance. On occasions, we were accompanied by other government agencies, such as

Ken and Glen Teske – bogged on patrol

Camp out on patrol

boating and fisheries inspectors and the Army conducting exercises. Glen Teske and I are still good friends.

His tracker, George, had a brother named Tommy George, and although their names are different, they were full brothers. Tommy worked for many years on a cattle property outside of Mareeba. He was a ringer until he got too old for that job, and they then kept him on as a general roustabout and gardener. Every year, he would return to Laura with his yearly earnings. He would arrive neat and tidy and within two to three days, you would not recognise him as the same man.

He would hit the grog, something fierce. He would remove his false teeth, would not shave or comb his hair and in general, looked derelict. After his holidays were over and it was time to go back to work, he would refuse, so Glen would have to deal with it. He would inevitably be arrested for obscene language or other minor offences and conveyed to Cooktown. I would then drum up the magistrate that Tommy was back and refusing to go back to work. Tommy would front court, plead guilty and be convicted and fined $20 on each charge, in default two weeks imprisonment with no time to pay.

As he had no money, he would spend the time in the Cooktown Watch-house. The idea was to get him out of the horrors and have him return to work. He did not touch alcohol all year at the property, only when he returned to Laura on holidays. He was a man then in his 60's. Sober, he was a lovely man, a hard worker, very wise on the land, and a respected elder among his people. The property owners had that much respect for him that they would fly him to and from Laura in their aircraft at holiday times. Whilst he was in my custody, he was only locked up at night and had the run of the police station yard during the day. This was the case for many trusted and well-behaved aboriginal prisoners. The station and yard were always spick and span when Tommy was there.

Most afternoons after work, Tommy and I would sit and talk about life before dinner. I had a lot of time and respect for him and became very friendly with him. When it was time for him to be released and returned to work, I would call Glen Teske. He would organise the aircraft and I would take Tommy to the Cooktown airport. He would return to Laura, pick up his swag and possessions and return to the station property. This happened year after year, and the last year that I was at Cooktown and Tommy was a prisoner, I invited him to have dinner with three of my friends who were visiting from Brisbane and myself.

Tommy went into the station, got clean clothes and got spruced up for the occasion. He was such an interesting fellow that he held the conversation most of the night, relating his droving experiences over Cape York from a young age. The next day my mates left, and Tommy was due to be released. I had a serious chat to him about his drinking problem when on holidays and about getting and having respect from the younger aboriginals in his community. I also explained that as he was an elder, he should be leading

Trusted gardener in police complex

Ken, on front veranda, Cooktown Police Station

by example. When he was due for release, I informed him that I would organise the plane and he told me that he was not going back to work.

I was taken aback and asked why. He told me that he had thought about what I had said to him, had talked to some Hopevale aboriginals and had booked himself into the rehabilitation centre at Hopevale community to give up alcohol. He did this and refrained from alcohol consumption until his death, not that long ago. He lived a long life, well into his 80s.

Tommy and his wife were responsible for the construction of the Laura Aboriginal Cultural Centre. He ceased work at the station and became an aboriginal ranger in the area. He travelled to other parts of the world, giving talks in that capacity and I believe was awarded the Order of Australia Medal.

I left Cooktown after his release and did not see him again for several years. On the last occasion prior to his departure from Cooktown, he caused me some embarrassment after he had been released. He had been clearing vegetation from around the Watch-house and had made a garden. One day he helped me burn some marijuana in the incinerator. These bushes were from a crop where the offenders were not located and had been kept in the exhibit room.

After burning the plants, I stacked the bags of compost at one end of the cells. Unknown to me, Tommy had dug the compost into the garden bed. He told me before his release, to water the bed now and again as he had planted paw paws. Unfortunately, I never found time to water the garden and I had forgotten all about it, until the clerk of the court came into my office one morning, grabbed me by the arm and told me he was making a citizen's arrest. When I asked why, he led me to the garden site which was between the Watch-house and a path leading from his home to the Court-house. Low and behold, there were about 30-40 healthy marijuana plants, about 30 cms in height. I had not even noticed them.

I told Tommy about this many years later and he laughed for a long time. The last time I saw him was in 2011, when I was at Laura and attended the Cape York Aboriginal tribal dance festival with my wife. I noticed Tommy on stage, welcoming the dance troupes in to the arena and farewelling them when they had finished their routine. My wife and I went to the rear of a building containing the stage and knocked on a rear door. The announcer, a younger aboriginal man, asked me what I wanted, and I told him that I was a retired police sergeant once stationed at Cooktown in the 1980s and was an old friend of Tommy George.

He told us to wait and then went and spoke to Tommy. Tommy looked around and a look of delight showed on his face. He said something to the announcer, and then two chairs were placed beside him and we were invited to join him on stage. The announcer, his grandson, then introduced us to the crowd as his grandfather's honoured guests. I was so honoured to be treated in this way that I had tears in my eyes. We remained there with him for some time and had a good old chat. Tommy was in his 80s at that time, and it was the last time I saw him.

During our many conversations, Tommy informed me that he was born near Lakefield, and both he and his older brother, George Musgrave, as young children were about to be removed from their tribe by police and welfare officers. The property manager, a 'Mr. Fred Sheppard', hid them in big mailbags. Thus, they avoided the trauma suffered by many Indigenous children of that era, when they were forcefully removed from their families and relocated to an Aboriginal mission where their life was controlled by a white manager and staff.

Tommy George

Tommy George was a renowned stockman, tracker, land right's activist and co-founder of the Laura Aboriginal Dance Festival. He was the sole custodian of Awa Laya, the language of the Kuka Thaypan people. Tommy and his brother George Musgrave were awarded honoury doctorates by James Cook University for their help in documenting language and Traditional fire management of land. He famously took on Billionaire Gina Rinehart, leading her to abandon plans in 2014 to dig for diamonds in the rock country around Laura, 150 kilometres west of Cooktown, and helped secure indigenous management of the national parks on Cape York. Tommy was a great storyteller, and he loved to make a joke and liked to keep everyone in line. He and his brother were raised in traditional ways by their family while living and working on Musgrave Station, on Cape York. Tommy co-founded the Laura Dance Festival and campaigned to protect the World renowned Quinkan rock art near the township. Dr. Tommy George passed to eternal rest in the year 2016, at the age of 87 years.

Courtesy: Laura Aboriginal Cultural Centre.

Early in my time at Cooktown, I became aware of two brothers in one family who, in company with others, would frequently assault local males, but no complaints would be forthcoming as the victims were frightened of retaliation should they make a complaint. There were numerous false rumours as to what had happened to people 'thinking' of making a complaint against them. One Saturday night, whilst I was away from Cooktown and staying overnight at Lakeland Downs with my family, this group of youths assaulted a tourist who did make a complaint to police.

The constables attended and located the offenders outside the Cooktown hotel. The offenders, about six in total, then challenged the police. One of the officers was forced to produce a firearm and instruct them to leave, which they then did. I was contacted and advised of the situation. I instructed the officers to get statements from all witnesses and not to go near the offenders until I returned the following day. All offenders were arrested and charged with the assault the following day.

All offenders pleaded guilty and, to their surprise, were all given a custodial sentence. They never committed another assault and no longer thought that they were beyond the law. A couple of days later, a group of young aboriginal males came to the police station and requested to see me personally and individually. All had the same message — that they had witnessed the incident involving the constables and the group of local males, and that should the police ever need assistance, then, all they have to do is call on them to assist. I relayed this information to my constables. This showed the respect that the aboriginal people had for the local police.

On the subject of prisoners, I had to modify the steel mesh on the main exercise yard to be able to pass a plate and cup through the door to feed the prisoners, because quite often there were no police present to perform this task at mealtimes and my wife had to do it. My wife and I were also responsible for preparing the prisoner meals, and they were always fed well. On a couple of occasions, one cell was used for housing rogue crocodiles. If one was creating a problem to the boating fraternity moored in the river, the appropriate authorities were contacted, the crocodile captured and secured, then placed in the cell to be kept cool until vessel transportation could be arranged for its removal.

There was a building in the police yard in front of the Watch-house, between the Court-house and the police station that had been modified by the state works department into a self-contained unit. This unit was often utilised by various government employees for short term accommodation. One morning, before commencing duty, I visited the Watch-house to see how many prisoners were to be fed breakfast.

There were two aboriginal males sitting in the doorway to a cell and they were practically white. I asked what the problem was and one replied, "Croc Boss." I said, "What do you mean?" He pointed to a frangipani tree nearby, in front of the exercise yard, and there was a three-metre crocodile, tied by the snout with rope leading to the mesh at the front of the exercise yard.

The croc had a wet, hessian bag over its head. A couple of national parks guys came out of the donga and said that they had arrived late, checked in to the donga and then went in search of the rogue croc which they located and captured. They had to keep him somewhere, so they tied him to the front of the cells. I told the prisoners not to worry, as the croc was only a watchdog. The aboriginal prisoners were not locked in the cells at night for a couple of reasons. One it was much cooler and two, they had a good view out through the exercise yard of the park and the river.

There were three main cells behind the exercise yard and two separate cells outside of the exercise yard. One was utilised as an exhibit room, the other, a padded cell. There was no toilet in the padded cell and a bucket had to be used for that purpose. As the Cooktown hospital did not have facilities for keeping mental patients, they had to be kept in the padded cell at the police station until we could arrange transport to Cairns.

This occurred about two to three times a year. The cells had been constructed in the 1800s and were of historical value. The cell used for exhibits still had the chain shackles fixed to the interior block walls. During the Palmer River Goldrush in the 1800s, Cooktown was a major port and a large town. The Court-house went up to the Supreme Court, and some convicted criminals were hung on the gallows located on the existing police land.

The police station was a district station with a Sub inspector in charge. The population of Cooktown was around 90,000 and the Palmer River goldfields, 16,000. During my time in Cooktown, the division population was about 4,000, including both aboriginal communities, and 2,000 in the town area. While O.I.C Cooktown, I was involved in Little Athletics, the S.E.S. and the R.S.L. The latter was only a sub-branch and, when I arrived in Cooktown, traded only on a Friday night. Unlicensed club permits were obtained for the sale of alcohol. All duties were performed by volunteers. Due to my military service, I became a full member and assisted in a volunteer capacity. There were no other licensed clubs in Cooktown at that time. The only form of entertainment was at the three hotels.

At one meeting, I recommended we hold a family afternoon BBQ every Sunday afternoon in addition to Friday night trade and I would be the cook. I would provide the BBQ, and the women's auxiliary would organise the food. This commenced and grew from about 30 people to around 120 over a period of two years. The club had to build a large barbeque area to accommodate all those meals. I did most of the cooking up until I left.

I also held the position of Secretary for three years. A couple of times per year, the admin officer and I would visit the Cape Flattery silica sand mine located in a remote, coastal area, about 100 kilometres north of Cooktown,

Cooktown RSL, front entrance

Ken cooking Sunday family BBQ

and conduct driver's license tests, mainly for trucks and semi-trailers being driven at the mine. The company would fly us to and from the mine in their light aircraft, which was piloted by a former-Queensland police pilot, Sergeant Ron Rourke.

There were several eccentric people living in and around Cooktown, but one person in particular and his wife caused me immense problems. This person thought that he was Jesus Christ after his wife told him that he was. He called himself Saint Ulfus and harassed local state politicians so much that he was granted a one hectare, 99-year lease on an ocean front parcel of land, just south of Cooktown.

He and his wife ended up having 12 children, and all of their names started with a J, after disciples. He never worked whilst living in Cooktown and drove a Mercedes Benz car as well as a light truck. Some months after arriving in Cooktown, I had cause to arrest him one evening and place him in the Watch-house. Whilst we were busy transporting his wife and a number of the children back to their house, he broke out of the Watch-house, broke into the police station, and destroyed some files and property before leaving. He was later located that evening and charged with several offences.

He pleaded not guilty, and the matter went to the District Court where he was convicted and fined on all charges. From the time of his arrest, he claimed that I was the devil and caused me numerous problems from then on. Over my six-year term in Cooktown, he and his wife wrote hundreds of letters of complaint about me and my staff. He addressed the original to the Queen and sent copies to the Prime Minister, Premier, Police Minister, Police Commissioner and the District Officer. He would frequently telephone the District Officer, who would then contact me and want to know what was going on. The letters were written by his wife who had a Bachelor of Arts degree in education.

They refused to send their children to a state school, built a classroom on their property and she self-taught them. They were vexatious litigants and all the letters were lies, but still I was investigated on numerous occasions as a result of these letters, until one investigating Inspector depicted them for what they were and cleared my name for all the accused wrong doings.

I attended many jobs that could bear mention but will only relate to some. One being that I received a call stating that a male person had been forcibly removed from a prawning trawler in Princess Charlotte Bay, several hundred kilometres north of Cooktown, due to his threatening behaviour. He had been placed on an isolated small sand island in the bay and given enough water and supplies to last until police arrived to deal with him. He was also given a tent and swag.

As this person was a big person and was possibly mentally unstable, I departed Cooktown with a constable to investigate the matter which by now had attracted international media coverage. We had to drive to a remote river east of Musgrave Station on the Cape York Development Road. Upon arrival, we were met by the skipper of the trawler who was alone in a 10-foot tinnie. He told us that he had to anchor the trawler in the bay at the front of The Kennedy River.

The river he was in was the Annie River. We had to travel some miles down the Annie River, then another mile or so out the Kennedy River, to reach the trawler. The water was too shallow for the trawler to proceed any further. Once at the trawler, we had about one hour steaming time to the island in question. The waters in that area are infested with sharks and crocodiles. We ascertained that the skipper had needed a deckhand and advertised in Cairns and Brisbane for one.

This guy on the island had applied and stated that he had previous experience. The job initially was for six weeks, and this person was flown to Cairns and then to Princess Charlotte Bay by float plane at the expense of the skipper. On the first night out fishing, it was found that he had no previous experience, and he could not deal with being spiked by bullrouts and having to remove sea snakes from the net.

After one night, he demanded that the skipper arrange for his return to Brisbane. The skipper refused, and this person then threatened the life of the skipper and the safety of the boat. When they finished work and the deck hand had gone to sleep, the skipper requested assistance from another vessel via radio. Upon their arrival, they all then removed him to his current location. He had been stranded for about two days prior to our arrival.

I motored the tinnie in towards him on our arrival at about 4pm and told him that he would be picked up early the next day, as we did not want to have to guard him that night on board. He was collected the following morning and we headed back to the Kennedy River. Again, we were not able to anchor in close due to the depth and the outgoing tide, the current of which was fairly strong. By the time the five of us boarded the tinnie, there was about six inches of freeboard. Not much if he began to play up. At this stage, he was contented as he believed that we had arranged his return to Brisbane, and I was not going to tell him otherwise until on dry land.

It took us a long time to return to the police vehicle due to the outgoing tide. I considered that we were doing two to three knots per hour. Once at the vehicle, we had to return to Musgrave, where I had arranged for the Royal Flying Doctor plane to meet us. When I arrived at Musgrave, I then advised him that he was being detained under the Mental Health Act and was being conveyed to the Cairns Base Hospital.

The constable would be accompanying him on the journey. He was not happy but accepted the fact that he would be fed, have a bath and a clean bed for the night. I slept the night in the back of the police vehicle, somewhere off the road between Musgrave and Laura, due to the time of night. I had built a bed box in the police vehicle behind the seats and in front of the cage.

The box had three compartments, containing cooking and eating utensils; a ten-man army ration pack and recovery equipment. This was made for times like this or when not able to cross flooded creeks. I arrived back in Cooktown at about 12 noon the following day. In all, this job had taken five days to perform. The constable returned from Cairns by police air wing also that day.

Cooktown was the last town on the east coast and the end of the road for anyone heading north to a major town. For that reason, we used to get a lot of strange people arriving and staying for a time in Cooktown. One such person arrived in Cooktown. He was a third-year university drop out who had been studying Law and also was an ex-drug user.

He had no fixed place of abode and would sleep out anywhere in the close proximity of the town area. He was known to frequent the local churches, sit in the front row and argue with ministers giving the sermon. Another habit was to pat women on the backside in the town area, but no person would make an official complaint. As he had long, fair hair and a beard, he was nicknamed 'creeping Jesus' by the town people.

Most people in Cooktown had a nickname. I had told him on several occasions to pack up and get out of town, only to receive a lengthy spiel about how he knew his rights and that he had "studied Law and there was no offence that I could get him on" and so on. I told him that this was not the city and we handled matters our way in the bush to try and bluff him to leave, but, to no avail.

One Friday afternoon, I received a call that there was a bad smell coming from a small yacht moored in the river in front of a cafe. There was a rubber zodiac tied to the rear of the yacht and no occupants had been noticed coming or going in recent weeks. I went to investigate, borrowing a dingy from the café owner and rowed out to the yacht, where I discovered the partial, skeletal remains of a tall male person on a bed of cushions in the bow of the yacht. The smell was unbearable, and his body fluids were several inches deep in the well of the boat. The deceased's skull, lower arms and legs were skeletal and the remainder intact. He was lying on his back. His skin had dried to the extent of that of a dead, roadside animal.

I returned to the station, called out a constable on overtime to assist, and then went first to the auxiliary fire brigade to get two sets of breathing apparatus and then to the hospital to get protective clothing and gloves. I had nothing to cover our footwear. I then returned to the yacht in company with the constable. We again entered the yacht wearing the items I had borrowed, slid a tarp under the body and carried it out and placed it in the zodiac. By the time all of this had taken place, the sun had gone down.

The local undertaker who had the government contract arrived in his short wheel-based Toyota Land Cruiser and refused to take the body due to its decomposed state. Naturally, this caused me a problem. The café owner had an old, rusty Ford pickup utility. I asked him if I could use it on the condition that I give it a good clean afterwards. He did so and the body was placed on its back in the truck. I then decided that I would cover the body with the cushions and bedding from the yacht.

I took a container of petrol from the rear deck of the yacht and decided that I would take the body via the dump, burn the bedding and cushions and then convey the body to the hospital morgue using back dirt roads on the outskirts of town. I did not need the constable for this, so he then ceased duty.

I was driving up the main street in this old rusty blue, pickup truck with the body in the back, and as I drew level with the bottom pub and opposite the post office, the cushions blew out of the truck onto the roadway, leaving the body exposed with the forearms up reaching towards the sky. As this happened, I stopped to retrieve the cushions and right at that time, three aboriginal women who had been at the post office making a telephone call, walked around the back of the truck, looked in and then began screaming.

Everyone in the pub ran outside to see what was happening and started to cheer and make all sorts of comments when they saw the body. After I threw the bedding back over the body, I couldn't get out of there quick enough. I went to the dump, burned the cushions and bedding and then drove back onto the main road to head to the morgue. I had only gone a short distance when, as luck would have it, low and behold, who should be hitchhiking into town, no other than 'creeping Jesus'.

I stopped a couple of car lengths back, and he ran to the truck, stuck his head in the passenger window and was about to speak when he noticed me driving. I said, "I have told you on many occasions to get out of town". He then began to give me the same old spiel, I said, "No more. I'm sick of listening to you. I told you we do things differently in the bush. Look in the back. You're next." I left him on the side of the road with his mouth down near his knees and never saw him again.

On another occasion, whilst the Cooktown races were on, we received a call that a family with a young baby were stranded in swampland in a remote area, some three to four hours north of Cooktown. There was a river nearby, the tides were getting bigger and they were afraid of crocodiles. They were nearly out of water, food and baby food as they had been there for several days. They had eventually got a message out on their HF radio.

The mayday call had been received in Albany, Western Australia. We had additional police from Cairns to assist with the races so Constable Teske from Laura and I attended to this recovery. It took us several hours to locate them, and when we did, were surprised to see the tourist had bogged his vehicle in a salt pan after doing do-nuts. He had broken through the hard crust and sunk in mud to the chassis. He had tried to dig around the vehicle only made a lake of water around it. There was a dry, sand island, about 10 metres in diameter, located about 30 metres from the vehicle.

On the island he had erected a tent, and all around the tent he had piles of wood to light at night to keep the crocodiles at bay, as the tide had been coming right up to the sand island. He had joined about three lengthy fishing rods together and placed copper wire to the rods and the battery for an aerial. With the use of two vehicle winches, one portable winch and additional cable, we were able to winch him out over several hours. We were all covered in mud by the time this was done.

We drove to a windmill with water troughs on this cattle station and had a bath in the cattle troughs, before returning to Cooktown. It was very late when we arrived back, and I put the family up in the donga for a couple of days until his vehicle was cleaned up. They were from Western Australia. He never offered us any thanks for our troubles, although his wife did.

About one month later, both Glen and I received a snatch strap for our troubles. I still have mine, some 35 years later.

During the preceding three-month period prior to my departure from Cooktown on promotion, I was responsible for the operational control of several incidents which attracted both national and international media coverage.

These incidents included:

- A large-scale air/ground drug smuggling/Asian child prostitution operation code named operation "standby", which led to the apprehension of two aircraft at different locations in the division and the arrest of four persons.
- A sea plane crash on the Endeavour River, Cooktown,
- The discovery of a body in the Endeavour River near the wharf - Suspected murder.
- A successful, four-day search for a 22 month-old male child in dense tropical terrain at Helensvale, south of Cooktown,
- The discovery of 7 x 44 gallon drums containing approximately 350 kilograms of packaged, compressed cannabis, found at various locations along the coastline within the division after a lengthy air search,
- A drug related, shooting/murder investigation of a woman at Archer's Point, Cooktown,
- A crocodile attack on a fishing boat in the Annan River, Cooktown.

All of these events occurred in addition to the normal, lesser occurrences which occurred on a frequent basis within the division.

With reference to "Operation Standby", the operation was commenced upon receipt of information that an aircraft was due to arrive in Cooktown with a cargo of narcotics from Asia, and that another aircraft was to depart the Atherton Tablelands and rendezvous with the first aircraft somewhere in the Cooktown Division. A suspect vehicle containing two persons was also involved and was to meet with the aircraft. Numerous inquiries made resulted in ascertaining descriptions and locations of the suspects, the aircraft and the suspect vehicle.

Due to a well-coordinated operation by the local police and others assisting, both aircraft were located at separate airfields and the pilots detained. Both pilots were armed with concealable firearms, which was a known fact prior to their apprehension. The vehicle involved was intercepted, and the two male occupants detained. Further inquiries revealed that these four persons had conspired together to import both narcotics and child prostitutes from Asia to Australia.

No drugs were located, as the mission had been a training run in preparation for the smuggling operation. All four offenders were charged with several offences. Further investigations made by federal police in relation to this operation led to the arrest of other persons of Asian origin in southern states. This operation caused considerable strain on police resources as, once again, the annual Cooktown race meeting was being conducted on those days and all available police had to be utilised on this operation.

The most rewarding and gratifying job that I have attended during my career was that of the missing toddler, Eric Arthur Taylor, as briefly mentioned prior. Eric, 22 months old, went missing late in the afternoon, from his dwelling in Helensvale, some 30 kilometres south of Cooktown. By the time police were alerted and arrived at the scene, it was close to dark. His home was in a remote area, which consisted of mountainous, tropical terrain, densely timbered, with several running creeks nearby. Grave fears were held for the safety of the child.

A large scale search was commenced at daylight the following day. Other strategies were put in place on the first night. I was the search commander for this search, which eventually became the longest, most publicised, successful search of its type in Australian history and possibly still is to this day. The search went for four complete days, resulting in finding the child alive, naked and covered in scratches but in reasonable condition. He was about two kilometres from his home, above an escarpment where horses could not even travel.

At its height, there were about 260 persons involved in the search. They comprised of local volunteers, S.E.S., Army and local police personnel. I appointed Sen. Const. Wayne McGilvray as the field commander. The S.E.S. helicopter and pilot were made available for the search. I flew in twice a day for briefings and outside of that, operated from the S.E.S. headquarters in Cooktown, organising resources and supplies. I did not have much sleep in those four days.

The logistics for this search was enormous. Tents had to be set up for the searchers for sleeping, dining, cooking, and in addition, toilets and showers. All these facilities were out in an open paddock. The searchers remained on location for the entire search and had to conduct the search in shifts. One cannot describe the emotion of the searchers and all those involved when

Media Release — Ken at Cooktown hospital nursing Eric in company of his mother, Maryanne Taylor the morning after being found

word came in that he had been found alive. Tough, hardened people were all brought to tears.

I was at the S.E.S. H.Q. at the time. One of the hardest tasks to perform at that time was that detectives were about to interview his mother in case of foul play on her part. She was an emotional wreck. Word then came in over the radio that he had been found, but we did not know if he was alive. I interrupted the detectives, and we all went out to the radio when shortly after, we were advised that he was alive. I turned to his mother, she looked at me and then ran and hugged me, and we both then broke down and cried, as did many others in the room. I will never forget that moment.

As the high school at Cooktown only went to grade 10 and my eldest son was in that class, it was time to leave Cooktown. He had been an inaugural student from grade eight, when the high school first opened.

Maryborough

I was transferred to Maryborough on promotion and arrived there in September 1988. My role there was that of shift sergeant. I was also the licensing inspector for 23 Hotels in the division. I did notice on my arrival that the arrests in the past 12 months for that Station, which included a C.I. Branch, were not many more than Cooktown, and we only had five uniformed officers, including myself, and one detective. For the preceding nine months at Cooktown, we had 158 arrests on 212 criminal charges and 214 arrests for drunk. That showed how busy Cooktown was.

In late May 1990, we obtained information from a Forestry Department Manager based on Fraser Island that a major anti-logging protest was being organised for action on Fraser Island to disrupt logging operations. This forestry officer, Mr Andrew Millard, had been at a Roma Street forum in Brisbane the previous Sunday, where activist groups were talking about a planned blockade to stop logging on Fraser Island and were handing out pamphlets asking for volunteers to join the protest. Andrew brought a pamphlet in to the police station.

I then notified the district Officer, Inspector Stan Rossow of this. He then had me prepare an Operational Order to police the protest. I compiled the operational order and, in consultation with Maryborough police prosecutor, Sergeant George Pope, addressed every possible act for offences that may be committed by the protestors. This became an attachment to the operational Order. This order was distributed to several police establishments and to the premier's department. At the time, the labour government was in power in Queensland.

I later learnt that the conservation movement involved in the proposed protest action had a complete copy of that order before heading to Fraser Island to commence protest action.

A group of approximately 50 demonstrators arrived on Fraser Island in early June, 1990, and set up camp in readiness for future action. When we became aware of this, Inspector Rossow appointed me as field commander for the police contingency to be sent to Fraser Island to police the protest.

Initially, arrangements were made to accommodate the police at a forestry establishment, Dilli Village, on the southern part of the island. This village had accommodation, a dining area, a kitchen, and a cook to provide meals. 16 police, including myself, from the Maryborough district, were dispatched to the island.

Four of those officers had just been sworn in. We were then all based at Dilli Village. As no protest action had commenced at this stage, the first week was spent teaching officers how to drive four-wheel drive vehicles in sand, along with bushcraft and orientation of the logging area. The forestry department had divided the island into 14 logging zones; the first in the south, and then running north to the 14th.

These zones were all in the centre of the island which consisted of dense rainforest and steep sandhills. About one in forty selected hardwood trees were logged. There was one contractor and three cutters conducting the operation. At the time of our arrival, they were working between zones seven to ten. In the first week, we worked 8 am to 4 pm shifts. After work, those interested would go fishing in front of the village, on the beach as the tailor were running. All of the fish caught were prepared and cooked for meals.

Once the protest commenced, protestors walked into the work site and disrupted the cutters by blowing whistles. There were some professional activists at the commencement who were very troublesome in their actions and some arrests were made early in the protest. Shortly after the protest commenced, I received instructions from the regional commander that the police presence was mainly to uphold the peace and that we were not to make any arrests unless they were for offences of a serious nature.

Forestry officers were to take any appropriate action. We could assist them in moving the protestors out of harms way or by dismantling anything that they had constructed to halt the timber operation. I created some controversy when I requested this instruction in writing. Any inaction by the police would not be acceptable to the local population in Maryborough, as a lot of people's livelihood would be at stake.

After receiving this instruction, I formed the opinion that this protest had become political and that the government did not want another problem similar to that which occurred in Ravenshoe; when logging was stopped,

Commissioner Newnham, police and forestry officers on his visit to Poyungan Creek, Fraser Island

Police and forestry officers apprehending protestors during "Operation Logging"

many people lost their jobs and the community in general was financially affected.

I felt that we could have closed this protest down very soon after it had commenced, if we had been permitted to make arrests under the acts that we had researched. As this was not going to be the case, I then adopted a policy of having daily meetings with all involved, including the protestors. The protest was full on for the first six weeks. Many shifts exceeded 12 hours due to travel times to and from Dilli Village to the work site.

On many occasions, we could not traverse the beach due to tide conditions and the inland tracks were very rough. Most of the work was occurring in the forest, inland from Happy Valley, a fair distance from Dilli Village. Due to a large usage of overtime, I made the recommendation that the department rent three adjoining houses in Happy Valley. This was approved. Some personnel moved into these houses, and we obtained accommodation at two other forestry houses, one at Poyungan Creek on the western side of the island near the contractor's house and workshop, and the other at Lake Allom. This way we had a police presence close to where the protestors may target.

The protest lasted for two days short of one year and for a greater part of that year, the contractor could operate in any of the 14 zones. Should the protestors blockade a log haul road, we would move to another location without their knowledge, thereby stretching their resources. A common action they adopted was that of erecting tripods in the middle of the roadway. This consisted of three logs joined together by thin twine at the top and the legs spread apart. A protestor would then use a rope ladder, climb to the top and sit in the apex of the tripod.

Should anyone try to remove them and lift one of the legs, either the rope holding it together would break and the tripod topple to the ground or the tripod would twist and fall to the ground, either way; possibly causing injury to the person sitting on it. Unknown to the protestors, we practised dismantling tripods that we had built ourselves where no harm could be caused to the protestor. We did not have to put this into practise until we had no other choice.

Erected tripod blocking road

Police practising dismantling tripods

Early in the protest, a professional protestor arrived at their camp and introduced actions that were difficult to deal with. One in particular was for protestors to lay down on the ground when approached by police or forest officers and refuse to move, thereby forcing those officers to carry them out. This was often in difficult, hilly, dense, tropical terrain. This fellow whose name was Brian was a big man who liked his food. He was always polite, but it was obvious that he was the brains when action was planned.

The protestors operated by a majority rule principle, in that they never had a leader, and should future action be proposed, then they would have to vote on it. They appointed a different spokesperson daily to talk with police, media etc. I devised a plan that whenever we had a problem with the protestors in the field, we would always ask to speak with Brian and explain that we had a good relationship with him. If in view of other protestors, we would offer him some food, which he always accepted. After a couple of days of this, they thought that he was trying to run the show and was too friendly with the police, so they sent him off the island, not to return. He could not understand why this had happened.

The police worked the same days as the loggers. A three day break every second week, those being Friday, Saturday and Sunday, and every other Sunday. We all returned to our homes on the three-day break or, if some desired, on the other Sunday. Once we moved from Dilli Village, most staff were rotated on a fortnightly basis. Some sergeants did three months straight. We received meal and living away from home allowances and had to purchase and prepare our meals. Most of this was done by me and the sergeants. We were also responsible for maintaining the rental houses, vehicles and equipment. I remained as field commander for the entire 12 months, having two shorts stints of leave in that time. By now, some police personnel were coming to Fraser Island from other districts within the region.

After many months, the government restricted logging to zone nine only and authorised persons only were permitted into those areas. Once this occurred, the protestors blockaded all roads leading into that area with tripods. It was now time for us to dismantle them, which we did in a safe and effective manner in the presence of the media. They did not construct any further tripods.

There were times during the year that both police and protestor numbers varied. At times, there were only two police and two to three protestors present. During the protest, Mr Tony Fitzgerald Q.C. was appointed by the government to conduct an inquiry into logging on Fraser Island. He and his colleagues had dinner with us at our residence on one of his visits. Once I commenced daily meeting with all those involved in the first two months of the protest, the protest then continued in a peaceful manner.

For the entire 12 months of the protest, the contractor only lost five working days due to protest action and obtained his annual quota of timber. There were no persons injured in the protest and very few complaints made against the police. In June 1991, the government handed down its decision that all logging on Fraser Island would cease. All those employed in the industry, the contractor and the department of forestry employees, were compensated in various ways as a result of this decision. During the 12 months that I spent on the island, it was the only time that I can recall having no fish in the freezer at my home.

The only time that I went fishing, after the training period at the start of the protest, was on my day off on the Sunday or at times on a Friday after work. Some Friday evenings, we would get together with forestry workers on the beach, have a fire, and whilst some were hauling in fish, I would clean them and cook them straight away in beer batter on the back of the truck. You cannot get fresher than that. Any remaining fish was eaten by the police working and living on the island.

In February, 1992, whilst relieving in the position as officer in charge of Maryborough station, Her Royal Highness, the Duchess of Kent, visited flood victims in Maryborough shortly after the township was in flood. Also, part of her itinerary, two days later, was to travel to Lake Allom on Fraser Island to officially declare the area world heritage. She was to fly in to Dilli Village, then travel by motorcade to Lake Allom where the ceremony was to be conducted.

I made some inquiries and ascertained that her movements would not be possible. Dilli Village airstrip was waterlogged, and no aircraft could land. The motorcade would not be in a position to travel on the beach, as strong winds and high tides were making the beach impassable. This information was relayed to the tour organises, and her schedule was going to be altered for her to return to Maryborough the following Sunday to again speak with flood victims. As this was the last Sunday in the pay fortnight, many police would have to be utilised for the visit on overtime.

For this reason, I had a discussion with the district officer and advised that I could arrange an alternate plan for her to visit Fraser Island by boat and conduct the ceremony at a different location. This proposal was granted, and I was given the task to make these arrangements. In consultation with the Duchess's Aid, a British Naval Commander, National Parks Management and the Officer in Charge of Hervey Bay, Senior Sergeant Guild, we set about altering Her Royal Highness's schedule. Approval had to be first obtained from Buckingham Palace, which was done.

Senior Sergeant Guild organised vessel transportation, by way of the Water Police vessel and the Department of Marines vessel. I contacted the owners of the newly completed, but as of yet, not opened, Kingfisher Resort on Fraser Island and proposed that the vessels tie up to their jetty, should their approval be granted. They were delighted with the idea of having royalty visit their resort prior to the opening. A young National Parks Officer, formerly of the Fraser Island Forestry Department, was placed in charge of the official ceremony, luncheon, guest list and their transportation to and on the island. When the Duchess and her official entourage travelled to Fraser Island, they would be met by four-wheel drive vehicles and escorted by police; to firstly Lake McKenzie and then on to Central Station for the official ceremony.

Two police vehicles would be used in the escort and I would be in charge of the police. I then travelled to Fraser Island to do a recognisance and timings. Upon my return to Maryborough, Marc and I worked throughout the night to finalise arrangements before returning to the island for the event. We both worked for 36 hours straight with very little sleep. The Duchess was greeted on the jetty at Kingfisher by the wife and daughter of the owner, who had flown in from Melbourne for the occasion. The weather was fine, and the tour passed without incident.

Prior to the Duchess's departure from the island, she requested to speak to me personally. We had a lengthy conversation. She was a very astute lady and told me that she knew how hard it would have been for me to organise a change to her schedule at short notice. She also knew that I would have had little sleep. She thanked me for my efforts and stated that her visit to Fraser Island had been the highlight of her Australian tour.

I relieved as officer in charge of Maryborough, until my promotion to Senior Sergeant and transfer to an administration position at Maroochydore.

When I arrived at Maroochydore in September 1992, there were three Senior Sergeants, which included the officer in charge. I had very few weekend shifts allocated to me in the annual budget. I was given a small office of my own, and my main role was to adjudicate on all criminal offence reports and detail each one to the respective officer or section for further investigation. This task could have been performed by a senior constable and was inappropriate for an officer of my rank.

I complained to a commissioned officer and the position was then given to a sergeant. I then planned all major events occurring in the division and performed some district duty officer duties. Soon after my arrival, the district introduced some major operational changes. A district Watch- house and communications centre were established. I was placed in charge of the newly formed district communications centre and had to establish that centre from the outset.

I was part of a team from the north coast region selected to undergo training in Brisbane on the first enterprise bargaining agreement 'E.B.1'. Our team travelled to the northern region and evaluated staffing resources in that region suitable for operational duties that were to receive the operational shift allowance 'O.S.A' in lieu of penalty rates. This took several weeks, and we visited many remote stations.

Another role that I took a major part in was the introduction of civilian communications room officers 'C.R.O's'. I was a trained panel selector and panel convenor for civilian positions and police positions up to, and including, the rank of sergeant. I worked in Brisbane as part of a team,

ΓER FOR ENVIRONMENT AND HERITAGE

ɔomben, MLA
for Windsor
ɔor 160 Ann Street, Brisbane
ɔx 155, NORTH QUAY QLD 4002 · Telephone (07) 227 8819 · Facsimile (07) 221 7082

- 3 APR 1992

Mr R Dargusch
Assistant Commissioner of Police
North Coast Region
61 Esplanade
MAROOCHYDORE QLD 4558

Dear Mr Dargusch

I would like to express my appreciation of the assistance provided by your officers at Maryborough and Hervey Bay. They provided invaluable logistical and organisational support with respect to the recent visit to Fraser Island by Her Royal Highness, the Duchess of Kent.

Unexpected weather conditions required a complete reorganisation of Her Royal Highness' Island visit.

Sergeant Ken Salmon of the Maryborough Station played a crucial part in analysing the Island situation to advise my office of the problems associated with the visit, developing an alternative program and organising the detailed transport requirements of two vehicle convoys and three vessels. All of this was done at short notice and under considerable pressure.

That the Island visit was conducted without incident and on schedule is a credit to Sergeant Salmon's organisational and liaison abilities.

I must also acknowledge Sergeant Jim Guild, Sergeant Francis and the crew of the P W Cahill who provided the efficient land and water transport for the official party.

Their courtesy and willingness to participate in last minute arrangements was essential in making the occasion a success.

I would be grateful if you could pass on my thanks to your officers for a job well done.

Yours sincerely

PAT COMBEN

Letter of Appreciation from Mr. Pat Comben M.L.A
HRH Duchess of Kent visit to Fraser Island

selecting many initial C.R.O. positions for state communication centres. I was also panel convenor for most C.R.O. and sergeant communications coordinator "Comco" positions at the Sunshine Coast Communications Centre.

I spent a lot of time researching and submitting proposals for future communications centres in the Sunshine Coast District. I relieved on a couple of occasions at commissioned officer level but made it known to the district officer that I had no desire to advance to that rank until the remainder of my children had completed high school. I requested that others be given that opportunity until I was ready. In the interim, tertiary studies for promotion to Commissioned rank were introduced.

I was then in my late 40's and made a decision that I would not complete those studies. I had completed, in all, 36 weeks in Chelmer Police College on various management courses and was only granted an exemption from one tertiary subject. This helped me to come to that decision. I continued to perform additional work in my position as O.I.C. Sunshine Coast District Communications.

Command Centre, at Hyatt Regency resort Coolum during CHOGM

Portable air conditioned, 2 story command centre CHOGM

In March, 2002, I performed duty in the command centre for the Commonwealth Heads of Government CHOGM) summit, held at Coolum on the Sunshine Coast. In early 2004, I was selected to take part in a project team to evaluate the viability of the New South Wales Police Assistance Line, which was similar to the now police link system. I was flown to Sydney with the project team to inspect their system and gave some input to project team members based on my communications experience.

I retired from the police service in July 2004 after 36 years of service.

I was awarded the Queensland Police Service medal
The National Police Service medal
The National Service medal
The Australian Defence media

Danny Murdoch

I first met Dan Murdoch when we were both attached to the Criminal Investigation Branch, Brisbane, and then again in the year 1987 on my first day as District Officer at Ipswich I was advised that Dan was the officer to head up the investigation into the unfortunate death of Pamela Bain, which occurred early one morning on the Warrego Highway, west of the City of Ipswich. The Pamela Bain investigation is documented in Dan's story in this volume of keeping the Peace. Throughout my tour of duty at Ipswich in the late 1980s, it was apparent to me and others that Dan was a most competent criminal investigator of serious crime, and an officer who displayed outstanding loyalty to his superiors and his work colleagues. In June, 1992, I was in charge of the South Eastern Police Region and based at the Gold Coast, when I promoted Dan to the rank of Detective Senior Sergeant to head the Gold Coast Juvenile Aid Bureau. He did the Service proud in that role and spent the last two years of his service with the Police Department as an Acting Detective Inspector at Logan Criminal Investigation Branch. Unfortunately for the Department in the month of December, 1996, Dan resigned and now operates his own successful business.

Laurie Pointing

The Danny Murdoch Story

My name is Danny Murdoch, commonly known as Dan. Regarding my age and other personal details, I will have to spend a bit of time to recall those details due to advancing decades and intermittent memory losses. I say this with slight humour and wishful thinking of a youthful past. So, I will get back to you shortly on that.

Early Life

My parents were separated very early in my life which was unusual for the times, but I was raised in a loving home with my wonderful mother (Mum), Grandfather (Pop) and Grandmother (Gran). I recall we lived in a garage with no electricity on land, in what is now the thriving suburb of Corinda. There was farmland all around and 'down the back', which lead to Oxley Creek and then to the now Rocklea Markets. Little money was at hand, but strict love was aplenty. Pop had a milk run with a horse and cart delivering to households in the area; I recall fondly either sitting between the horses' legs or atop the sulky with Pop.

My mother worked hard for Atlantic Oil in Brisbane City, who later I believe changed their name to Esso, and Gran ran the small household with an iron but compassionate hand. Sundays were special. I remember that they normally started out with me and my cattle dog, simply called Red, going for a half wander/crawl around the farmland and the edges of the creek, something parents would not allow a toddler to do in this day and age, and then returning slowly to the garage where there was a 'lean-to' made from canvas tacked onto the garage. This is where we had our dining table and chairs, a bit cold in winter but great in summer.

The wood stove and ice chest also adorned this area. It was also where Gran would religiously give me one tablespoon full of castor oil every Sunday before lunch, demanding that it was good for my health. I hated it — if ever this concoction was forced down your young throat, you will know what I mean. Some year's later pop had a stomach-ache and Gran gave him her remedy, castor oil. Pop doubled up in pain and fell to the ground. The Queensland Ambulance Transport Brigade (QATB) were called, and he was diagnosed with a burst appendix, caused so they said by Grans' wonder drug. Gran cried remorsefully and that was the finish of the castor oil treatment. Pop survived.

Pop sold the horse and cart milk run and moved to Labrador, where we ran a small shop on the old Pacific Highway with Gran making apple pies, meat pies and cakes on a wood stove (again under a canvas lean-to) out the back of the shop exposed to the elements. It was where I first started school at the age of four years and nine months, proudly walking a couple of miles to school on my first day, alone. We moved again to a fruit shop in Cavendish road, Coorparoo, opposite the State School and just down from the then Fire Station.

I recall we had an old Morris utility, and Pop would get the fruit and vegetables from the markets every morning. We moved again and again, as was our life at the time; from Coorparoo to a home at Tugun, this time on a dirt road called Wyberba Street, near the old Tugun train station. Pop obtained a job managing the Tugun general store. He then changed jobs and worked at the Currumbin Bird Sanctuary, opened back in 1947 by Alex Griffiths, working in the milk bar and helping to feed the birds. I also got part time work there, giving people rides on Shetland ponies with my young

Currumbin Bird Sanctuary – as a young fellow – circa 1957

friend who kept horses on the family farm behind where the Currumbin Bird Sanctuary is still situated.

I also tried to assist in feeding the birds.

Now it needs some explanation as to why so many moves disturbed a young fellow like me — at a time when he needed stability. The First World War is the reason. You see, Pop was in the Light Horse Brigade, I think it was the first Brigade, but I am not completely certain. On returning from the war, he just could not settle; his brother was killed in close quarter fighting in the European campaign and Pop saw tragedies he could not and would not speak about. Only later in life he seldom talked in quiet tones with short sentences of the horrors he witnessed as a young soldier.

I understood his need to keep moving, which he continued to do until the end of his life. Gran, Mum and I followed him.

Gran stood by him resolutely. A memory branded into my mind forever is seeing Gran at 4.00 pm or so every afternoon, dressed up in her best frock, wearing a broach and necklace, grooming her hair to perfection and placing on lipstick, which was the only ladies' makeup she would allow herself. She would wait at the top of the backstairs for Pop to arrive home in his Ford Consul (another car change) from work and greet him. I believe that witnessing loyalty and love like this as a boy, together with the strong upbringing, started to fashion me as a person.

Schooling

To think about school brings back some memories, thank goodness. Particularly, my personal credentials. My name is Danny (Dan) Murdoch, and I was born on the 2nd. April 1947 in Brisbane, Queensland. I have lived since that time in many places around Queensland, elsewhere in Australia and other parts of the Asia Pacific Region, such as Singapore and Thailand. I have worked and travelled to some far-flung corners of the globe and have witnessed many things. So, in retrospect, I regard myself as lucky, fortunate and honoured in so many ways. I live by a philosophy that yesterday is gone and tomorrow is new; in fact, yesterday simply taught me about tomorrow.

My personal motto is that *'life is a journey from birth to death, fighting selfishness.'*

I also believe that I, and in fact all of us, can make a difference no matter who we are, no matter where we are, and no matter our age.

So, I walked myself to school on the first day. That was the way we were brought up, and I wasn't letting anyone embarrass me by actually walking me to the Labrador school to start my independent adventure. I then attended schools after Labrador at Coorparoo, Currumbin, Kedron and The Gap. Halfway through my Sub Senior year, my Auntie Heather who worked at Parliament House, secured me a job at the Lands Department in George Street as a Clerks Assistant. I was 15 years of age.

So, this is where it all started.

Work — The Start

I remember as a young fellow, seeing the older men, as there were no women or girls there at that time, in the Files Section where I worked racing to the Lands Office Hotel in George street at lunchtime 1.00 pm, and throwing down a few 10-ounce beers before they had to start again at 1.45pm or 2.00pm or 2.15pm. I also recall with humour seeing one or two of those very keen lunch time drinkers laying down in the Map Room in one of the map drawers and having a camp (sleep). The Map Room had these very large and deep drawers you could pull out and get into (with some drunken ease), and then close shut, just leaving a gap for some Map Room fresh air. They reckon it made a nice bed for an afternoon nap.

So, I got out of there as quickly as I could and transferred to the Rural Fires Board, with my boss being a Mr. Healy. At that time, we had small offices in "The Mansions", down the bottom of George Street near Parliament House; a wonderful heritage building.

At this time of my life, I had left Mum, Gran and Pop's home on the South Coast (now Gold Coast) and moved to Newmarket, Brisbane to start work and live with my other Grandmother, Grandma Meade. I had a spot on the open veranda of her home with my bed and small table, which was semi enclosed by timber slat blinds which were broken. Every time it rained, I had to sleep with my raincoat on and a south wester (rain hat) to keep out the rain. So, there must be something about me as a young fellow, always having to either have a 'lean-to' over me or having the elements greet me every so often.

Again, events and circumstances teach you, don't they? I briefly give you this background of my life as a youngster simply to explain my origins.

Work-Clerk of Petty Sessions

I missed the beach and surf on the Gold Coast and would travel back each weekend to stay with the family and surf. So, I started to look around for options that may have been available for me to return to the Coast and work and, of course, let me be able to surf. I loved living at Newmarket with my Grandma and members of the family like Arthur and Heather and their young boys, who were also drawn to the surf in those days.

So, I was lucky and received a transfer to the Clerk of Petty Sessions (now the Clerk of Court or the Magistrates Court) office at Southport. Later, I transferred to the Magistrates Court at Townsville as the Depositions Clerk, and then finally to the Magistrates Court at Coolangatta. Thinking about Townsville, the head Magistrate in Townsville was a Mr. Henderson. I recall (with a smile on my face) a couple of events in Townsville at this time that one could get away with in those days, although not likely at all today.

As a depositions clerk I had to type all proceedings down on a typewriter – actually, it was a special model for the task, called a Remington Noiseless.

Now, my special model had three keys which used to stick, the C, K and S keys, and this made me swear quietly under my young breath whilst in Court hearings, and I was finding getting a new typewriter by official requisition impossible. The actual main Court room in those days was a wonderful ornate timber filled room with a very high spiral set of stairs leading to the Bench where the Magistrate sat.

The Depositions Clerk (yours truly) sat prominently halfway up those winding stairs on a less prestigious but still 'high up' smaller bench; a wonderful position to view the offenders in the dock and the entire proceedings. It also gave me a vocal vantage point when I had to stop the witnesses halfway through an evidentiary sentence because my typewriter keys got stuck again. I got sick of it.

So, one day as I was taking evidence on my special Depositions Clerk Remington Noiseless typewriter, the machine ever so slightly started to move towards the edge of my 'high up' bench and, unfortunately, I had trouble stopping it from falling quite some distance to the Courtroom floor below, after bouncing on a couple of the beautiful timber stairs. It broke, and we had to remand the case due to the Depositions Clerk (me) having no spare typewriter. As I recall, a new Remington Noiseless was sent by train up from Brisbane to allow important criminal matters to once again flow normally.

I still have trouble understanding how that typewriter slid from the bench.

Part of the duties of the Magistrates at that time in Townsville was to take turns in visiting the Stuart Creek Goal (now Correctional Centre) to hear and determine cases occurring within the prison. I would tag along as the Depositions Clerk with my friend, the Remington Noiseless. The old prison, as I recall, had several watch towers where armed guards would be constantly on alert, and was where the Magistrate and I would enter the main complex.

The instructions during that period were for the Magistrate and I to look up to each tower in turn and wait until the officer on duty stood at attention, saluted and called out in a loud, official and stern voice "Sir"; the Magistrate and I then had to acknowledge with a similar official look and silently salute back.

Not sure if that is still the way things are done — I doubt it, but it has stayed in my mind as a military style of procedure which was important, as it displayed and maintained an air of discipline, respect and importance to the entry of the Magistrate into the hallowed prison ground. If they don't do this now, they should.

Anyway, back to the Gold Coast and the Coolangatta Court House. I was getting a bit older by this time and starting to enjoy life; especially in those days, in the wonderful, but more sparsely populated, Gold Coast.

The surf was good; the girls just as good, work was great, and life was wonderful.

I had just passed the age of 21 and the time was the late '60s, I was made a Justice of the Peace as part of my role in the Magistrates Court. I remember fondly that the Coolangatta Court Office was in the same compound as the Coolangatta Police Station and, of course, the Court House itself. In fact, the Police and Court complex covered a large block of land bordering Griffith Street, Warner Street and Marine Parade. We worked in close quarters with the Police and all banded together socially.

The local Detectives going into the '70s and beyond were 'Street smart.' Characters such as John Meskell and Roy Fursman, together with other competent plain clothes officers. Now I know history has written a lot about this period and of officers like these two; however, all I can say is that I witnessed first hand that nobody came into Coolangatta and the southern Gold Coast area during that period without Meskell and Fursman knowing who they were, what they were doing there, where they were from and where they were going. This to me was real policing.

If there was a crime, they knew where to look. I always remembered that.

I also recall vividly events like Police or Court House staff send offs and Christmas parties. In those days, you would get your favourite brew in a wooden five or 10-gallon keg (remember?), but the big difference is that we used to prop the keg on the Magistrates Court Bench top, hold it up with a piece of timber on either side to stop it rolling off and spike the wooden stopper with a nail and hammer. If we could not find any timber suitable, we would respectfully use the Criminal Code and the Bible from their rightful places on the Bench to assist in the important securing of the keg. As part of my duties I had to 'sit on the bench' of a Saturday morning as the JP, together with one of the 'good citizens' of Coolangatta, to hear and determine the simple offences and to decide bail hearings on the misdemeanours and crimes committed the night before. Normally I would wear a pair of board shorts and rubber thongs, but with a white shirt and tie of course, as one had to get ready for surf after Court.

While I am in the mood for relaying things as they were in these times with a degree of honesty, I recall with a taste of shame, or perhaps gleeful bravado, one Friday night in Coolangatta, when as a youth it was customary to attend the Cabbage Patch Hotel for a few cold ones.

On this particular evening after the liquid dinner was consumed, a friend of mine and I decided it was right and proper to attend at the Coolangatta Post Office at the top end of town, climb onto the roof and with our legs dangling over the side of the front of the building from a less than safe height, and sing the well-known advertisement jingle called *"The Milky Bar Kid is strong and tough."* Now, in the 1970s, it was necessary for all Detectives who interviewed a suspect and gained a statement from him or her via typewriter to have the suspect sign the document in front of a Justice of the Peace; and this weekend, it was me.

Halfway through the song, the Coolangatta Detectives car pulled up outside the Post Office and out steps Detectives Meskell and Fursman. How they knew I was there is the 8th wonder of the world, but as I said previously, they knew who was who in the town. Meskell called out to me in a half official and half humorous voice, *"Can you get down from there, I need a statement witnessed."*

The Milky Bar Kid

So of course, I did as he asked and attended to official Police business. That is the way it was in those days.

They were great days, and good training for my future and for my life in general. I lived on a farm by this stage, at the back of Tallebudgera, where my friend bred cattle and horses. We also had cattle on the adjoining wilderness areas between Currumbin and Tallebudgera; travelling to work each day. I honed my horse skills with the breaking of many youngsters and was learning to be quite a handy farrier.

I had changed by this time from owning a red cattle dog (Red) to a blue cattle dog (Bluey) as a friend I could rely on.

Farm Management

Getting Pop's itchy feet, I left the Magistrates Courts office in Coolangatta and drove to South Australia, looking for adventure, and found work as a farm hand and then a sub-manager of a 5,000-acre property on what was the 90 Mile Desert, near a town called Tintinara. We ran sheep, a few cattle, and grew lupins on the property, and I handled young horses in the local area for some of the adjoining properties. Good job, good people, but freezing cold, as I recall.

I kept life interesting by heading up to Adelaide every couple of weekends to look around and relax.

The property I worked on was called Sheleba Downs. I lived in a shed with no heating, but I had running water which was a plus, and I used to keep warm at night with newspaper placed between my blankets. Minus six plus degrees some mornings, and I had to crank up the Suzuki and drive to the many water troughs, cracking the ice covering the top to let the cattle and sheep drink. Fencing on Sheleba Downs was hard work; hand digging and about a foot down you hit sandstone.

I only stayed on this property for a reasonably short time before the loneliness and cold got to me a bit. I liked the tractor work, digging up the rabbit warrens and ploughing the paddocks, and the horse and cattle work of course, but those sheep and the cold were a bit tough. I could never get used to sheep — don't know why, maybe something about logical thinking.

I worked in a pub in Adelaide for a time, at a place called the Feathers Hotel. Then I guess I was like my Pop and was getting itchy feet again, so I decided to head back to the Gold Coast, maybe I missed my friends and the surf. I worked around the Gold Coast and Northern Rivers areas as a farrier, breaking and training young horses and as a waiter for some time. A former Coolangatta Police Detective who had joined the Commonwealth Police in Sydney spoke to me at the Tweed Heads RSL where I worked part time and talked me into submitting my application to join. So I did

Farrier: A person who cares for the hooves of horses and fits them with horseshoes.

Commonwealth Police

Thankfully, I was quickly accepted and was stationed after training at the Commonwealth Police Redfern office for a time, before being transferred to the Lucas Heights Nuclear Reactor site operated by the Australian Atomic Energy Commission. I did basic guard duty in vehicles and on foot, but I made it interesting by chasing the activists "Friends of the Earth" who were a group of protestors camped in the scrub adjacent to all sides of the reactor.

Shortly after, I was moved to Plain Clothes duty back at Redfern on the notorious 7th floor in the General Crime Squad, and then in the Immigration Squad, locating overstayed persons, criminal deportees, and conducting some Interpol enquiries.

I was with the Commonwealth Police when the changeover occurred to the Australian Federal Police in October 1979. Even though the State Police in NSW and elsewhere at that time in history had a low opinion of the Federal Police, I enjoyed it a lot. I worked in the main department with a former London Policeman called John Jones. We worked in a plain clothes area doing Family Court matters and in general crime investigations. John taught me a lot about how to be a Police Officer.

I worked on well-known cases such as the Greek Conspiracy case, where 181 members of the Greek community in Sydney were arrested and charged with defrauding the Commonwealth Dept. of Social Security by making false claims. Why I recall it well is that I was typing the interview between the principal investigator, myself as co-oberrator and the suspect, when the possible offender picked up the typewriter and threw it out of the window,

Dan Murdoch — Commonwealth Police Raid Preparation 1978

which was closed. I was then on the 8th floor of the Redfern office, and the road beneath was always busy with commuters' going to and from the nearby Redfern train station.

The typewriter smashed into a million pieces and missed everyone. A miracle I reckon — and this may have been a sign he was innocent.

My other duties included a security team member for dignitaries, such as the Australian Prime Minister Malcolm Fraser and his wife Tammy, other Heads of State from overseas countries and HRH Prince Charles on a couple of occasions. HRH Prince Charles gave me a royal tie pin. I recall it as being purple and gold very small, but unique and a prize for sure. I went and lost it.

I had married with a young family, and Pop's itchy feet kicked in again. I decided to go back home to Queensland and join the Queensland Police Force; I guess this is where the real fun started.

Queensland Police

I did my six months training with efficient, roguish, lack of humoured, but wonderful, Police trainers like Wayne Bennett, the big Welshman and wrestler Bill Turner, and many others, such as Sergeant Keith Bowen and Sergeant John Hetherington. I was fortunate to attain dux of the class as well as the leadership award for my squad of which I was extremely proud.

Terry Lewis was the Commissioner at the time.

My initial posting after graduation was Clayfield Station under Sergeant First Class Kevin Guteridge, who steered me on how to do things on my first day, by sending me to a major traffic accident at the famous Albion five-ways. Naturally, I was panic struck when I saw the pile up in the middle of the road, with no one to assist me. I learned fast, did some hand motions to the traffic, which they had showed me how to do for a minute or two at the Police Academy. Also, a bit of the pushing of vehicles, radioing operations for towing assistance, made some notes in my official Police notebook, kept my hat on straight and got through it somehow.

After my three-month stint at Clayfield, I was assigned to the Police Beat in the City, working out of Police Headquarters. Baton in the right-hand pocket, handcuffs in the pouch, with the notebook and Bic biro firmly in place. I stayed there for a month or two until I was called to attend to the Hotel on the corner of Roma and Ann streets opposite King George square, I cannot recall the name, but it is the now the Mercure Hotel.

Dan Murdoch — swearing in — Commissioner Terry Lewis

I was informed that the Head Chef had apparently stolen some meat, which was found in his backpack by security as he was leaving the Hotel for the evening. He was complaining a fair bit due to his management status at the Hotel, but in the bag was in fact the meat. So, after a short 'fire side chat', I arrested him, which is what I thought one had to do due to my thinking that I was the Policeman, and he was a suspect.

I got into quite a bit of trouble from my shift commander when I radioed in the job to him. Apparently, I should have called in the CI Branch. Anyway, I told the commander that I had already arrested him, and I was marching him to the Watch-house. The end of my shift that day was a good dressing down by both the commander and the CI.Branch 0fficer then on duty.

So, in their wisdom they transferred me – to the Brisbane CI.Branch.

Brisbane CI.Branch

I had the privilege in those days to work with or to simply observe excellent detectives such as George Sharry, Pat McCall, Ken Martin, and tough men such as Barry Morgan, who used to move a large pile of dirt around his backyard in suburb of The Gap to keep himself fit. If Barry shook your hand, you knew it. I worked in the General Crime Squad, housed next to the Break and Enter Squad on the Ground Floor of Police Headquarters for some time, and was then posted in 1981 to the Mounted Unit at Oxley with Police old timers and legends, like Sergeant Des Goan and Gordon Close.

This brings back an unforgettable embarrassment.

One fine day we had to do a Mounted Unit parade at a police recruit swearing-in day to be held behind the Police stables on the Academy sports grounds. Now this particular event was really special for some reason, not like the normal swearing-in parades. There was the Premier, Special Ministers of State, everyone who thought that they were in the Queensland who's who list.

Now I was given a new horse to handle. He had been used only for tent pegging before, so was not very good at parades. Anyway the "boss" of the Mounted Unit wanted me to get him used to parades and get him used to actually standing still. You see, tent pegging is where you go flat out with a lance in one hand and then lean over to one side of your horse and try to spike a wooden peg that is sticking out of the ground. So, the horse gets to know only one thing. Walk to the end of the paddock, turn, and gallop in a straight line to the other end of the paddock.

So, I got the job of riding the tent pegging horse. I can't think of his name, but he was black in colour and not a very handsome chap.

The Mounted Unit was all dressed up in their best parade gear and down we went, in what they call a "troop formation" to the parade ground. We were wearing our pith helmets, parade uniform, and leggings, and we all carried a lance with a small flag on the top. The pith helmet was white with a chin strap and a long metal shiny point sticking toward the sky out the top of it.

I remember well that we had to make our entrance when all of the distinguished visitors were seated, the TV cameras were ready, and the newly sworn-in officers were on parade, ready to be officially inspected. So, we did in fact, eight of us in four lots of two, side by side. We all looked great. The sun was shining, and it was a brilliant afternoon for a swearing in; all the VIPs were there looking flash and important with their wives, girlfriends, and attendants.

Our troop was in perfect formation and walked with mounted elegance to the southern end of the parade ground, then had to turn in formation and stand in one line facing the northern end of the parade ground. We were like decoration, and everything went well until the formation turned at the southern end, and as did my horse, who thought he was on a tent pegging run, so what did he do? What he was taught to do so well: he took off at a flat gallop. Down the full length of the parade ground, absolutely and totally uncontrollable; there was no stopping him.

I had the lance in my right hand and the reins in my left. The pith helmet slid down over my face and the metal shiny point was now pointing straight ahead. However, the pith helmet stayed in place due to the chin strap now firmly attached by my teeth.

The lance lowers itself into tent pegging position. I could not see a thing, so down the paddock we went, lance and flag waving, pith helmet over my face like its own mini lance. So, I raised the lance and threw it.

At this time, as I knew later, I was about in line with the distinguished guests. Channel Seven was also in an excellent position.

I grabbed the reins with both hands now and tried to make some leverage on my black tent pegging horse but no, there was no stopping power to be found. He had his mouth wide open; he was going to the end of his run. The pith helmet was still stuck over my face like glue.

Then he stopped at the northern end of the paddock, thinking he had done a great job. I pulled the pith helmet from my face and dismounted. Halfway down the paddock was the lance stuck in the ground like some Olympic javelin, still swaying from the impact into the ground. It looked wonderful.

All eyes from the parade participants, distinguished guests, men, women, and children had their heads turned left, toward me.

I led my tent pegging horse from the parade ground and back to the Mounted Unit stables alone. I didn't ride that horse again.

However, on a happier note, I was fortunate to ride my own Police Horse 'Rosso' as one of the 'coach horses' when Queen Elizabeth visited Brisbane for the opening of Parliament and the Commonwealth Games in 1982. At the official walk past in George street when she was inspecting the 'troop horses', she spoke to me and said, *"Oh you have a lovely horse"* in an upper-class regal English tone. I was thrilled Her Majesty liked my horse. I really wanted to say to her something like: *"Your Majesty, your son Charlie gave me a tie pin, but I lost it. You wouldn't have another one, would you?"*

However, I refrained from doing so.

That same year I was transferred back to the Brisbane CI.Branch and got the first of my two stints relieving for extended periods in the Brisbane Stock Squad. I met good Bushmen like Detective Sergeant Graham Pike, Jock Beale from out Mungallala way, and Ted McIntosh, Gary Richards and Jim Wilby. I worked with some of these men on the Mungindi stolen sheep muster in an area where the Barwon and Weir Rivers met and were in full flood at the time, and other stock related cases.

Taringa CI.Branch

My next posting was in 1983 to the Taringa CI Branch under Detective Sergeant First Class Bob Dallow. All I can say about Bob is that he was a wonderful mentor for a junior Detective and a loyal manager to the men and women under him. In those days, Taringa was the centre of a high crime area with a large geographical area of policing responsibility, stretching from the inner City near Milton to the newer settled areas of Kenmore and Pullenvale. This lends itself to almost being impossible for a Detective to get low arrest figures on your Crime Statistic sheet. It was at Taringa that I recall fondly Police Constable Peter Jackson as a skinny pimple faced young man, working out of the Indooroopilly Station. A friendly keen proud young man, who later played State of Origin Football and for Australia.

I remember him coming into the CI.Branch office at Taringa with offenders grinning like a Cheshire cat silently saying, *"Look what I got Dan."*

Equally I remember Peter's life spiralling out of control through circumstances he was unable to control, and tragically he passed away in 1997. Memories of events that occurred to him as a youth in school were the trigger to his self-passing.

I recall with pride that in that era of Policing, it was normal for uniformed Police and Detectives in general to regard crimes against citizens personally, and the more serious a crime, the more personal it became. While I was in the Taringa CI.Branch, I learned under Sergeant Bob Dallow the importance of knowing the area I was responsible for, who the good folk were and who were the villains. To do and understand this was real community and genuine proactive policing. Years later they used these so-called 'initiatives' as a new way for the future of Policing. To Detectives at the time, it was not new, it was just what you did naturally.

Taringa CI.Branch cannot be remembered without recalling an investigation which encased taking crimes personally linked with the themes of Community and Proactive Policing. It was a case of a local St. Lucia girl who was mentally disadvantaged being viciously raped in "The Valley", near the Brunswick Street Railway Station adjacent to the rear of the Wickham Hotel.

The rape included the use of a 76cm slither of timber.

One may wonder why Taringa took on this case. The father of the victim attended one Saturday morning at the Taringa CI.Branch when I and my partner Detective Dennis Horne were on duty. He was crying. We were told of an event that occurred and that his disabled daughter was in a serious condition at the Brisbane General Hospital, and that he had informed Police but could not get assistance. This was possibly due to the fact his daughter could not verbally relate her ordeal.

Detective Horne and I worked for 14 days straight, sometimes without sleep or sleeping with a couple of chairs in the Police Station placed together to take a quick nap. We infiltrated the locals in 'The Valley' until finally an arrest was made of two persons for the rape of this girl. During the interrogation, or 'interview with a purpose', one of the offenders gave us an almost perfect verbal version of the legal definition of rape. This disturbing case was made even more difficult due to the victim not being able to talk to us at all, and she could only display her horrible injuries as a starting point for our enquiry.

They were convicted and sentenced to a lengthy term of imprisonment. The victim's father cried again, as we all did, when Justice was done.

I give this case only as an explanation of the themes of Community and Proactive Policing; Police then did it automatically, and now in a different world and time, still try to do.

There were moments of a slightly less serious nature, although laced with high importance and danger. One such day I was on an early shift with Detective Dennis Horne, and we decided to go down to Logan, which was way out of our area, and clean up a fraud file which had been sitting on our desk for some considerable time. Luckily, we found the suspect at home and were delivering him back to the Taringa CI.Branch for questioning,

Constable gains highest police award

A PLAIN clothes constable policeman yesterday gained the highest award the Queensland Police Department can bestow.

Danny Murdoch, now attached to the Ipswich CIB, was presented with a Favourable Record by regional superintendent Merv Hoppner.

The citation, awarded conjointly to plain clothes constable Michael Horne of Brisbane CIB, arose out of an investigation.

The probe resulted in the conviction and imprisonment of two offenders for rape and other serious offences in Brisbane on March 9, 1984.

It had been hampered by the victim being admitted to hospital for surgery as a result of her ordeal and was unable to be interviewed.

Despite this difficulty, Murdoch and Horne through their extensive inquiries, initiative and resourcefulness, were able to locate the scene of the crime at the rear of a Fortitude Valley hotel. Technical officers subsequently gathered valuable evidence at that location.

During the next two weeks Murdoch and Horne tirelessly pursued their inquiries and on March 22 were able to interview a suspect.

This suspect was later identified by the victim as one of her attackers. During interrogation the suspect made a full admission and implicated an accomplice who was subsequently apprehended.

The citation read in part: "By their outstanding and highly professional police work, the members are most deserving of this award . . . presented for intelligence, tenacity of purpose and dedication to duty displayed throughout an investigation."

Constable Murdoch, in accepting the award, said the horrific injuries suffered by the woman had made him and his partner "pull out all the stops to catch those responsible".

District inspector Laurie Pointing said it was gratifying to see good police work recognised by the Commissioner of Police Sir Terence Lewis.

Superintendent Hoppner also praised the Ipswich CIB for their excellent clean-up record of major crime.

• Danny Murdoch — centre — receives his Favourable Record award from regional superintendent Merv Hoppner — right — and district inspector Laurie Pointing at the Ipswich Police Station yesterday.

Taringa Rape Investigation — Award

and to enable his lack of memory to be revived. We were near the Walter Taylor Bridge at Indooroopilly when a Code One came over the radio: *"Any car in the vicinity of the ANZ Bank at Indooroopilly please attend robbery in progress."* Detective Horne was driving. I responded to the call, and with great haste we proceeded to the Bank; the time being just after 10.00am.

My first vision was of a male person carrying a TAA airline bag, running down the long front concrete stairs leading from the front door of the Bank down to the footpath; he was in a distinct and urgent hurry, like he was fleeing. After advising the fraud suspect to please lie down on the back seat for safety, I asked Detective Horne to stop the Police vehicle. I alighted and started to give chase and due to the fact that this was a Code One, and a Robbery was in progress, I retrieved my snub nosed .38 revolver from my ankle holster in case things turned bad. The street outside the bank and leading down to the Indooroopilly train station area was flooded with pedestrians. I remember I started to call out to this robber in a loud, official and urgent voice:

"Stop Police, Stop Police."

He was carrying the TAA Bag, and I was running after him with the gun held high in the air like in the movies; Detective Horne and the fraud suspect were following in the Police car slowly, observing. I managed to catch up to the suspect, holstered my gun this time in the belt of my trousers, and without saying a word to him, marched him the very short distance back to the Police vehicle, which had the passengers side window open. The suspect kindly placed his head and upper body through the open window with his torso remaining outside the car, Detective Horne was holding him in a Police hold possibly taught at the Academy. The suspect was trying to speak but in a spluttering type of manner and could not be understood. He dropped the TAA bag, which I picked up from the gutter and opened excitedly with the thought of retrieving the money stolen from the ANZ Bank. We were heroes.

Inside the bag, I saw one ham and cheese sandwich wrapped up in grease proof paper, one train ticket from Indooroopilly to Darra and a note. The note said this: *"If anyone finds xxxx please advise xxxx."* At the same time as this wonderful police work was being displayed to the general public, a further message came over the Police radio: *"All units attending the ANZ Bank at Indooroopilly please disregard, false alarm."*

I spoke to the good citizen apologetically, while placing him nicely in the front seat of the Police vehicle; he was looking bewildered from his encounter with the heroic Police, stammering and stuttering a little less. I hopped in the back seat with the fraud suspect, and we drove to the Indooroopilly Railway Station, making sure our robbery suspect caught the correct train to Darra, and then made our way to the Taringa CI.Branch office.

The fraud suspect confessed as I recall.

Unrelated of course, but sad to say, my partner Dennis Horne died in private but unfortunate circumstances some years after. He was a friend, a good Policeman and an honourable man.

I had purchased a small farm near Ipswich and was breeding Quarter Horses by this time and gained a transfer to the Ipswich CI.Branch, initially under various Detective Senior Sergeants, such as Norm Bryant, Ken Morris and Dave Beakey.

Ipswich CI.Branch

Anyone who has ever worked in Ipswich as a policeman or woman in those days or prior would know that it was a tough town, with nests of crime minded individuals and groups intent on committing both local and more widespread armed robberies. Apart from these crimes with a number of homicides thrown in, Ipswich was known for a high rate of major drug offences, break and enters, and car theft. Street crime was run of the mill.

I can only write with pride that in working alongside my competent colleagues, Detectives leading the charge, crime in Ipswich was cut down. District Officers such as John Yarrow, Ron McGibbon, Laurie Witham, Laurie Pointing and Peter Slater displayed graphs and figures commensurate with the local Police work and commitment. Detectives such as Detective Sergeant John McGill, Neil Armstrong (Moonie), Peter Barron, John and Glen Pointing and the list goes on, were the backbone of the CI.Branch.

My pride in working with these men was that major crime at that point in time was normally solved. Ipswich in those days carried on the traditions I observed from watching the methods of Detectives like Meskell and Fursman so long ago, and proudly following the leadership of the calibre of the Morgan's, Pointing's and Morris's of the Force (Service). No mention of

Ipswich in that era would do justice unless I gave credit to a public servant who worked in the CI.Branch as the Intelligence Officer. This is prior to sworn in Intelligence Officers being stationed within the Police Service itself.

His name is Jim Curley. Now the reason I mention Jim is that in those days, if Police stopped a person or vehicle for any suspicious activity, or just came across them in the course of their duties, they would (hopefully) fill out an 'activity card' with the details of the person they spoke to.

These days they may call this type of intelligence gathering 'profiling', but it actually meant that if a crime was committed, we knew where to look.

Jim collated these cards and the data they contained manually, with paper and pencil so to speak, and patiently placed them in his filing drawer. When there was a crime, we asked Jim and he would know 'who was who in the zoo.' These early lessons I had learned from observing Jim, taught me the value of manually doing things, personal thinking, and knowledge. The key word is manually, and I will refer to this further when I give an account of my current work activities.

It would be slightly pretentious to go through and list the crimes that we were confronted with and solved in Ipswich; however all Detectives should be proud of their record of keeping the good folks safe from an onslaught of armed robberies, systematic car thefts and what they loosely term now 'home invasions' and to throw in the mix, some unsettling homicides.

To talk about these crimes individually, particularly where the loss of life was involved, would be unsettling and disrespectful in many ways. Suffice to silently be proud of all Detectives at Ipswich CI.Branch in their commitment and dedication. Everyone assisted Detectives and uniform Police alike in keeping the people of Ipswich safe.

One crime did stick out, mainly because it should never have happened, and an innocent lady should not have lost her precious life. Her name was Pamela Bain.

On a Wednesday, the 15th. July 1987, Mrs. Pamela Florence Bain, aged 65, and her husband Donald William Bain, aged 70, were travelling west on the Warrego Highway near Ipswich, heading to Toowoomba to visit their family. They were driving their Ford Falcon sedan and towing a small caravan.

As the vehicle passed an unused quarry at Tivoli, a bullet shattered the passenger window of the Falcon, striking Mrs. Bain in the lower part of the neck and killing her. Her husband quickly pulled to the shoulder of the highway and hailed a passing car, and an Ambulance was called.

Ipswich Police were also notified of the shooting.

Queensland Police Scenes of Crime, local uniformed officers and Ipswich Detectives arrived to investigate the shooting and conduct a search of the vacant land bordering the Highway adjacent to the scene. A new Ipswich District Officer, Laurie Pointing, had just been appointed and it happened to be his first day 'on the job.' He immediately attended the scene and took charge of 'fine combing' the vacant quarry, mine area and nearby scrubland.

A full search utilising dog units, helicopter, water Police, Police cadets and the tactical response group were used to secure and search the area and nearby scrub land, while Detectives interviewed local residents.

The entrance wound Mrs. Bain suffered indicated that the bullet had been fired from an elevated location, giving Police their first clue. All avenues of enquiry were considered, ranging from it being a deliberate act to a careless act using a firearm. The search continued for the rest of the 15th. and into the next day the 16th. July.

Detectives heard stories of persons on trail bikes armed with rifles in bushland near the site of the shooting, the death of Mrs. Bain also caused a degree of fear among Ipswich residents.

We started to reach an opinion that the shooting may have been the result of indiscriminate firing of a weapon in the direction of the Warrego Highway killing Mrs. Bain.

The search resulted in the finding of nine 6.5mm cartridges that came from an old-style military weapon, similar in type to a Swedish Mauser. The location of the cartridges was some 700 meters from the Warrego Highway and the site of Mrs. Bain's death.

The cartridges matched the bullet retrieved from Mrs. Bain's body.

Ipswich Detectives broadened their investigation to include persons of interest, resulting in many persons being interviewed. Police were still considering all options, including deliberate actions and the possibility of a group of persons target shooting.

Police appealed to the public for assistance. Detectives believed that intense Police enquiries and their activity in these areas would prompt action by witnesses or even the offenders themselves. Politicians also started to campaign for the strengthening of gun laws. This started a lively debate publicly regarding the availability of firearms in Queensland and claiming Queensland as a State not strict on gun laws.

On the evening of the 17th. July, together with Detective Glen Pointing, I spoke to two young men at the Ipswich Police Station, and subsequently visited an address in Karalee. We located a 6.5mm Mauser rifle buried at

Pair face trial over death of a tourist

TWO Ipswich men were yesterday committed for trial over the death of a 65-year-old Victorian tourist killed by a bullet on the Warrego Highway at Tivoli on July 15 this year.

Robert James Kington, 22, now living at Coopers Plains, and Christopher Gerard McEwen, 19, of Lyndon Way, Karalee, pleaded not guilty to conjoint charges of unlawfully killing Pamela Florence Bain, of Vermont, Victoria.

Mr Bill Pullar, SM, found sufficient evidence after committal proceedings in the Ipswich Magistrates Court yesterday to commit the men for trial in the Brisbane Supreme Court on November 23.

(Mrs Bain was passenger in a Ford motorcar, with a caravan in tow, travelling west on the Warrego Highway toward Toowoomba, when she was shot in the neck. She later died).

Mr Pullar granted both defendants bail without any conditions of reporting to police.

On lesser charges of discharging a firearm over separate private properties on each side of the Warrego Highway, Kington and McEwen were remanded until February 3, 1988.

The charge of unlawful killing carries a maximum penalty of life imprisonment.

Prosecutor Constable Michael Robinson presented 37 written witness statements, a video-taped recording of police investigations at the Tivoli scene and 66 exhibits. Four witnesses gave evidence at yesterday's hearing.

Exhibits included a high powered Swedish Mauser military rifle, ammunition, discharged cartridges and a four-litre paint can.

Ipswich Detective Danny Murdoch identified (from photographs and videotape shots of the Warrego Highway) a gumtree in a disused colliery used as a shooting target which was 675m from the site. Nine spent cartridges were found 21m from the base of the gumtree.

Det Murdoch said Francis St residences were about 100m behind the target tree.

He told Brisbane public defender Michael Shanahan, appearing for Kington, a disused quarry was between the tree and the accident site. A school was also located nearby.

The night after Mrs Bain died, Det Murdoch interviewed Kington and McEwen after they had gone to police. Both defendants had been extremely co-operative, sad and distressed.

He said Kington and McEwen had shown him the gum tree target and another target across the road where they had been firing the rifle on July 15.

Police scientific officer Michael Bennett Kellar told the court highway traffic could be seen from the firing range.

Ipswich City Council surveyor Thomas Wyatt Shannon, as third witness, said it was "a downhill run" from the target area to the highway.

Mr Shannon said there was "a slight amount of foliage in the area, but nothing significant" obstructing vision between the target and the highway.

Ashley Phillip Burchett, a tyre fitter of Red Hill, said he had sold his Swedish Mauser rifle to a group of four young men about two months before Mrs Bain was shot.

He could not identify either defendant as the purchaser of the rifle he sold for $150.

Mr Burchett said he had offered the rifle for sale after hearing four men discussing buying a second hand rifle for pig shooting.

During the transaction, he said he had explained the use of the firearm and listed its three safety features to lock the rifle bolt and trigger.

Burchett said during cross examination that he had advised the men to make sure they fired into the ground or the base of a big tree.

"They needed a background, something so the bullets were not going to go too far," he said.

He had given the advice because "it was a rifle and it would be dangerous to shoot it any where else".

STRAY SHOT CLAIMS LIFE

The undertaker removes the woman's body as police continue [illegible]

By BOB DUTTON

IPSWICH police are hunting a thrill shooter whose stray bullet yesterday killed a 65-year-old Victorian tourist at Tivoli.

The woman, Pamela Florence Bain, of Vermont, near Melbourne, was a passenger in a Ford Falcon sedan travelling on the Warrego Highway.

Ipswich District Police chief Inspector [illegible] Pointing said she was on a three-month holiday with her husband, Donald William Bain.

The couple had just left Ipswich for Toowoomba, towing a small caravan, when the tragedy struck about 11.30am.

Insp Pointing said Mrs Bain died instantly when the bullet shattered the passenger side window and struck her in the lower part of the neck.

He said she slumped forward in her seat and her husband quickly pulled off the highway, rushed to the passenger side and discovered his wife had been shot.

[illegible]

• Flashback to the highway shooting

Queensland Times 2nd. October 1987

the rear of the property. Two local men, Robert James Kington aged 22 years and Christopher Gerard McEwen aged 19 years, were interviewed and charged with the Unlawful Killing of Mrs. Bain.

The two men were remorseful for their actions and the death of Mrs. Bain.

On the 2nd. October 1987, the two men were committed for trial for the unlawful killing of Mrs. Bain.

It was not until 1996 that Queensland along with the rest of Australia strengthened their laws relating to firearms.

While I am recalling notable events that occurred in Ipswich, I am reminded of two other crimes. Both occurred on days when a normal working detective may think, *"this is a nice quiet day, nothing happening."* Then all hell breaks loose.

One of these days was Saturday the 21st. October 1989. I was working with Detective Fynes-Clinton out of the Ipswich CI.Branch, and it was mid afternoon and close to knock off time. We were aware of a horrific crime that had occurred that previous evening at West End, Brisbane, when a man called Edward Baldock was murdered. As I remember events, uniform Police advised us that a young woman by the name of Lisa Ptaschinski was at the Police Station and wanted to speak to Detectives. She was ushered into the day room of the Ipswich CIB wearing white; I mean sparkling crisp white, everything from head to toe.

Surprising to us, she advised us that she wanted to talk about the death of a man in West End the previous evening, which as things turned out was in fact Mr. Baldock. After speaking for some time about many unusual and disturbing things surrounding death, the drinking of blood and activities related to her friends, we engaged with her and she finally told us about the death of Mr. Baldock in detail with a clear and focused mind. Detective Fynes-Clinton and I suddenly realised the importance of the description of the crime that she started to outline to us in cold, disturbing detail.

We started to record the conversations and immediately called Detective Senior Sergeant Pat Clancy of the Woolloongabba CI.Branch, and advised him of the unsettling facts we were hearing from this 'woman in white', Lisa Ptaschinski. We subsequently drove her to the Woolloongabba CI.Branch and into the hands of Pat Clancy, relaying to him an outline of what she had explained to us, including the horrific details. We handed her over as well as the tape recording.

I will not relive all of these details here of the "Vampire Killers" case, as it is known and can be researched and has been told in many articles and newspaper reports, including visual and audio representations. However, I know that the evidence we produced in this case, as told to us by Ptaschinski on that quiet Saturday afternoon, assisted in refining and aligning the facts as to what actually occurred that evening.

Another day as I was thinking again, *"this is a nice quiet day, nothing happening"* was back in time to New Year's Day, 1988. My partner and friend, Detective Glen Pointing, and I were starting our shift at the Ipswich CI.Branch, right on 8.00 am, as it was not correct or polite to be late (ever), even though there could have been an excuse as it was just a few short hours after News Year's Eve. Detective Senior Sergeant Morris was also on duty that day. We received a report that there was a domestic situation in Leichhardt with an armed man threatening residents. By the time we arrived, he had abducted an 18-year-old girl and made off with her according to a witness, in a Valiant sedan heading towards the Cunningham Highway.

So, our *"nice quiet"* New Year's Day was escalating into a problem.

Luckily, we quickly located the Valiant slowly making its way along the Cunningham Highway; we could see the female hostage driving and the male person pointing a gun to her head. I should now set the escalating scene for some clarity. There was the Valiant with the suspect and the hostage driving slowly, Detective Glen Pointing and I in one vehicle behind, Detective Senior Sergeant Ken Morris following in another vehicle. Then unexpectedly, a Honda sedan arrived as the fourth car in this slow procession and atop the roof was a large, mounted camera. The media had turned up.

Excellent perception of the unfolding events by Ken Morris led him to make a quick decision to have the local Kalbar Police Constable attempt to somehow block the highway just before Aratula, which he managed to do by commandeering a semi-trailer as an effective tool. However, as all good plans sometimes do, they go slightly off track; our procession of vehicles led by the Valiant slowly arrived at a slight rise in the road just before Aratula, and we saw two cars which had managed to get through the roadblock before it became effective.

The suspect in the Valiant quickly observed what was happening and somehow swerved across the roadway in front of these two vehicles. He alighted from the Valiant and ordered the occupants out of the cars, all nine of them including children.

The problem was now turning from a problem into a nasty one.

Ken Morris used magnificent negotiating skills over an extended period of time, discussing options over a 'load hailer' with the suspect. By this time Channel Seven had arrived in their helicopter, which was quickly sent on its way by Ken. His words worked thank goodness, and the agreed plan was to let the nine innocents leave, and the Valiant with the suspect and the female would be allowed to continue their journey to an address in Warwick.

• Southern District deputy commander Supt Lawrie Witham presenting Ipswich detective Dan Murdoch with a commendation for bravery.

Ipswich seige-negotiator awarded special citation

ONE of three Ipswich detectives who defused a nine-person hostage seige and abduction at Aratula in 1988 was yesterday awarded a police citation for bravery.

Det Sen Constable Dan Murdoch was yesterday presented with his commendation for "courage, dedication to duty and initiative" in the January 1, 1988, drama by Southern District deputy commander Supt Lawrie Witham at the Ipswich police station.

Det Murdoch, along with former Ipswich CIB chief Insp Ken Morris and plain clothes constable Glen Pointing, were called to a Leichhardt home on information that a family dispute had prompted a 44-year-old man to threaten residents with a .22 calibre semi-automatic rifle.

The man, who was armed with a 13-round magazine of ammunition and a further 200 rounds of ammunition, abducted an 18-year-old girl and attempted to drive to Warwick.

The three detectives commandeered semi-trailers to create a road block on the Cunningham Highway where the man and two other cars were trapped. The 44-year-old took nine hostages.

After delicate negotiations, the hostages were released and the man drove to Warwick with the 18-year-old girl.

On arrival, the man took up position behind his vehicle but was finally coerced to surrender.

Ipswich Siege — Award

After a short interlude while driving to Warwick in our vehicular procession, Ken Morris contacted the duty Police Commissioner to order the local District Officer to allow us into his District. That worked. So now the procession included the Valiant sedan with the suspect holding the rifle still towards the female hostage driver, Detective Glen Pointing and I following, Detective. Senior Sergeant. Ken Morris next, the Kalbar Police vehicle and the Honda with the large camera on the roof. We slowly made it to the address in Warwick, where the street had been blocked off by local Police and the residents evacuated or locked in their homes.

Once again Ken brought out the 'loud hailer' and started to negotiate with the gunman, who had now alighted from the Valiant and was standing in the driveway of the address, holding the hostage and menacing her with the rifle. The Kalbar uniform Officer, a trained Police marksman, had his issued Ruger rifle ready, Detective Pointing and I had our little snub nosed .38cal Smith and Wesson ready in case we needed to throw them at something, and Ken did the talking. He was again brilliantly successful, and after a period of time the offender lowered his weapon and released the hostage.

The offender, John Gary Keeley, was then arrested, and the drive back to Ipswich and the Watch-house was at a rather quick pace.

While stationed at Ipswich, I was fortunate to gain promotions to Detective Senior Constable, Detective Sergeant, and then through a transfer and promotion to Detective Senior Sergeant at the Juvenile Aid Bureau on the Gold Coast.

Gold Coast JA.Bureau and CI.Branch

The Assistant Commissioner at the Gold Coast was Laurie Pointing, who I previously worked with briefly in Brisbane and then at Ipswich when he was the District Officer. The Region's Management team included Granville (Grannie) Pearce and Bob Hays. I commenced as the O.I.C. of the Gold Coast JAB, which was a very busy office.

This period of Policing in Queensland was difficult for many reasons; the Fitzgerald Enquiry had well and truly finished, and the aftermath was filtering through the rank and file, who in reality had no connection to the events that were uncovered in the Enquiry. My understanding and belief was that the sad uncovered stains placed on the Police were cloistered within a small group and the wider Police Officer had no knowledge or insight into what had been occurring. However, the Enquiry affected all Police in many different, and sometimes sad, ways.

As a leading Barrister said to me at the time the Enquiry was at its judgmental pinnacle: *"Dan, I have never seen any of these people giving evidence in the Supreme Court of Queensland, so they have not had much of an effect on the crime of this State."*

Maybe his words had meaning.

A short time after I commenced duty on the Gold Coast, I was assigned the first of long stint as the A/Detective Inspector of the Gold Coast CI.Branch. It was a time that called for protection of sorts of the classic hard-working Detective on the Coast, and vigilance for disruptions brought by hardships and the sometimes-angry attitudes caused by the Fitzgerald Enquiry.

Mingled with this difficulty was a Gold Coast riddled with crime, ranging from OMG (Outlaw Motorcycle Gangs) to Homicides and serious Armed Robberies on a systematic and targeted scale. There were some prison escapees hiding in the sunshine of the Coast and committing violent crimes to sustain their high-rise lifestyle. These types of problems laced with the ever-popular Gold Coast crime loosely termed Fraud, handed Detectives crime listed in all pages of the Criminal Code.

Any Detective who worked on the Gold Coast during this time of suspicion and upheaval should be proud of the way that they conducted themselves with dignity and with the overall objective of justice for the victims of crime. As part of the changes made, Detective Senior Sergeant John Pointing took over the operational leadership of the CI.Branch.

So, to myself as the Acting Detective Inspector, John Pointing as the Detective Senior Sergeant, and all CI.Branch Office Sergeants from Southport, Surfers Paradise, Broadbeach, Burleigh Heads, Nerang, Mudgeeraba and Coolangatta stations, it was satisfying to see the commitment by these men and women in those difficult times.

However, the annual Indy 300 car racing events did break the stress I must say, which we attended with a well-deserved ring side seat.

Logan CI.Branch

Similar to the Gold Coast in the early to mid-90s, Logan District was going through a time of change with local internal investigations which permeated the Logan CI.Branch, and once again affected the lives of the Detectives working there.

During this time, I was transferred to Logan as the A/Detective Inspector and once again found the core group of Police there loyal to the ideals of policing, protection of the victims of crime and legal persecution of the criminal element. Once again, a difficult and high crime area was made that much safer by the men and women working there.

The latter part of the 90s saw a change in my life, and I took early retirement to pursue a career in private business concentrating on Fraud matters and similar enquiries. This was the start of an interesting career and lifestyle.

I could only do a few things with any confidence and credibility, and they were policing, training horses and picking on my guitar. So, I choose a path closely aligned to my policing knowledge.

Dan having a play.

Currently – Making a Difference

In 1997, I commenced a business called Dan Murdoch Risk Services, concentrating initially on Fraud investigations. However, within a short period of time, a personal contact of mine I had known previously, and who was then doing investigative work in Australia and South East Asia, contacted me and asked me to accompany him to Asia on an investigation. The investigation centered on intellectual property crimes and had at its core elements involving counterfeit software.

The complainant was the world's leading software company, and the suspect company was on the first board of the Singapore Stock Exchange. The financial consideration at stake was a Civil Court case involving $50Million USD.

My reason for mentioning this short period which lasted two years in my history is that during the time we roamed Asia completing the enquiry, I built relationships with serving members of the FBI and law enforcement persons stationed in Bangkok and other Asian locations. I used these contacts in Law Enforcement to finally bring the original intellectual property matter to a successful conclusion.

I was then asked by an old friend to return to the Brisbane area and manage a Quarter Horse Stud he was establishing, which I did until I received a phone call from one of the FBI colleagues from Bangkok who had since left the FBI and was working for a pharmaceutical company as their Asian Product Security Manager. This was about the year 2000.

He simply said words to the effect of: *"Dan, we are trying to locate the manufacturers of counterfeit medicines and find it difficult due to the fact that it is easy for them to remain anonymous on the internet, can you work out a way to find out who they are, where they are, and gain evidence against them so we can launch criminal prosecutions."*

So, I once again re-established my company and used the knowledge I had learned from the years working in law enforcement to use a simple but effective method of uncovering these perpetrators and bring them before various Courts globally.

The idea was simple.

I set up pretext companies in various locations worldwide and let the manufacturers and wholesalers of these counterfeit medicines come to me and make their offers; it was then that I used objective and subjective skills I learned from my days in the Police to attract these sellers away from their computer screens into a real-life situation or a face-to-face meeting. The face-to-face engagement meant that we could now start to collect real evidence with a real person in a real location.

Using this simple but in practice difficult methodology, I have been successful in obtaining enforcement action and conducted undercover operations in various countries around the world such as Hong Kong, China, Singapore, India, Turkey, the United Kingdom, France, Belize, Panama, Malaysia, the Philippines, Thailand and in many States of the USA. I am privileged due to this work to have a special relationship with law enforcement in the USA, where even though a formal complaint may have been lodged regarding a possible offender, law enforcement allows me to continue to operate and gain evidence for their production in Court.

The undercover component to what I do currently is complicated for a variety of reasons, and can have high elements of danger, due to vast profits and unusual geographical locations which are not always concerned with a person's security.

Some insight into counterfeit medicines and what we currently do cannot be understood until some reality is brought to the table in facts and figures. For instance, the world Police agency Interpol has stated "*more than one million people die each year from counterfeit drugs.*" Since that time, I have also seen the profits to these criminal groups rise substantially; they have changed their focus from fake antibiotics and men's health medicines to Cancer medicines, HIV and hepatitis medications and other expensive medicines, such as current Covid 19 remedies, ensuring a high profit margin. It must be remembered that in some countries, particular types of these medications can cost between $4,000.00USD to $25,000USD for one vial, which is just one treatment.

The temptation is therefore great, and their activities kill many people.

The reported profit from fake medicines is hard to quantify but has been placed at $200 Billion USD conservatively. I believe it could be more. The startling thing is that these medicines have the potential to enter, and have entered, the normal medical supply chain in various locations globally.

I and my current staff now mainly concentrate on the uncovering and evidence collection of the counterfeiting of cancer medicines and also some Covid 19 medications worldwide. This is a global problem. In most instances the medicines we uncover have no active or very little active ingredients, so in my classically Police trained mind that is tantamount to murder. So, this is why I do what I do and will continue to do so for as long as I can. I and my staff conduct our initial intelligence manually, just like Jim Curley used to do back at the Ipswich CI.Branch so many years ago.

Of course, no old Policeman's story can be complete without a *'war story or two'* so I will share a couple that I am at liberty to relate.

Houston — Texas

From 2017 to 2019 I worked in an undercover capacity, gathering evidence against a group of Ukrainian individuals counterfeiting cancer medications and supplying them to consumers in various countries globally, including the USA. After gaining sufficient evidence to gain US law enforcement commitment, we worked in tandem with Federal Police from Houston, Texas to have the two main suspects travel to the USA to meet in an undercover capacity with a business plan meant to offer them a USA partnership.

The meeting was arranged in the presidential suite of a leading hotel in Houston, suitably fitted out with video and audio equipment and with Federal law enforcement also securing the adjoining room as the monitoring room. The meeting was conducted between the two suspects, myself and my son as the undercover operators, and then joined at a later time by Law Enforcement undercover officers, to complete the members attending this high-level undercover business meeting.

All was successful, and the suspects made startling admissions supporting the evidence we had gained during the past two years. Now once they outlined their extensive global network and their criminal behaviour, the plan was then as follows. We were to leave the meeting and proceed by motor vehicles to a pretext warehouse where the two suspects were to inspect our facility. On the way there, there was to be a traditional traffic stop, and the suspects would then be quietly removed from the vehicle and taken away for formal questioning.

However, this is what happened.

On the route to the pretext warehouse, a helicopter hovered above, and then an armoured vehicle(s) was spotted close to the vehicular procession containing the suspects, making the scene unusual to say the least and certainly far removed from the original plan. Then suddenly, a 'flash bomb' was thrown by one of the armoured vehicles to the close vicinity to the vehicle containing the suspects. Tactical Response teams appeared out of nowhere and the scene turned into a Hollywood action movie scene; the suspects were removed from the vehicle and hurried away in combat style urgency.

There was a debriefing later that day on the undercover operation and the subsequent arrest of the two suspects, and I asked one question of the Tactical response leader:

"What was the reason for the flash bomb?"

His reply was simple

"Practice".

God Bless America.

Belize

There is a country in Central America called Belize, which used to be called British Honduras back in the days prior to 1973. It is or was well known as the cocaine smuggling stop off point between Colombia and Florida in the USA. I went there to do an undercover mission with my handler (my former FBI friend), and the task was to meet with a seller who we knew was using Belize as a trans-shipment location to send fake medicines into the USA. We had been talking with this seller who had Indian connections for some time and had gained his confidence to the extent that he agreed to meet with me in Belize.

I together with my undercover controller, entered the country using our own identity and then changed to using a pretext name with my own set of fake ID documents. My real ID was locked in a safe at the Hotel we were staying at. Also, to facilitate the meeting and visit to Belize, we engaged with a local agent who would act as a guide and bodyguard in case security issues arose. He also booked a Hotel room in a separate Hotel in my fake ID name. The local agent was heavily armed at all times due to the nature

Dan – Belize 17th. August 2005

of things that occur within that country.

So it seemed simple; I have $10,000.00USD, and I have to go to an address at so and so Street Belize City, hand over the money to this person I had been happily engaging with for some time and take from him a large number of fake medicines. I was then to hand the medicines over to the local agent for evidence keeping, return to the pretext Hotel with the agent, wait in that vicinity until things appeared clear and then take me back to my real Hotel, where I would resume my real identity and leave the country. I had no idea of the name of this pretext Hotel at this stage.

To attend this meeting I had a red backpack. Inside was my fake ID, the money, a pretext local phone and a comb because one had to look cool, and nothing else.

My controller waited at the real Hotel. The well-armed local agent and I attended the address at 11.00 am in his 4WD, parking a comfortable distance down the street. Now the street is not like a normal suburban Street, but like out of a crime movie with small derelict houses and no persons visible outside. The area just looked and felt dangerous. I walked a short distance to the address and knocked on the timber railing outside. The door opened. Now this door was not a normal door, it was about eight to ten inches thick I recall, made of solid steel like a bank vault with what looked like a ships' steering wheel apparatus used to open it. The person who answered was about six foot six inches tall but to me he looked eight-foot, black skin and just one mean looking fellow.

My backside started to twitch.

So, I popped into full undercover mode and happily started my introduction after I entered the Bank vault door, which he closed and locked behind me. He asked me to go into a side room and there I saw a complete set up of medicines of all descriptions, obviously waiting for shipment out of the country to their various destinations. I cannot recall his name; I was just worried internally about how I going to get out of there safely. By the time of entering this fake medical wonderland, he had taken my red backpack inspected it all and had given me a general but roughish personal body search. He obviously was not the Indian person I had been talking to for the past 18 months gleefully agreeing to our meeting at this location, and at this exact time.

Using all the things I had observed and had been taught and witnessed in the Police and elsewhere, I started to use my best Australian accent to continue with the deal as though things were normal, trying to be Ozzie humoured within a tense and worrying environment. I finally demanded the medicines I had come for, and he produced a large plastic bag full of what looked like my target drugs. I handed over the $10,000,00USD inspected the medicines quickly, extended my hand to this huge species of a man and smiled and said, *"What is the best Bank in Belize? I want to open an account; I hear it is a good place to safely store money."* I said this as I started walking towards the door. He gave me limited directions.

I was relieved when he opened the front (safe) door with this huge wheel without saying goodbye. At least I was outside in the slums of Belize. My safety net being the 4WD and my bodyguard were nowhere to be seen, I had the red backpack full of fake medicines, fake ID and no idea where I was in relation to my pretext Hotel or real safe Hotel. I started walking and rang my controller, who then attempted to contact by phone my so-called local bodyguard. I also noticed that some 25 to 30 meters behind me was a vehicle with two men inside, driving very slowly.

I was told by my controller who was safely in his real hotel, that my bodyguard had been chased out of the area by two armed men in a vehicle who appeared in the street outside the house I was doing the deal in. The local bodyguard, even though armed to the teeth, decided to leave me to my fate and just get out of the area. The only thing he told my controller was that my pretext Hotel, which in fact was a local Turkish run Casino I was booked into, was near the ocean, about one kilometer from the address I was at. All I could see was a tall building in the distance and the one car behind me. No one else was visible.

So, I started to walk quickly, and then more quickly, heading in the general direction of the tall building, hoping it was the Casino. I noticed one of the men got out of the following vehicle, holding something in his hand. I could not see what it was, but it made me move even quicker, not an easy task for an old fellow. I made it to the tall building and at least the bodyguard was correct — it was the pretext Hotel he had previously booked me into, the name was the Tropicana Casino Hotel. I hid by mixing with people in the gambling floor of the Casino. After a while and using my fake ID, I was able to secure the room key and hibernate, hoping my controller or the bodyguard would retrieve me.

However, for reasons of fear or fearful local knowledge, no one decided to come. By this time, it was around 5.00pm and I had to get back to my safe Hotel, which I had figured out by now was about 10 miles away. Now in Belize, you don't just walk down to the concierge and a taxi is waiting; you have to walk into the Street and hopefully you will find a real one who will not see 'a foreigner' and drive you to your fate in the slums where I had just come from. Anyway, I had no option, and this is the route I took. Playing tough and talking strong to the taxi I found, I finally got back to the safe Hotel and safely, with my red backpack, my fake ID and body intact.

Belize City at that time was filled with dangerous areas and was run by drug running Rastafarians, and with no genuine law enforcement to secure safety, it was actually the Wild West in the modern era.

Anyway, I had a meal, a stiff drink, a lie down and got out of there the next day, snarling at my handler for being too frightened to come and get me.

What I was taught, and what I observed my fellow Police officers do while I was a member of the Police, gave me the skills, confidence and knowledge to carry out the work I still do in 2021, and it is with gratitude I say thank you to all of those men and women.

I was proud to be a Queensland Police Officer and I am still proud of what I do today, I feel privileged to have served in the Queensland Police Service — a Police service which allowed me to *"have a go"* at whatever I wanted to attempt. For instance, I *"had a go"* at the Mounted Unit, the Stock Squad, walking the Beat, the CIB, the JAB, did some prosecutions at times, attended the Commissioned Officers courses and *"had a go"* at relieving in higher duties.

I say thanks for giving me a go.

Awards

Sure, awards are nice to receive, and they are a visible thank you for some action that you have taken, the work you have done or training you have received. My way of thinking is that some of the greatest rewards and awards have come from achieving an outcome for a victim of crime, no matter whether the crime was a stolen pot plant or a stolen loved one, the gratitude of the victim simply saying thanks is wonderful, and the only award a Policeman really needs.

However, for the purpose of openness and a pinch of vanity, here are some of the awards I have received.

Police Awards

- 12th. March 1987 **Favourable Record** – Intelligence, Tenacity and Purpose in the arrest and convictions of two persons for Rape and other offences.
- 28th. March 1989 **Commendation** – Efficiency and Dedication to Duty throughout a Protracted Fraud investigation.
- 18th. February 1991 **Commendation** – Courage Dedication to Duty and Initiative during a Hostage/Siege situation.
- 24th. March 1994 Assistant Commissioners Certificate – Capture Armed and Dangerous Prison Escapees.

QPS Training

- Dux of QPS Training Academy Squad.
- Leadership Award QPS Training Academy Squad.
- Crime Investigators Course.
- 1st. Queensland Drug Investigation and Law Course.
- 1st. Economic Crime Course.
- High Distinction for a paper on Economic Crime.
- QPS Commissioned Officers Course Human Resource Management Strand.

- QPS Commissioned Officers Course Management Strand.
- QPS Commissioned Officers Course Operations Strand. Media Liaison Course.
- Promotional Panel Convenor Course.

External Training

- Assoc Dip. Justice Administration
  Principles of Management
  Criminal Justice System
  Policing and Society
  Police Law 1
  Police Law 2
  Queensland Police Administration
  Basic Communication at Work
  Software Applications
  Accounting Fundamentals
  Behavior
  Psychology

Glenn Andrew Teske

Glenn grew up in the North Queensland bush, in what could be described as 'The school of hard knocks.' His experience as a youth working on large cattle properties and living and working with Indigenous men and women and older seasoned and experienced stockmen was to earn him the knowledge that very few police officers acquire in modern day policing. While he may have been described as a 'bushie' when he entered the Police Academy at Oxley at the young age of 19 years, he was much further advanced in his knowledge of everyday life than most young men and women. He quickly adapted to city and suburban life and gained considerable uniform experience and a knowledge of criminal investigation techniques. His tour of duty at Landsborough when the old Bruce Highway ran through that division, saw him become an experienced police motorcyclist and a competent investigator of fatal and serious road accidents. Throughout his career, he performed duty at Laura police division in our Gulf country as the Officer-In-Charge, the Brisbane Traffic Branch, Kingaroy Stock Investigation Squad, Mareeba Stock Squad and Criminal Investigation Branch. His country background assisted him immensely during his tour of duty at Laura, where he developed an outstanding working relationship and understanding with members of the Indigenous community. Glenn was an outstanding worker who expected his colleagues and superiors to exhibit the same high standard of performance to their daily duties as he did. However, on occasions this was to his detriment.

Laurie Pointing

The Glenn Andrew Teske Story

Early life prior to Police Academy, Oxley.

I was born at Toowoomba on the 24 March, 1959, and my earliest memory of my childhood is a vision of a tall muscled bronze individual carrying a large plank of timber across his shoulder. He was just one man who stood out to a small three-year-old child, such men were preparing to channel, kerbing and bituminize our suburban Thompson Street, Geebung. My recollection is of me standing awestruck on our veranda (they were called verandas back then, decks had yet to be invented). To a three-year old, everything was of interest and of course everyone was taller stronger and more coordinated. These memories persist to the present day. I recall very little of my early school years, however there are a few surviving black and white photos of a small child always wearing a very large straw hat.

My father secured a job with a large pastoral company in Northern Queensland as a Station Manager and my mother and our family followed.

My schooling was now through the school of the air, via wireless to a teacher in Cairns. Every morning my mother would make sure I was ready with the radio correctly tuned to the station.

At the pre-determined start time, we would all call in individually, "Good Morning Mrs. Paterson", we would then stand and recite the "Lords Prayer" before singing our national anthem which at that time was "God Save Our Queen".

After this we could be seated, and each member of our class would read out aloud via the wireless the lessons we had learnt the previous day before starting new lessons. (I found out later that my mother would receive these lessons via the mail, and she could help me.)

I just thought she was a wizard and knew everything. Our lessons involved Math's English, History, Geography, touching on the news of the week.

This was a world where Aboriginal people were camped and fed by the Station management. They were paid under the provisions of the Aboriginal Protection Act, which was overseen I believe, by the Officer-in-Charge of the Local Police. These families were fed, cared for and sheltered by the Station. Working age youths, both male and female, were first used in the "weaner camp." The stockmen, mainly aboriginal men would be employed in one of three stock camps. Each man would have his plant of horses, ranging from four to six horses each.

There was on average 10 or so individuals per camp together with a stockman in charge. Each camp of stockmen/women would have areas of the station to muster. These areas had names and were in general unfenced and covered enormous areas. They would normally move out to these areas with all their horses together with the camp and cook; transported in an ex-army vehicle and pack horses.

An indigenous stockman was normally tasked with looking after the horses and he was known as the horse tailer. He was responsible for the fitness of all the horses and would find the horses of a morning by listening to the sound of bells fitted to the lead horses in the unfenced wilderness, unhobble them, and bring them back to the stock camp. Each rider would then choose their horse for that days mustering.

It was my mother who was tasked with the responsible for the feeding of the station staff, issuing rations to the aboriginal families and caring for the sick and injured. These mustering camps would muster semi wild/wild cattle and bring these mobs into a large open area, where the breeders with calves were drafted off together with any mickies and clean skin bulls.

This drafting process comprised of the head stockman or manager moving into the mob on horseback and cutting out the required cow and calf. A great deal of skill and horsemanship was required for this. The sport of camp drafting I believe was derived from this. My father generally attended to this task and if I was lucky and had no schooling for a couple of days, I would accompany him.

Once the mob had been drafted, this mob would then be walked back to the main station yards where the calves were drafted off. The process was repeated over and over by each of the individual stock camps throughout the dry period and sometimes in the wet. All these weaner cattle had to be educated to handling, as to humans and horses so the "weaner tailers" were engaged. The "weaner tailers" comprised of older stockmen, women and the younger youths utilizing mainly older station horses. It was into the "Weaner Tailers" I was put as a youngster.

I was usually with aboriginal youths older than me and older aboriginal men and women. These individuals spoke English in a manner very different to normal English, a variety known as pidgin English. It comprised of English words sometimes interspersed with the local dialect, made into phrases which were as best described as being noun backwards. An example of this would be "Little bit long way" which would mean in English 'Not far now but a bit further", or "Yarraman little bit long way walk for today" which would mean "horses are a fair distance away perhaps a day's ride".

All such members received remuneration, food and care. At the end of the mustering season, when the "Northern Wet" was prevailing, most of the able-bodied members of the aboriginal station community would break into their family clans and move to the coast where they would live in a traditional manner until the "wet" finished, and then they would move back onto the main station to start the season afresh. It was into this world I was thrust, picking up the language and mannerisms of those I most frequented with.

Then came the day I was returned to Brisbane for my secondary schooling. Unfortunately, my scholastic abilities did not match my sporting abilities and although I was picked and played for a number of representative and state sides, my focus on other forms of education was lacking to say the least.

I had no desire to remain classroom bound with a feeling of useless isolation, so I decided that schooling was not for me. So I left, and eventually found my way out west working on a cattle property as a "ringer". Although the work was familiar to me, the actual "class" system was not. There were a number of jackaroos employed on the property together with an older ringer and a cook. To my surprise, I had to eat my meals when at the station with the older "ringer" and the cook in the cookhouse, while the "jackaroos" and the manager and his family would dress in ties and eat their meals in the "big house".

One day the local police officer called at the Station, and as a result I was placed on the mail train and returned to my older sister's residence in Brisbane. I think both her and her kind husband could see that I was like a fish out of water and I was soon a passenger on another Mail train, heading back to my beloved north.

I returned to my home property and commenced working under the guidance of a white stockman who no doubt was under certain instructions from my father. This stockman "Bluey" was my role model. He became my friend, mentor and later my best friend.

I was working my dream job on a very large Cattle Station, under the guidance of a man I had on a pedestal. Working in these conditions, I learnt so much. I was already an accomplished tracker and horseman, and with the guidance of "Bluey", I learnt how to handle rough horses and work wild cattle.

My parents had moved back to South East Queensland, purchasing a property of their own and I was content where I was. Then the cattle depression in the '70s hit, and hit hard.

The management of these cattle properties was almost in financial ruin after the removal of aboriginals from the stations due to equal wages. Aboriginal families were relocated from the stations and these displaced individuals, entire families in fact, were moved to the closest towns where they commenced to live in disgraceful ghettos. These people had only rudimentary accommodation, no means of employment and nobody to look after them and their medical needs. They were close to alcohol and all the problems associated with this.

Lord Vesty, an Englishman who had interests in the Pastoral Industry, foresaw these problems. It has led to these aboriginals having their family clans broken up, domestic violence, murder and the disintegration of their cultural beliefs and ties, not to mention their language and traditions. Such disturbances remain to the current day, with drugs, alcoholism, domestic violence, crime and unemployment endemic.

It also resulted in the different cultures being mixed up, languages being mixed and traditional historical stories being either lost or tainted. Don't get me started.

The "Great Cattle Depression" gripped the entire nation. Cows and calves became worth $30 or even less. The cost of moving mobs was greater than the value of the mob. My mate "Bluey" was by now the Station Manager and my parents were running their own property. It was in this era that my Station was run on a shoestring budget. Very little mustering was taking place, especially in the outer areas, which went totally wild with clean skin (unbranded) cattle far outnumbering the branded cattle.

Back on my parents' property, they were struggling, and before long I was asked to return home to help on the home place. A journey which saw me again on the Mail Train, saddle, swag and a suitcase containing my worldly possessions.

I had paid a very emotional farewell to my mentor "Bluey". His promise still echoes in my ears that "when things come good, I could come back anytime". I knew my duty was to my parents but the bond was strong and so it was with a heavy heart I returned south.

Sometime after this, I was informed that my dear friend had taken his own life and our parting was the last time I saw this wonderful man. He had gifted me his mother's engagement ring and his beloved rifle. The ring I gave to my now wife who wears it proudly, and every time I see the ring I think of my long-departed mate.

Back on my parents' property, things were tough — no money, struggle street, really only those that have been at this point can understand. It was into this crazy closed world that I should have known that both my mum and my dad were severely stressed with the worsening pastoral conditions and financial positions

It was under these worsening conditions that my parents sat me down one morning and had a conversation with me that was to change to course of my life drastically. I can still visualize this conversation to this day. Both mum and dad were quite serious, sitting me down between them. Mum provided tea and pikelets, and I recall surveying the scene and becoming somewhat uneasy.

My parents believed that the cattle depression was going to go on for some time. They had exhausted all financial avenues and the future for them was quite bleak. Under these circumstances, I should look for "other" work as they termed it. What "other" work was there in this world? To me that meant fencing, yard building, dam sinking or anything along those lines.

My parents had higher ambitions — a government job! Maybe a police officer or a schoolteacher? Oh, those type of "Government" jobs. After further discussion and having drunk all the tea and polished off the pikelets, I promised to think about it.

My parents eventually asked me again if I had made a decision as to whether I wanted to be a teacher or a policeman. Having not thought about it at all, I quickly determined that as I hated school when I attended so I would not like being a teacher, so I said I have decided to be a Policeman!

I was once again on the mail train to my older sister and her husband's house in Brisbane. I stayed as their guest until the day I was put on the train into Roma Street, Brisbane, where I sat an examination at the Police Headquarters. After this examination, I was later recalled to undertake a medical examination by the Government Medical Officer.

Bluey: a name usually reserved for a male with auburn or red hair.

Lord Vesty: The English Vesty family for decades held large portions of pastoral leases in the Northern Territory and Queensland.

Jackaroo: a young, privileged male employed on large cattle properties. He lived in the main homestead with the owner or manger and ate his meals with the family. It was recognised that he would one day rise to be a manager after gaining the necessary experience.

Ringer: A male stockman employed on a large cattle and horse property who mainly worked with cattle and horses. He usually was only employed during the mustering season.

Cleanskin: An unbranded beast.

Mickey: A young bull not yet fully developed but capable of impregnating a female beast.

Scrub Bull: An unbranded mature age bull. This animal has been missed in musters for several years and becomes a very cunning animal, avoiding men on horseback and mustering helicopters. A bull such as this can grow large pointed sharp horns and can be very dangerous to humans.

Weaner: A male or female beast after being taken from its mother in the eight to ten months age bracket.

Weaner camp: At the end of the muster, the weaners would be taken to a different location and placed in a holding yard and fed on hay. Each day stockman would herd them onto pasture and at evening again place them in the holding yard. This would apply until they settled down and become used to humans and did not concern themselves with being absent from their mothers.

Tailing out: Days spent herding young cattle on horseback once separated from their mothers.

Horse tailer: On large cattle runs a ringer would be given the responsibility of looking after the stock horses. He would hobble them out at night if necessary and at daybreak ride out, unhobble the horses and bring them into the cattle camp for the ringer's to select their respective mount for the day's mustering. He would then spend the day finding suitable feed for the remaining horses.

Hobbles: A chain about six inches in length with a swivel in the middle. It had a greenhide or leather strap at each end which buckled round the horses' legs in the vicinity of their fetlock.

Greenhide: A hide taken from a beast that had been slaughtered, salted down with course salt and conditioned for a period of time. The hide could be used for several purposes. Making hobble straps, greenhide ropes, greenhide whips and many other bush items.

Wet Season: The first couple of months of each year in the north of the State (Gulf country) Queensland, and the Northern Territory. During this time, all cattle work on cattle stations cease.

Queensland Police Academy Oxley

Then came the day I received my notification to present myself to the Police Academy at Oxley and on my first day, dressed in newly purchased "civilian" clothes and a tie; I attended the Academy together with about 50 other male and female hopefuls.

On being introduced to a very tall, ruddy-complexion Irishman, we were told in no uncertain terms to line up in ranks of three. "Ranks of three" — what sort of pidgin English was this, "ranks of three"? From nowhere appeared three gentlemen dressed in white sports shorts and white polo t-shirts (Wayne Bennett), who began yelling and physically pushing us into three lines of three.

These government types had a funny way to me as a "bush kid" — why not explain it all first! I quickly learnt the "government way" — "Hurry Up and Wait" and "Don't ask questions, just do as you are screamed at!" This was to be the day that I was to make two lifelong friends; Trevor Thompson and Greg Stiles.

Although Trevor is no longer with us, having been killed in an accident while riding a Police motorcycle, I am still firm friends with Greg. I quickly found that safety was in numbers and to be different was making a target for yourself. Those that didn't conform or obey were singled out and made to "duck walk", do a series of "push-ups", or "march on the spot with your arms either above your head holding a Lee Enfield .303 rifle or more painfully, both arms outstretched in front holding a similar rifle in each hand."

This process eventually weeded out those that did not possess the right temperament, fortitude or the moral fiber to be Police Officers. The training and the men and women that were our trainers, primed us with the skills that we would rely upon to save not only the lives of civilians, but also the lives of each other in the uncertain situations we would later face.

The skills I learnt at the police academy were so deeply embedded that years later when called upon to utilize such skills in the course of my duty, they came quite readily and smoothly. A credit to those techniques of training and the individuals that utilized them to train us. One of training days was reserved for a visit to the morgue and to witness a Post Mortem. There were about 20 of us together with an instructor, and we were seated in an auditorium with the deceased lying on a stainless-steel table out in front.

I found myself seated in the front row, perhaps two meters if that, from the deceased and the doctor performing the exhibition. While witnessing a Medical Practitioner performing a Post Mortem examination was not a pleasant experience, it was good grounding for what was to follow over many years as an operational police officer.

On being sworn in as a constable in a small ceremony held at the academy, my signing "Commissioned Officer" Superintendent Morrie Hales after the ceremony approached us, took my father aside and enthusiastically shook his hand.

My father later informed me that they had both been "train drovers" together in a younger life, and this may have been the reason why I was frequently called to the Mounted Police Section to shoe police horses and educate problem horses.

Maurice Spencer Hales retired with the rank of Assistant Commissioner, Personnel

Brisbane Traffic Branch (Training)

After swearing in as a Probationary Constable at age of 19 years, I was sent to the Brisbane Traffic Branch, where I was performing uniform patrols. From watching how more seasoned members spoke to our "customers", I was able to finesse my own version comprising of the best methods I had seen my mentors use.

I very quickly learnt that if another member was in trouble and needed help, everything would be dropped, and all haste made to help out. It was into this working life that I was thrust and into an arena where the "bikie groups" were flexing their muscles and making a general nuisance of themselves.

Needless to say, a lot of our efforts were directed at ensuring that the bikies were kept under control. It was an era where these blokes road large Japanese road bikes, such as the Kawasaki 900 and 750 and Honda 750s. They moved onto these machines as their traditional machines, such as the Harley Davidson's and British bikes, could be outrun by our Ford V8s.

I recall an incident where we had a "Rebel" mounted on a Kawasaki 900 run from us near the Chermside Hospital; he travelled onto the large Rhode Road roundabout and couldn't work out where he wanted to go, so he just went round and round with us following. After a number of circuits, he dropped the bike and skidded into the curb where he sustained a fractured leg. My adrenaline was pumping, but being with a seasoned Senior Constable, I learnt something.

I learnt two things that night: (1) you don't rush into things, you take your time and properly appraise things, and (2) if they are crying out in pain and are vocal and moving around, they do not generally have a life-threatening injury. This was to remain with me later on in my career and is a lesson I still make use of today, but generally those injured receive my immediate attention.

I was told to search the rider while we waited for the ambulance to get on scene, and during this search approximately 500 grams of white powder (heroin) and a number of sheets of paper stamped with numerous shapes was found (LSD tabs). The young bloke had a small number of large Australian bank notes also on his person and no identification.

I was instructed to accompany this person in the ambulance and during our ride into the Hospital, I gave him the appropriate warning according to the "Judges Rules". On politely asking him further questions, he told me that he was only delivering the drugs on behalf of his mates and that the money we had found on him was payment from a previous delivery. He declined to tell me who he was working for or to whom the drugs were being couriered.

On arrival at the Hospital, I saw my partner already there with two detectives, who told us we had done a great job and that they would now take it from there. I later charged this offender with a number of traffic matters, including Dangerous Driving of a motor vehicle.

I gave evidence at the Committal hearing, where the offender was committed to stand trial in the Brisbane District Court later on in the year. I subsequently received a call to attend this trial where I saw our offender neatly dressed in a suit and tie and with most of his tattoos covered up. He certainly bore no resemblance to the young ruffian we had located all those months back. The jury duly found him guilty, with the judge sentencing him to four years imprisonment.

Sandgate Police Division

I was sent to Sandgate Station as a trainee constable, and it was at Sandgate where I first investigated a sudden death. The deceased, an elderly male, had passed away quietly at home in bed with his elderly wife. For those not familiar with this duty, it is quite stressful talking with the deceased's wife, helping her get in touch with their children and friends, but at the same time trying gently to extract the full antecedents of the deceased, while waiting for the Government Undertaker to arrive and convey the deceased to the city morgue.

Fortitude Valley Police Division

From Sandgate, I was sent to Fortitude Valley where I was placed on beat duty, walking one of four routes through the centre of the Valley. Friday nights we worked 24 hour shifts and other times we worked until 3 am.

I walked the beats through our allotted zones with an experienced Sergeant in a marked car as our supervisor; if we made arrests, we would call the "drunks van" and the sergeant would convey the arresting officer to the Watch-house which was on South Bank those days.

We walked those beats rain, hail or shine, and I recall vividly the nights after the Valley emptied and only the alley cats, rats and coppers were about. I recall thinking, "Here I am in the middle of Brisbane and I am lonelier here than I was in the vast bush of Cape York." Things were about to change, though.

This was of course in an era where "brothels" and "gambling dens" were somewhat prolific in the Fortitude Valley area. As beat constables we were never told to avoid such dens of iniquity but as they were often on the course of our respective beats, we would patrol past such venues.

I must point out that I never had any problems eventuate from such premises during my entire time I was at the Valley. I was aware though that these venues were kept under control by both the "Vice and Consorting" Squads. This was a time of heavy narcotic usage and transactions and also more importantly, the era of the violent "armed robberies". I knew through experience that these issues went hand in hand and that a large amount of information in relation to these issues came to hand through the work of the "Vice & Consorting" Squads.

I know that quite a large number of very dangerous criminals were removed from society through the actives of members of these squads.

I was detailed to perform duty in the "drunks van", operating with a seasoned constable First Class. Our job was to patrol the streets in a Falcon Panel Van, waiting to be called for transportation of various prisoners arrested by the beat crews. We attended numerous brawls.

My partner lived in the Wickham Hotel, which at that time had a patronage of totally Aboriginal Clients who also at times had severe disagreements amongst themselves which we attended. With living there and knowing most of the customers and my country background, we made a formable partnership. It was my partner who introduced me to the 101 of Narcotics. Under his guidance I became very adept at spotting "druggies" and all their secrets.

My next training tour of duty was with the Fortitude Valley "Dead Body, Fire and Domestic" car. Again, I was working with a new partner, this time a very seasoned Senior Constable.

My duties there involved general patrolling until either a fire or a death or a domestic disturbance was reported, then we would spring into action. The Royal Brisbane Hospital, now known as the Royal Women's Brisbane Hospital, was in our area. All sudden deaths at the hospital (Without a Cause of Death Certificate) and all victims of various types of accidents that arrived either DOA or died shortly after, would have to be investigated.

Together with the "Dead Bodies", our duty also entailed being the first on the scene for initial investigations into fires which occurred within our District between the hours of 12 midnight and 8am.

Our other duty of course was the "domestic disturbance" calls. These were most prevalent on Friday and Saturday evenings, and mainly involved husbands, male partners, knocking off work and attending their favourite licensed premises and having too much to drink.

I have lost count of the number of times I saw the female battered and bruised. The common thread of these arguments was either along the lines that the husband drank too much, thus spending what little money there was in the household, or that the husband was having an affair.

I was to learn quickly that you never arrest the husband for assault, as this would nine times out of ten have not only the "battered" wife becoming violent towards you but also the children. However, should an arrest be made, the prisoner would be conveyed to the Watch-house where he would have four or more hours to sober up. He paid the princely sum of 10 cents "bail" which would be forfeited, and he would return home hung over and all aggression gone until next week.

As the months passed, I returned to the Academy to undergo further training and examinations before obtaining my Appointment Certificate, having successfully passed through the 12-month period without too many blemishes.

It was during this period that the "Right to March" protests were held in the City Centre during peak hour times. Such demonstrations caused massive disruption to people either coming to or leaving work. The Premier at the time, Sir Joh Bjelke-Petersen, decreed that such demonstrations were to be stopped due to the severe disruptions it caused

These protesters could have lawfully obtained a Permit to demonstrate easily enough if they wanted to hold their demonstrations outside of Peak Hour but no, they believed it was their right to illegally hold such demonstrations and cause widespread disruption to everyday people going about their lawful business. I was one of hundreds of Police Officers called in at short notice to Police the law. Such demonstrators were principally student aged protesters going to University or unemployed marching down the roadway.

Such protesters had no idea of what life was about due to their young ages and were mainly driven by ideology, not experience.

Chermside Police Division-Relieving Duty

I was sent relieving to Chermside Police Station, performing general duties and patrols and local inquiries. I was attached temporally to this Station while the permanent member was away on leave. It was here I met Senior Constable Ken Salmon, who I would follow around the state and we become firm friends.

The members at this station were a dedicated mix of male and female officers with a gruff, tough Senior Sergeant in charge, who lived with his family in the Police Residence next door.

Day shifts normally involved counter duties, issuing licenses, taking complaints, attending traffic accidents and arresting shop lifters from the nearby Chermside Shopping Centre.

I completed several months here relieving the various permanent members and thoroughly enjoyed myself. Cattle prices had come good and for a while I considered returning to the "bush" to the cattle camps of the north. Thanks to my mate "Ken", who over several months convinced me to stay where I was.

Zillmere Relieving-Then Permanent

From Chermside Station I was then sent to Zillmere Station relieving. This was a small station with a staff of four and a Sergeant as the boss. He lived in the Police residence, which was above the station on the ground floor. The family had very little privacy owing to the construction of the police residence and the police station office. My duties at Zillmere were very similar to my role at Chermside.

I spent some months there before receiving a permanent posting to that station. I later learnt that the Sergeant First Class had represented both Queensland and Australia playing rugby league football.

Due to the limited number of staff, I found that of a night we often worked by ourselves, with the shifts comprising of 8 am to 4 pm and 4 pm to 12pm, with Fridays working a 7pm-3am shift. The Homestead Hotel was in our area and was a constant source of complaints with brawls and serious assaults.

I had the unfortunate task of investigating a fatal accident where a Torana sedan driven by an elderly lady failed to give way to a motor cyclist. I was working by myself and attended to the scene and tried my utmost to assist the motor cyclist who was middle aged and wearing a wedding ring.

My Endeavour's were fruitless despite my constant prays and he passed before the Ambulance arrived.

I was completely blindsided when I was interviewing the elderly driver of the Torana. On learning my name, I found she knew my parents quite well and had been our neighbour at Geebung and that I had played football with her only son.

I found that the deceased was returning home from work at Evans Deakin Industries. He had undertaken this journey for over 10 years, was married with his wife expecting their first child in a matter of weeks. I can recall a very subdued young officer returning to the office late in the night thinking that the cattle camps were not that bad although the pay was awful.

I recall one morning, with just the boss in his office and me working the counter issuing licenses etc., when a well-dressed man in his early 30's approached the counter. I saw he was sweating profusely, and I thought perhaps his tie was a mite too tight. On asking how I could help, he informed me he had been stabbed in the back by his wife and that he needed help.

On further questioning and not believing him at first (how many people can say they have been approached at the license issuing counter with a man claiming to have a knife in his back), he turned and sure enough he had been stabbed, with the black handled "Wiltshire Stay Sharp" protruding from below his shoulder blades and a steadily widening patch of blood forming on his nice white shirt.

The ambulance was summonsed and transported our victim to the hospital. I believe Detectives from Nundah CI.Branch later arrested the wife who had been upset about her husband's nocturnal activities.

It was at Zillmere that I undertook a simple task that haunts me to this very day. I was working night shift alone as usual, when I followed vehicles inbound along Robinson Road that was travelling at a high rate of speed. I followed this vehicle for perhaps 1.5 kilometers and found the car to be travelling at about 87k/h. On stopping this vehicle, I saw that it was a very well-manicured HQ Holden Monaro with wide wheels and a five-liter 308 cubic inch motor with four speed transmissions. The vehicle contained a young male "P" plater who was the driver and a young very attractive girl.

I learned that this was the driver's girlfriend and that he was taking her home. The vehicle was his but registered in his father's name. During the course of our conversation, I found this youth to be arrogant, opinionated and overconfident, traits that do not mix well with a powerful car.

No matter what I said he would never admit his speed and stated that he knew how to drive and had he wanted to, he could have simply accelerated away from my six-cylinder patrol car. Not wanting to engage this youth any further, I issued him with a $20 three-point speeding ticket and sent him on his way.

This was not to be the last I heard of this matter! Being another late shift the following day, I was advised when I arrived at work that the youth's father had been into the station demanding my name and number. He was rather rude but claimed that he knew politicians in high places and that he would have me sacked! Yes indeed, some days later I received a phone call from my Inspector in the Valley wanting to know just what the hell had transpired.

I told him briefly what had occurred, and he advised me that he was getting some flak from the Assistant Commissioner who in turn was getting an ear full from a certain politician. He instructed me to furnish a complete brief of evidence as the matter was obviously heading to Court and when I handed the Brief in, he would handle it from there.

I thought I may have been in some strife, having never before incurred the wrath of neither an Assistant Commissioner nor a politician.

He calmed me and said the following, which I have always remembered: "Glenn don't worry, I am not concerned in the least. I find that if my men are getting complaints made about them spasmodically, I know they're working well. I am more concerned about members who get too many complainants or no complaints." With that, I quickly completed my Brief of Evidence and handed it to my Inspector, who then looked over it and seemed satisfied.

A month or so passed, hearing nothing and knowing that this was going to be a hotly contested trial, I waited with some trepidation. I learnt from a neighboring station crew that earlier in the week they had attended a serious road accident, involving a single vehicle in which the driver had lost control, colliding with both a Street light pole and then careering into a power pole, snapping both off, with the vehicle coming to rest in almost two separate pieces.

Both the occupants, a young girl who was the passenger and the driver a young "P" plater, were killed instantly. They were the very same couple I had stopped earlier. I often wondered if I had of written another ticket, thereby revoking the youth's license, whether this accident could have been prevented.

I was somewhat melancholy about this entire episode but was told by older more seasoned veterans that he had pleaded not guilty, so he had use of his license until after he was found guilty. There was nothing I could have done to prevent this. I have always wondered though, that perhaps if the father had a different attitude and approached things differently, his son and the young girl would still be with us today.

I was working one morning when we were called to a suburban house in Boondall. The information from operations was sketchy at best, but we gather that a woman had shot herself in the house while the rest of her family, consisting of her husband and two teenage children around 14 years to 16 years, was having breakfast.

On arrival at this house, the father and children were quite distressed and told us that the wife/mother had suffered from a stroke sometime earlier and was extremely depressed as a result. That morning she had prepared breakfast as she normally would and then retired to the bathroom for her morning shower.

This morning was different in that after having prepared the breakfast, she went into the bathroom, closed the door, and they heard a loud bang come from that room. The husband admitted he had a 12-gauge shotgun that he kept in the bedroom. He stated that they had tried to open the bathroom door but were unable to. The husband stated that although he knew what had just occurred, he didn't want to go into the bedroom and see if his shotgun was still there.

On forcing the door open, it was quickly apparent that this poor woman had placed the muzzle of the weapon into her mouth and as a consequence ended her troubled life. We cancelled the ambulance and called for the Government Undertaker and Scenes of Crime Photographer instead.

While we were waiting, and after advising the family that their worst fears were confirmed, my partner and I returned to the victims' house to await the arrival of those who we had summonsed.

Things never seemed to be quiet when I was on shift, and one Sunday I received a call while working by myself on day shift. The call was to a house near the Zillmere Primary school, where a young couple had found that their six-month-old daughter was lying in her cot, not breathing. As I was only a short distance away, I arrived on scene very quickly, finding that once again I was the first on scene. I entered the house and found the couple inconsolable beside the cot in which lay this little six-month-old girl, dressed in a nappy and a cotton smock.

She had passed, and on inquiry found that she had been placed in the cot some four to five hours earlier for her routine nap. Her doting parents had checked on her from time to time and found nothing of concern. On once again checking on the infant, after realising that she should have been awaken by now, they found her cold and lifeless. I did a check of the little girl's body and found no marks of violence or anything to suggest that her death was suspicious. As this was the couple's only child, I let them stay with the infant until the Ambulance arrived. They confirmed that the infant was indeed deceased.

Towards the end of my tour of duty at Zillmere, I will relate one incident I found quite amusing. I was working alone, patrolling some standalone shops at the top of Church Road, Zillmere, when I heard through the stillness of the night air a very loud moaning and the words "Oh God Please" being repeated. On hearing this noise, I determined it was coming from a vacant allotment next to the Windsor Zillmere Australian Rules football grounds.

On driving towards the source of this noise I expected to come upon a scene of a savage assault, but all my spotlight could pick up towards the back of this vacant block was an orange XB Ford Falcon taxi. The "sounds" were still coming from this vehicle and not fully understanding exactly what was in fact going on, I stopped next to the vehicle and shone the spotlight into the rear compartment of the taxi, only to see a naked female sitting atop of another person.

On shining the light into the vehicle, both persons immediately stopped what they were doing and got out of the car. The "naked" middle aged female then aggressively demanded to know what right I had in interfering with their discourse, or should I say, intercourse. The male was saying nothing and was frantically searching for his clothes and putting each item of clothing on as he found them.

The female meanwhile was still verbally abusing me in her "birthday suit"; her only fixation was getting stuck into me for disrupting their actions. As this woman was middle aged and somewhat obese and left nothing to my imagination, I tried where I could to explain to her that all and sundry could hear the goings on and that even the granite world war 1 soldier on the plinth down the road was complaining about the noise.

I was not making any headway with this woman, so I turned to the male and told him that both could be arrested for "disorderly conduct" and that as this liaison was being conducted away from either of their residences, I suspected that one if not both were married, and that the consequences of being arrested may not sit comfortably with their respective spouses.

The male driver completely understood and managed, after not a little persuasion, to silence the woman and get her dressed. On leaving the scene, I wondered how on earth I was going to explain this in my "duty log" outlining what I had done that night. I thought then that there are just some things that you cannot explain.

Landsborough Police — Division February 1981

My old District Officer was now in charge of the Nambour Police District, and he called and offered me a position at Landsborough Police Division. He explained that it was a two-man station with the Officer in charge being a Sergeant Brian John (John) Knapp and that as there was a large section of the Bruce Highway to administer, there would be a Police Motorcycle available for me to ride.

This was in the days prior to the completion of the new section of the Bruce Highway, the Inspector knew I was a keen motorcyclist. On my arrival at Landsborough, I met Sergeant "Brian", a most likeable chap almost twice my age. I was at this time the ripe old age of 21 going on 22. Our office was located in the one building, with our office and the "Clerk of the Courts" office being at the very front of this building.

Behind our respective offices was a courthouse, with the "bench" on our common walls, facing towards the back of the building and with the "bar" tables centered in the room. Towards the rear of the building was a very small storeroom, a single toilet, and a meal and "witness" room.

On taking up my duties, I inherited a rather old, yellow stained K4 Honda 750 Police bike. The bike was both aged and unloved but had very few kilometers registered.

My Sergeant informed me that I was to always remain contactable when on patrol duty as our division had 30 kilometers of highway to police and a very high rate of serious and often fatal road accidents.

Apart from the highway patrols, my duties also involved the renewing of licenses, issuing of licenses, and the associated office duties. Further, although we had the responsibility of the highway, we also had to undertake policing of the towns of Beerburrum, Glasshouse, Beerwah, Landsborough, Mooloolah and Peachester.

There was an Ambulance base at Beerwah at which was stationed two officers. The nearest fire brigade was Caloundra. Our nearest Police Stations, should we require assistance, was from Maleny, Caloundra or Caboolture.

So, there I was on a Police bike, patrolling the Bruce Highway. Early one morning I was awakened by a loud pounding on my door. On opening the door, I saw the boss fully dressed, telling me to get dressed and get the Police bike down to the bridge south bound of the township as there had been a major accident.

On my arrival the boss was already at the scene, and I observed that a semi-trailer loaded with bricks had collided head on with a furniture truck; the furniture truck then colliding with a near new XD Falcon sedan containing an elderly couple.

The entire outside skin of this Falcon was missing, from the front mudguard through to the rear mud guard where it had come into collision with the furniture truck. Unfortunately, the driver of the furniture truck was deceased. This was my first "highway" fatality. My boss became my idol, even though he wasn't aware of this fact. I was like a sponge and enjoyed every minute I was with him. I'm not sure whether or not he trusted me, but he was always by my side, apart from when I was patrolling on the motorcycle.

His philosophy was that we share in the jobs and also the accidents. Even though I was the constable, we would always take it in turns to do whatever job presented, even the fatal accidents.

I was quickly learning that serious accident investigation was going to be a necessary requirement to undertake my position successfully. I had a very amiable and knowledgeable tutor. After ceasing duty for the day, I was always invited over next door to the Sergeant's residence to enjoy cold ale (home brew) and often a bar- b- que.

I found that patrolling the highway was a sort of "cleansing karma" and although I averaged some 12-15 tickets a shift, I enjoyed what I was doing in keeping the highway safe. I can happily relate that there were never any serious accidents that occurred while that Police bike was actively present on the highway.

Some shifts I would cover some 400 kilometers on that bike, patrolling our section of the highway. I found that a lot of the serious accidents occurred when traffic backed up behind slower drivers or drivers towing a caravan and that this "tail back" could be kilometers long.

Drivers following would become impatient and overtake, crossing double centre lines and invariably have a head on collision with an unseen oncoming vehicle. Being a small country station, any sudden deaths, including road fatalities, required the deceased to be removed by the Government Undertaker to a morgue located at either Caloundra or Nambour Hospital.

There was the normal procedure, which I was entirely familiar with. What I was not familiar with was the fact that I would have to organize the Post Mortems and that I would have to be present when such autopsies were conducted, taking possession of any specimens during the course of such autopsy.

Such specimens would then be taken and placed in a small refrigerator at the station before being taken to Brisbane to the Government Laboratories. Here I was confronted with this procedure being conducted in a very small room with only the General Practitioner who was also the Government Medical Officer — and I was his assistant! This was another steep learning curve for a young police officer.

I actually found that through this procedure and asking the doctor numerous stupid questions, I was furthering my medical knowledge and through this I was becoming better equipped to administer first aid to victims.

Sometime after starting duty at Landsborough, I was detailed to attend a residence in Glasshouse Mountains where a mother of three young children had failed to return home from work on a nearby farm. Her husband had become concerned when she had not returned home that evening and despite numerous phone calls and a search through the night, he had failed to find and any trace of either her or the vehicle in which she was in.

I took all the details and returned to the Station and called everyone on the husband's list. After putting a "BOLF" (Be on the Lookout For), describing the missing woman and her vehicle, I started a search of my own, riding every road, street in my area, but nothing. Several days past when I was summonsed early one morning by the Forestry workers based at Beerwah. They had found the missing woman's vehicle on a little used forestry track.

There was no sign of the missing woman. On arriving at the scene and organizing the forestry works, we set out in an "emu parade" around the vehicle. It was a short time later that the missing person was located, lying amongst the shedding debris of the pine trees. She was lying some 100 meters from her vehicle with a .22 calibre rifle beside her. She had a gunshot wound to the inside of her upper mouth.

Incredibly, this woman survived for a further three days before passing away. Neither her husband nor close friends had any inclination that this poor woman was contemplating such an action. She had displayed no overt behaviour to indicate that she was considering taking her own life. It was a tragedy; the husband was now without a wife, a farm hand on low income, bringing up three children all under the age of 12 years, occupying a rented house.

My Sergeant introduced me to "community policing", a term that was yet to become popular and a form of policing that was years ahead of its time. Every Friday and Saturday night, no matter what shift we had worked that day, we would get into our uniforms and drive to every licensed premises in our area, walking into the front and back bars, "showing the flag". We would always stop at the main bar of the premises and order a sarsaparilla for the boss and lemonade for me and engage the locals in conversation.

When I questioned the boss as to why we were actually doing this, he patiently explained to me that as I was well aware, most of our problems on those nights came from the overindulgence of alcohol, mainly drink-driving or domestics, so by showing everyone in the licensed premises that the Police were indeed out and about and active, it had a cautionary effect on the locals.

I do not recall having ever had to attend a traffic accident nor domestic dispute on either of those nights or nights where we "did the rounds". It also had the added benefit that the locals could see we were approachable and just normal guys going about our business, and this in turn gave them the confidence to approach either one of us and confide in us information of a criminal nature.

During this period with my boss, we attended a large number of fatal accidents, sometimes with up to three deceased.

I can recall during this period that I was introduced to the fast "ambulance escort". This came about if one or more of the victims were clinging to life and were in need of urgent medical attention to prolong their life. Depending on the extent of the injuries and how precarious the victim/s was clinging to life, it meant escorting the ambulance to either the Nambour Hospital or the Royal Brisbane Hospital.

The Nambour escort was generally straight forward; however, should it be determined necessary to travel to the Royal Brisbane Hospital, I would take off with 'blue lights and siren" ahead of the ambulance, "clearing the way" so that the ambulance had a fast as possible journey to the hospital. My boss would always call Brisbane Operations and advise them that we were coming and thus members of the Traffic Branch and Mobile Patrols would close off all the intersections ahead of us, enabling a clear fast passage.

Tranistion Training Onto The Kawasaki Z1000

After a period of time, I was summoned to the Depot at Petrie Terrace in the heart of Brisbane to exchange motorcycles.

It was a sad journey south, one last ride on the bike that I had grown to love. Yes, it was old and from a bygone era, but none the less, I feel that when that model was first introduced it was a revelation. I handed over the Honda keys and was in return handed the keys to a bright and shiny Kawasaki Mark 2 Z1000.

Having owned a similar bike, I thought I knew what to expect. I rode this machine back to Landsborough with my head held high and my chest puffed out. This machine had plenty of power and would easily wind the 180k/h speedometer past that point. The bike handled well, and had a different fairing, and was equipped with double disk front bakes and a single disc on the rear. It also came equipped with an electric siren, so powering the siren was not a burden on the engine and thus overall top speed.

Then came the day when my Sergeant took a short period of leave and left me in charge during his absence. Nothing out of the ordinary occurred during this period, much to my everlasting relief. It was a very happy junior constable who saw the boss's vehicle and van pull into his driveway.

Shortly after my Sergeant returned to duty, I received a wireless call advising me that there had been a serious accident on the highway near "Moby Vic's", then a well-known fuel and food stop.

My worst fears greeted me, quite unannounced. A fully laden tri-axle milk trailer had collided head on with a green Torana sedan, containing three males.

I was first on the scene and discovered that the green Torana had been overtaking while travelling south and when the overtaking lane ran out, the actions of the driver of this vehicle forced his vehicle into the path of the semi-trailer, with the Torana ending up underneath the trailer.

To say the injuries were horrific would be a total understatement. The driver who was deceased had suffered shocking injuries. Both the front and rear seat passengers were still alive, just. Thankfully, a nurse stopped and was directing me in what to do to keep the rear seat passenger alive while she worked on the front seat passenger, who I saw had horrific head injuries. We were soon joined by a doctor and shortly after an ambulance.

There was little any of us could do and sadly these two passengers passed away. My training kicked in, and after advising Nambour Operations that a Police photographer was required, I continued with the investigation.

I attended the autopsies of these three gentlemen and later took the specimens to the Brisbane Government Laboratory, then located in George Street Brisbane. When the results later arrived, the driver had an alcohol level of .270, the front seat passenger a level of .299, while the rear seat passenger recorded a level of .577!

Inspecting the vehicle in daylight, I found a large amount of spirits in the vehicle which had been stolen from various sporting clubs on the Sunshine Coast earlier that day. These young men, as I found out, were meat workers employed at the Cannon Hill Meat Works and were out of work temporally while the electricity strike was being settled.

The day came where my revered boss was promoted and transferred as the Officer-In-Charge of the Blackwater Police Division, leaving the Landsborough position vacant.

At the same time, the Clerk of the Court next door was also transferred, leaving me by myself with assurances from the neighbouring stations that they would be there in a heartbeat if I needed assistance. The Clerk of the Court position was the first to be filled. He was the only Justice Department employee at this little courthouse, engaging in the office duties as well as acting magistrate/coroner when called upon.

This gentleman may be described as a short, somewhat overweight man, with a full head of hair and a beard, and I was to quickly find him a thorough, down-to-earth gentleman.

I got to know him better as each day progressed, he would often pop into my office telling jokes and funny antidotes. There was a radio receiver installed in our office, over which could be heard the Nambour Operations staff calling out our call signs should we be needed. If there wasn't an answer, John would overhear the calls in the next office and call Nambour and advise them of where they could get me. Throughout my association with John, he patiently taught me the procedures of the "Clerk of the Court", a skill I was to find very helpful when relieving at centers where this duty was also incorporated with the Police duties.

John was a thorough gentleman, and somewhat of a keen fisherman. He had come to Landsborough from Normanton, which when growing up on the Station was our closest town apart from the fishing village of Karumba. There were quite a lot of lies told about our respective experiences in this frontier town. I also found out that he was born and raised in the western town of Barcaldine, which coincidently was the closest town to the station on which I worked after running away from home.

Time progressed, and my new Sergeant arrived on transfer from the Gold Coast and was a former Police Motorcyclist, no doubt he would be experienced in investigating series and fatal road accidents. How wrong I was!

I found that my new sergeant was very conscientious about the office but with any complaint being received either at the counter or the phone, I would be called away from my highway patrols to investigate any such complaints. I also found that on the report of a serious accident, I would always be the first of us on the scene, no matter how far away I was.

I feel the "point of no return" started as a multiple fatality involving four adults and two children, aged four and seven years. It was a head on collision involving only two vehicles. One vehicle, Unit 1, carried two young adults and the two children. The other vehicle, Unit 2, carried a husband and wife who had just reached retirement age and were on their first travelling adventure of their retirement.

For some reason, these two vehicles collided head on. The four occupants of Unit 1 either died immediately or soon thereafter. The male driver of Unit 2 died immediately, while his wife clung to life amidst the carnage. Despite out best efforts, this poor woman succumbed to her injuries and passed away.

I was totally clueless as to how had two vehicles collided head on a perfectly straight and well-sealed section of the highway. Unit 1, a small Japanese sedan, had incurred severe damage to the front end and both front tyres were deflated. Could this be the cause — a tyre blow out with the female driver losing control and moving onto the incorrect side of the highway and into the path of the oncoming vehicle? I removed the two front tyres and put them into the storeroom.

I later gave extensive evidence in the Coronial Inquiry at which the parents of the deceased young woman were in attendance. On finalising the inquiry, I left the court room and was approached by both, who thanked me profusely for the thorough investigation I had conducted.

I felt that had I been in their position and on seeing such a young Constable investigating such a major accident, I may have had serious doubts as to the outcome.

I recall another serious accident which involved a later model Valiant Sedan and an early model Volkswagen sedan. The entire front end of the Valiant was torn away from the firewall forward, a trait I was too often to see of this type of vehicle. The Volkswagen, with its fuel tank located in front of the driver, had ruptured. The sole female occupant of this vehicle had horrific leg and chest injuries and was trapped within the vehicle. Despite our best efforts, we could not get the occupant free from the wreckage, which soon caught fire. Spreading quickly, the fire took hold of the cabin and the sole occupant.

From a distance, we had to bear witness to this poor woman's agonising demise. Immediately prior to the fire taking hold, I had spotted and retrieved an expensive brief case lying on the front passenger floor of this vehicle.

By the time the Fire Brigade arrived from Caloundra, the flames had all but died down, so they extinguished what flames were left and departed the scene! I was left with the two tow truck operators to retrieve the burnt corpse from the wreckage and with the help of the Government Undertaker, took the deceased to the Morgue at Caloundra.

I was becoming hardened to all this death and suffering and was at my wits end to try and establish a method of controlling the carnage. Some of the scenes shocked me to my core, and so believing that photographs of some of these scenes may shock people coming to renew or try for their licenses, I placed upon the wall in the front counter area black-and-white photographs of some of the scenes.

I ensured that none of the victims were recognizable but made sure the numerous photographs got my point across. My sergeant at the time agreed with the reasoning and the general public upon seeing the "carnage wall", as that is what it was referred to as, were suitably shocked. The "carnage wall" was quite the talking point for a number of months, until our local state member called in, having heard about the "wall" on the grapevine. He viewed the "wall", saying very little before taking his leave.

Within hours we had a call from our District Officer in Nambour, instructing me the remove the photographs forthwith as they were considered too graphic! He sympathized with me and fully understood the reasoning behind my actions, but this politician thought it too ghastly for the general public to digest. Never mind that it was the "general public" who were out there on the highway killing and maiming themselves. How times have changed, now you see similar scenes with actors playing the part on "live television" in an attempt to reduce the road toll.

It was around this time that I was summoned from VKR Nambour to attend a serious domestic, not far from the small hamlet of Peachester. I was advised that an Ambulance was in attendance and that they were attempting to render aide to a victim of a stabbing. I was also advised that my Sergeant was also on the way to the scene, and that the offender was still on site and threatening the female victim and the sole Ambulance Officer with a large knife.

As I was at Beerwah, I set off blue lights and sirens to arrive at the scene a short time later on the Police Bike. I saw that my Sergeant was already on the scene.

The female victim was bleeding from a stomach wound, not as much blood as I imagined but nonetheless in great pain, pleading with her partner who was brandishing a large kitchen knife to allow the Ambulance officer to give her aide.

I approached the offender, talking calmly to him asking him to, indeed, pleading with him to allow his partner to get the medical assistance she so desperately needed. He made a number of guttural sounds, wide eyed and breathing heavily and sweating profusely. I formed the opinion that I might be in a bit of difficulty here as he was quite obviously under the influence of drugs.

With little warning, he charged at me with his knife raised. I shouted at my Sergeant to shoot him, pleading in fact for him to shoot, as I dodged about, avoiding certain serious injury. I had little area to work in and the offender soon caught up and a struggle ensued.

During the struggle on the ground, he lost the knife, and we were both on a level playing field. Adrenaline on my part soon took control and the offender was subdued in handcuffs. His partner was treated at the scene and I escorted the ambulance to the Nambour Hospital in very quick time.

I found through experience that while I was on that highway, patrolling and showing a visible presence, the accident rate plummeted. Over the public holiday periods, we would have not only the Brisbane Traffic Branch but members of the Transport Police (uniformed Police attached to the Transport Department policing heavy vehicles) assist with highway patrols.

We never had a fatal accident during any of these periods over the years that I was at Landsborough, which reinforces my beliefs that visible patrols reduce road accidents.

On any average day whilst patrolling the highway, I would average 400 km on a 30 kilometer stretch of the highway and issue around 15 traffic offence notices, and these notices were for predominately "crossing double centre lines". Out of all the accidents that I attended, there were only three accidents where alcohol was involved and no loss of life or injuries through failure to wear a seat belt.

The time came at Landsborough, when my Sergeant was promoted and transferred. His replacement was filled with a Sergeant from a small mid central western town.

On his arrival, I explained to him that this station was renowned for the number of fatal and serious traffic accidents and that at some stage he would have to investigate one. His response was: "No way, why have a dog and bark as well."

On taking up duty, my new Sergeant advised me that as he was in charge, he would attend to the office and it was my job to issue the licenses and attend to the counter and also the patrolling and any issues that arose. As I was to find out, he was correct in every aspect.

It was during this period that a rather large container vessel called the MV Anro Asia, ran aground on the northern tip of Bribie Island. I rode up to Little Mountain, just outside Caloundra, where I had a grandstand view of the beached vessel. In my mind, it was huge and heavily laden with containers stacked high on the deck. Attempts to re-float the vessel proved fruitless, and so a decision was made to utilize Chinook helicopters from the RAAF to individually lift each container from the deck of the stricken vessel until it once again floated free of the island.

This operation took several long days, with the helicopters removing each container and flying them to a park nearby the town of Caloundra. These containers were loaded onto semi-trailers and carted to Brisbane. When things started to get me down, I would ride up to the Little Mountain site with my binoculars and watch this fascinating operation.

John from the Court House organised some leave from the Court House, and I took leave from the Police. Together with John and his family, we travelled to his hometown of Barcaldine. I had just purchased a brand-new motorcycle, so I would accompany them riding to this township. We were to stay at his parents' house. You can understand my surprise when we pulled up outside his parent's house and there was my old boss "Poddy", the very same gentleman I had shot kangaroos with all that time ago.

What a reunion, and I recalled how "Poddy" had told me he had a son working in the Court system — what a coincidence, but a very happy coincidence. It was over too quickly, and on the way back I called into my old mentor's current station, Blackwater, and there spent some very pleasant days with his family before heading south and returning to Landsborough.

It was at this juncture that big changes were about to happen. My old original "boss" now at Blackwater had previously submitted a number of reports requesting an upgrade of manpower at the station, as the workload for two men was too large to handle and was getting heavier every week. The government wheels grind slowly so some three years later a further two officers were transferred to Landsborough.

These two extra constables, however, were for traffic duties only and would therefore share the one Police bike I was using. I was therefore relegated to a "general duties" police exclusively. This was all good and looked great on paper, but one of the new constables could not ride a bike! I was instructed to continue to ride the Police bike on the highway during the day shifts while the officer who could not ride attended to the Office duties. After his shift, he returned home out of the area and I was left to attend the call outs of an evening/night.

I decided it was time for a change, and I decided that I had gained sufficient experience to apply for a one-man station (now a one-officer station), so I submitted applications for every one-man station which became vacant in the state.

Laura Police Division Transfer 1983

The time finally came when I was advised by my District Officer at Nambour that I had been successful in obtaining a transfer to a one-man station. In my sheer delight, I had neglected to ask just where I had been transferred to. Finally, he told me that I had been transferred to a township called Laura, although he did not know just where Laura was as he had not had the time to look it up.

On asking my mate in the next-door office where the hell is Laura and meeting a blank stare, I proceeded to look the location up on a map of Queensland. Try as I might, I could not find the town anywhere. I remembered that I had applied for a number of western and central western small towns at the same time as applying for Laura, but no matter how hard I looked at every map I could get my hands on, I couldn't find it.

So, I telephoned the Promotions and Transfer section at Police Headquarters, Brisbane, and asked the million-dollar question, just where is Laura?

The lady on the other end of the phone politely told me to wait and she would find out. Great, I thought, even the Section that handles these matters does not know where Laura is. Sometime later she returned to advise me to look North West of Cooktown and there I would find the township of Laura. On further inquiry I was advised that the township comprised of a General Store, Post Office, Railway Station, Picture Theatre, Hotel/Motel, Primary School and Medical Clinic.

The main activities were farming and cattle grazing. The township was serviced by road, rail and air. Quickly finding it on a map, I was somewhat relieved that this town seemed somewhat bigger than the normal run of the mill one-man police stations in western and northern towns.

The business people together with the farmers in Landsborough, Beerwah and the Glasshouse Mountains, organised a send-off for both my partner and I. The event was held at the Beerwah Hotel and almost 150 Police Officers, Farmers and business people attended. I was stunned that so many people would attend. The speeches were overly flattering I thought, but I was genuinely surprised that I had touched so many people on our small community.

Prior to my departure, my old colleague from Chermside, Ken Salmon, advised me that he had just been promoted to Sergeant at Cooktown and he would be my neighbour. In my sheer happiness, I had neglected to ask him just what was at Laura and just how the road was getting into Laura.

Loading my XB Falcon sedan up, we head off on this great new adventure. I organised with Ken Salmon that I would meet him at the Laura Turn off, Lakeland Downs, on the evening of the third night of travel.

On meeting up with Ken Salmon, he told me just what was at Laura. For start, the railway ceased to exist in 1961, the General Store was also the Post Office, and the pub was a corrugated iron affair offering six beds and a main bar. The picture theatre consisted of a corrugated iron shed open on one side, in which pictures would be displayed on the hotel television once a fortnight after a video had been procured from the "mail plane" which landed every Tuesday fortnight.

There was a one teacher school, with around nine-10 students of varying ages. There was a "Medical Centre" as well, which was a modern air-conditioned building and was serviced once every two months by the Royal Flying Doctor Service who would run a clinic there. There were four white adults in the town, and now with my partner there would be six white adults, three white children of varying ages, and about 150 aboriginals living in the community.

On arrival at the Station/Residence I was met by the relieving officer, who politely asked "where had I been" and that he had organised a ride back to Cairns on the local carrier.

Here were the keys to the short wheelbase Toyota Land cruiser and here are the keys to the Station/Residence, and then he curtly bade me "Goodbye".

The telephone exchange was manned from 9-am-5pm Monday to Friday, the exchange being located within the Laura Post Office. Outside of those times, communication was by means of a small 25-watt Codan wireless. The aerial for this device was some 25 meters of small electrical wire strung in a tree. The device was powered by a small 12-volt battery.

Power, as I indicated before, was via a 240-volt diesel generator which was almost out of fuel and when switched off, the lights were powered by a bank of 32-volt batteries. At around 1 am, I was awakened by a mad hammering on the front door of the residence and told that I was needed urgently down at the hotel, as the place was being torn apart by drunks. I always thought that 1 am was some three hours after 10pm, the time at which all good publicans shut their doors and go to bed.

Driving the 150 meters to the hotel, which was the only brightly lit place in the entire town, I could see a mass of heaving black bodies brawling and a noise that would have the Melbourne Football Stadium weep. Peeling my way into this heaving mass, I eventually found the publican who pleaded with me to do something as they were destroying his hotel.

With him pointing out the ring leaders (I didn't know anybody), I arrested the main instigators and carted them to the single cell and locked them up for the night. I returned to the hotel and after not a little shouting and shoving, finally managed to get the remaining 20 or so people to return to their residence.

Unfortunately, this was a regular occurrence for a week or so until eventually I had had enough and advised the "Runner" that as hotels closed at 10 pm, there couldn't be any undue disturbances at the hotel, as it would be closed. I advised this 'runner" that IF there was a problem at the hotel, the publican could deal with it and I promptly went back to bed.

The next morning, I visited the hotel (prior to opening time) and had a pretty frank discussion with the publican, advising him that prior to 10.30 pm I would be of assistance, but after that time I would come down and deal with the situation and also take names and statements from the drinkers for a prosecution for trading after hours. I had no further call outs after 10.30 pm.

I did, however, have issues after this period, as the then publican sold the by now-well-known-combatants with alcohol, which they took back to their residences; consuming the alcohol on their premises commenced to fighting and arguing, which would eventually require me to attend the disturbance and arrest and lock up the offending parties.

During the ensuing battles, I was outnumbered on quite a few occasions and it was here that my previous training and instincts protected me somewhat. I got the usual biffing and resultant bruising, but I feel I gave as good as I was given.

In a short period, I had the respect of the town and also, more importantly, the respect of my "Tracker" George Musgrave. We developed a strong bond and I feel that I could and would place my life in his hands. This happened more than once, and I can gratefully say Tracker George was steadfast in the face of any number of dangers and life-threatening events. We were a formidable team.

As a result of this well-earned respect, George, who was also an Elder, gave me his fullest co-operation and assistance. He was also my early warning system, advising me when the men, who had come in from the mustering camps, had money and that there may be trouble later in the night. I found that this information was invaluable as I could head off the trouble before it started.

The local School Teacher left the teaching profession and bought the lease of the hotel. He was of similar thinking to mine and we formed a great friendship and working relationship. He had married a local girl, who on purchase of the lease became the cook. Every meal I had that she prepared was sumptuous.

The Post Office/Telephone exchange was operated by Aileen with her husband, Bill, operating the attached shop, selling basic grocery supplies. The shop also supplied Diesel and Petrol. Both these people were salt of the earth people and we became good friends. Bill was also the local Justice of the Peace. He was supplied by the local transport operator, John, who would haul the required goods, including petrol and diesel (in 44-gallon drums), from Cairns, suffering countless flat tyres throughout the journey.

The new School Teacher, Colin, arrived and being a single man at that stage, we took him under our wing. He was to become a lifelong friend. There was also a café on the main Peninsular Developmental Road, which was owned by the local indigenous community and run by Barry and his wife.

Approximately 15 kilometers east of town along the former railway line, was "Welcome Station", which was owned by Darryl and Iris. Iris would make the journey into town each day to bring their two sons and daughter into the school. The Station completely surrounded the township. I became lifelong friends with this couple and was soon assisting them with the mustering of their cattle.

The town had a Southern crossing of the Laura River and also a northern crossing. Both crossings were serviced by a wooden structure built during World War Two and during the "Wet Season" both structures would be inundated, cutting off the township by road for weeks at a time, with the only contact with the outside world being the fortnightly air mail delivery.

Inevitably during every wet season, the weirdos and "Cape Conquerors" would attempt to drive the saturated roads, forcing the Station people to care for them until the roads once again became passable. The roads were being cut to ribbons in the process. I lost count of the number of times I was summonsed to help these idiots.

Although originally being equipped with a short wheelbase Toyota, the vehicle was not equipped with a mechanical winch. It was supplied with a manual "Turfor Winch". (I was shown how this device worked at Cooktown by my friend, Sergeant Ken Salmon.)

The result was attaching my Toyota to a Coconut tree via a steel cable and inserting the cable into the device, inserting a long handle and pumping vigorously backwards and forwards, thereby pulling the vehicle forward. I would have to also say at this juncture that, Sergeant Ken Salmon was of such great assistance that my admiration of him knew no bounds. He was on that same pedestal as my good friend Sergeant Brian.

Sergeant Ken would call me for assistance from time to time. One of these instances was for Captain Cook's re-enactment of the first landing and claiming Australia for Britain. This was a fantastic weekend of festivities and re-enactments, with such an event still being held to this very day. On another occasion, I was called to give Sergeant Ken assistance, as an old World War Two mine had washed up on the beach north of Cape Bedford.

The location being about one and a half days drive from Cooktown. Together the two of us set out, arriving at the site the following day. On arriving, we were directed by some Hopevale natives to the mine. It was time for the people better equipped to handle this situation, so the Army Bomb Disposal was summonsed, arriving via Kiowa Helicopter mid-morning the next day. Attaching a small amount of explosives to the mine and moving approximately one kilometre down the beach, the explosives were detonated. The resulting explosion was most impressive as was the crater left in the beach.

I recall one such call from Ranger Ron from Lakefield National Park, complaining that three four-wheel drives had driven past the Ranger Station during the "Wet Season" without stopping and were currently somewhere inside the park. The roads north of Laura were also closed. I travelled the two-hour drive to the Park with great difficulty due to flooded creeks and boggy sections of road.

On arriving there, I was told of the circumstances and the suspicions that they were drug couriers. I was also advised to take the Rangers Nissan Patrol Utility as it had a winch. Ranger Ron was taking a 100hp all-wheel drive John Deer Tractor. I saw that the mustering contractor living in a residence on the Park had two 185cc Suzuki motorcycles. I approached this individual, Cameron, and his lovely wife, Doreen, and requested to borrow one of the machines. "Not doing," came back the reply and then, "If you're going on this adventure, so I am too."

With that, we set out on the motorcycles (our only weapons being my service .38 revolver and Ranger Ron's service .243 calibre rifle). Some four to five hours later after following the tracks, we came across the offenders near the turn of Jeanie Tableland, bogged completely in all three vehicles. Their claim was that they were fishermen, but a diligent search of their vehicles produced brand new fishing gear that had never been used, as well as brand new camping equipment, again unused.

The vehicles were HIRE cars out of Cairns. Using the tractor, we rescued each vehicle in turn and escorted them to the Ranger Station, where using the decrepit SSB Codan radio I undertook checks through VKR Cairns on the individuals. One of this crew had a lengthy criminal history and was wanted on warrants. He could be my passenger for a trip to Cooktown.

He claimed that he had never been to Cooktown and was most interested in visiting the town! I don't think he realised that the view from the station cells was not that great and I certainly didn't advise him otherwise! In fact, I gilded the lily somewhat and told him of the town's sights and attractions.

On taking my prisoner to Cooktown, I made a number of calls to the "Cairns Drug Squad" and also the BCIQ (Bureau of Criminal Intelligence-Queensland) and gave them the relevant information. It was my belief that a quantity of drugs may have been shipped either to the coast or dumped on the Jeanie Tableland's crude airstrip.

It was common knowledge around the area that these types of operations had been going on for years, and it was thought that the drug king pin "Trimboli" was involved. This information must have started alarm bells further south, and within days a RAAF Caribou STOL aircraft landed at the all-weather Laura strip with a request that I "rattle my hocks" and get aboard the aircraft. We were quite quickly airborne and heading north.

I suggested that as I had only limited knowledge of the area, we stop at Lakefield's all-weather strip and picked up Ranger Ron. (Due to the "wet season" I knew he would be in residence and itching for an adventure.)

Picking up Ranger Ron, we flew out onto the coast and followed it north. The scenery was breathtaking, although the noise from either engine was deafening. We flew up the coast and did a number of passes over the crude airstrip but found nothing.

It was after this that Ranger Ron made a request from one of the Pilots to fly over the "ranger out station" and check on the ranger and his wife and make sure all was well. The aircraft was thus diverted, and as we over flew the out station, we saw that both he and his wife seemed healthy, as they were spotted outside the residence

Being close to dark, the aircraft was made secure and we stayed and enjoyed the hospitality of Ranger Ron and his lovely wife Betty as well as their nearby neighbours Cameron and Doreen. I was duly dropped off at Laura the next morning, thinking that this would be the last I saw of the Cairns Drug Squad and members of the BCIQ.

Late one afternoon, I was listening to the "galah hour" on the Codan long range radio — what's the "galah hour?" "Galah Hour" is the session time prior to 8 am and after 4 pm, when the radio air waves become a free for all with every station, miner and contractor, attempting to call whoever.

The most powerful radios, that is the 100-watt radios, would drown out the lesser 25-watt radios, so I was content to just listen to the chattering, until around eight am of a weekday morning when "Cairns Charlie" from the RFDS would sound the "squawk" button, signalling the commencement of "Medical Hour" and the later business time on the radio.

After 4 pm RFDS would close, and "Galah Hour" would once again start until the sound of the far off Indian or Chinese fishing vessels would drown out all conversation. I say Indian or Chinese as I speak neither language, nor have I ever met anyone who could identify the conversations from these stations. You could always make out the language quite clearly and hear in the background the steady diesel chug of the boat's engine.

For distress calls outside these hours, one was required to press the "squawk" button for a minute or so, whereon Cairns Charlie would answer for any medical emergency and patch you through to a doctor. If it was dark, you had to tune your aerial to a lesser frequency and repeat this procedure. Even with the lower frequencies it was extremely hard to hear at times, especially when the doctor was prescribing urgent meds and their amounts.

As I was the keeper of the "Flying Doctor' box, it fell to me to be the First Aid operator. The doctor on hearing the symptoms would make a diagnosis and then prescribe meds from the box, such as Level C 10 or similar. The box was equipped with marked trays and with the meds numbered.

I was involved in the death of a small eight-year-old aboriginal boy, who had been fitted with the stint in his brain to help stop him convulsing. I had become quite fond of this little chap and often played him space invaders outside the Post Office. He was becoming quite good at the game. His mother came to me late one night with the poor boy fitting uncontrollably.

As this had happened before, I roughly knew the procedure and contacted the RFDS and told Cairns Charlie my dilemma. He in turn patched me through to the doctor and after explaining the symptoms, I was advised to give the boy a certain amount of meds via injection that would stop the convulsing. Having given the required amount in an injection, the poor lad continued to fit.

The doctor then instructed a similar injection be made up and administered. I duly followed the doctor's instructions, with no effect on the patient. I was advised to wait for the drug to take effect and after some time with little or no signs of recovery, I was advised to administer yet more of the medication via injection. I again administered the required amount of meds, which caused the young lad to stop convulsing.

I was told to monitor his heart and breathing rates and much to my alarm his heart rate became fast, then extremely slow, with his breathing becoming shallower and shallower, whereon his heart stopped altogether as did his breathing. I advised the doctor of this and was instructed to administer a different medication (adrenaline?) but to no effect. I had overdosed this little boy. I commenced CPR on the little chap with no effect — the boy had died.

I became extremely upset, watching the mother cradle his lifeless form in her grief. There was nothing further that could be done.

It was left up to me to transport this child to the Cooktown Morgue, some two and a half hours away. I allowed the mother to accompany me and she cradled her son the entire way. It was perhaps one of my lowest moments. I could only imagine what his grief-stricken mother was going

I was not permitted to attend the Post Mortem, which if I recall was attended by a member of the Cairns CI.Branch, as it was investigated as a suspicious death.

Life rolled on and waited for no-one, and later one evening I was again summonsed by the "Squawk" of the radio. On answering, "Cairns Charlie" advised me that a little girl from one of the outlying properties was gravely ill and in need of urgent medical attention. He advised me that the Station strip was unserviceable and that the RFDS plane would land at Laura. I advised Cairns Charlie that the Normanby River, through which I had to pass, was in near full flood and that there was no way of getting a vehicle through.

He advised me that the parents of the child had started out for the river and that I should try and assist as best I could, as the little girl was gravely ill. By the time I had loaded my Toyota with cables and scrounged extra rope and cables from Bill and Barry, I went to the School Teacher's house and obtained the assistance of Colin, and we set out for the Normanby River Crossing.

Just getting there was an adventure in itself, crossing flooded minor creeks and traversing boggy patches. I had been blessed, as some months prior after much wrangling, I had a brand new "Warn" 12000lb electric winch, fitted to the front of my short wheelbase Toyota. I felt that this valuable piece of equipment would come in most handy.

On reaching the crossing, I saw that the patient's parents were waiting on the other side and madly flashing the headlights of their vehicle. There was no way of communicating, but I could understand their worry with the predicament they were in. I resolved to do the best I could. The river was some 100 meters across and flowing quickly and around five to six meters deep. I comforted myself with the belief that no self-respecting crocodiles would be out on a night like this.

Tying a rope around my waist, I went up stream a considerable distance in the dark. My plan was to keep our headlights on the crossing, and I would swim across with the rope around my waist.

On reaching the other side, I would then use the patient's parents' Toyota to pull across the cables, using the winch to pull the cable tight after anchoring the free end of the Toyota. I would then take the child across on my shoulders to our side of the river. Easy!

On gaining the other side and making the necessary preparations, I was advised by the mother that there was no way her little girl was going to cross the river first and that I would be taking her across first. Yes, I could see her reasoning, but as she was a rather portly woman, I had my doubts. Using straps which tether the hind quarters of clean skin bulls, I fashioned a harness which connected us together and commenced to hand pull both of us across this river.

On reaching the far bank, I attached the small girl to me with the straps and placed her on my chest and pulled myself backwards across for the fourth time that night.

Having gotten both mother and patient across, we still had to travel back to Laura. We had neither towels nor dry clothes, with the four of us in the front of a shortie wringing wet. I stopped on the high bank of the river and throwing my wire aerial over a tree, advised "Cairns Charlie" that I had retrieved both mother and patient and I was about one hour away from Laura. We had to again return through boggy sections and flooded creeks.

Arriving back at Laura, I left mother and daughter with my partner, while Colin and I went down to the airstrip and lit the kerosene flares so the RFDS aircraft could land, as it was around 2 am. On hearing the aircraft, I returned to the Station, where mother and daughter had been given hot showers and given toiletries and a change of clothes. The young patient made a complete recovery later in hospital in Cairns.

An interesting accident which I was called to, involved an aboriginal family known as the “Darkens”, who were originally from Hopevale north of Cooktown, who had relations in Laura. It would seem that members of this family, six altogether, loaded themselves into Bedford Darkan’s Land rover Utility and drove from Hopevale enroute to Laura. Bedford, an elder gentleman, was the driver, with his wife and young daughter in the front, and his sons and nephew riding in the tray of the vehicle.

As they proceeded to travel down a steep incline heralding the approach to Kennedy Creek Bridge, Bedford lost control of the vehicle on the severe corrugations, resulting in the vehicle and its occupants falling over the side of the single lane bridge. The vehicle ended up on its roof at the bottom of the creek bed beside the wooden bridge.

I travelled to the scene with the shop keeper Bill and on righting, the vehicle managed to get it back onto the roadway in one piece. There was not a glass panel left in the vehicle, all having shattered during the accident. Miraculously there were no injuries.

On getting the vehicle back onto the roadway, it was found that all the oil and fuel had drained from the vehicle, and so being about 40 kilometers from Laura, I suggested that I tow the Land Rover back into town. As there was no room in the Police vehicle for any passengers, it was suggested that Bedford and his family resume their former positions in the Land rover while I towed it back into town. All went well and I travelled at speeds between 40-60 kilometers per hour, keeping what I thought was a watchful eye on the rear.

On descending a long downward slope approaching Coal Seam Creek, I was interrupted mid-sentence in our conversation by my passenger Bill, who stated, ‘Hey Sarge, you better get going, I think Bedford is trying to overtake you.” Looking into the side mirror, I saw the Land Rover almost level with my door, the horn blaring and Bedford wide-eyed, trying to control his vehicle.

As there were no windows left in the vehicle, Bedford’s eye sockets were black as was his passengers, but the rest of their faces was covered in a thick layer of dust, with their mouths momentarily skin-coloured as they frequently licked their lips!

The three men in the tray were similar in appearance and all had terrified looks on their faces, as Bedford, holding the steer wheel in a death grip, attempted to overtake while still attached to the tow rope. Accelerating moderately, I managed to stay in the lead. Back in Laura safe and sound, we managed to get Bedford's Landrover going and he went about his business, none the worse.

From time to time, it was necessary for me to transport prisoners I had arrested to Cooktown for their Court appearances. Frequently such prisoners would be sentenced to a term of imprisonment and I would have the return journey to Laura by myself. On one such occasion, however, my prisoner, "Monty", was fined and placed on a Good Behaviour Bond and so he returned to Laura with me.

Enroute back, a large python was crossing the road, and "Monty" begged me to stop so that the snake could be killed and taken back to Laura for a feast.

I adhered to Monty's request and placed the dead snake in the rear of the Police vehicle and thought no more of it. The snake was about seven to eight feet in length and about as thick as your forearm. I did however have a chuckle to myself about "Monty's" fear of snakes but his desire to eat them. On our return to Laura Monty, his relatives partook of a most enjoyable meal.

Life returned to normal once again, tourists getting lost or stuck, drunken fights in the Aboriginal Quarters, domestics — yes, the quiet life. The odd knife fight and serious assault aside, life was good again. I found that traffic accidents were happening when tourists would overload their vehicles (mainly Toyota Hi Lux's), hit the corrugations at speed and start to go sideways.

The inexperienced driver would then hit the brakes in a panic and over the vehicle would go, distributing occupants if they weren't strapped in and the vehicles contents over a wide arc along the roadway. Some of these accidents involved fatalities.

Some of these fatalities occurred up to two hours from Laura and I undertook the complete investigation, photography, criminal charges if warranted, as well as First Aid. I also had to convey the deceased to the Cooktown Morgue and later attend the Post Mortem.

One such accident occurred with a father and son going on a fishing trip, when they rolled their vehicle, throwing the father from the rolling vehicle.

The vehicle was completely destroyed and after making arrangements with the property owner to retrieve the vehicle and contents, I conveyed the deceased to the Morgue at Cooktown. The journey took four and a half hours and the deceased's son accompanied me throughout the journey.

The son was given a bed at the hospital and checked over, and Ken Salmon and I returned to the Cooktown Police Station

On another occasion, I was advised that a vehicle containing two males had driven off the Little Laura River Bridge, falling 30 or so meters to the riverbed upside down, crushing both occupants underneath. On arrival, we managed to extract both occupants, who were from the local Olivevale Station. Both young men were called "David". Using my trusty winch, we managed to pull the upside-down vehicle up sufficiently to extract the victims.

Both were still alive, and they were transported on a mattress in the back of a Toyota utility back to Laura. Fortunately on this occasion, a nurse had returned to town and the RFDS Medical chest was under the care of the Post Mistress.

Pulling up outside the Post Office, the nurse was summonsed while I spoke to the 'Cairns Charlie", requesting the RFDS plane for evacuation. Both "David's" were lying on their backs with their heads near the headboard of the vehicle. Unfortunately, the "David" on the driver's side was seriously injured and despite our best efforts, passed away not long after the drone of the "Queen Air" RFDS aircraft could be heard. I was later to meet the surviving David in Calvary Hospital, when I was taken there after a horse had rolled on me and I suffered a broken leg and ankle.

The deceased "David's" uncle was in the bed next to mine and the surviving "David" was across from me. It was David who recognised me. He had been hospitalised and was being treated some 18 months after the accident for facial fractures. A small world indeed?

Life at Laura was for the main part a "boys own adventure" that you only read about in books! I was often called up to attend both the Edward River Mission and also the Lockhart River Mission, as they were then known.

At that time, neither community had a full time Police presence. Both communities were in the Coen Police Division but as there were only two officers stationed here, there was no way they could be everywhere at once, so on occasions I was detailed to assist. Edward River was about five to six hours away from Laura and Lockhart River was roughly seven to eight hours from Laura. When being called out to these centres, you had to take all your own food and clothing for at least a week. The majority of the time you were on your own. Prisoners were flown out by Sergeant Ron Rook, "Rookie" the Police Pilot, in his 182 Cessna.

To say life was never dull when attending these centres would be an understatement. Periods of intense boredom interspersed with complete fear and adrenaline. You were always outnumbered. On one occasion having been sent up here by myself, a drunken riot had broken out after the "wet canteen" had been broken into.

The only safe place was the nursing sister's quarters, where about 15 of us hunkered down for the night. I recall walking around the quarters the entire night with my high-powered rifle, making sure no one approached and attempted to burn us out. Next morning with the commotion having died down, I went in search of the "ring leaders" and found a pair of red thongs inside the "wet canteen" that had been broken into.

Retrieving these thongs, I continued my search, when I came across a group of very hungover young males and on approaching this group and still holding the thongs, one member of the group said, "Hey Sergeant, where did you find my thongs!"

This was going to be too easy. Bundling the now remorseful group up and leaving them in the charge of the now appearing "community Police", I rounded up several more offenders, who were later flown out to face some quite serious charges.

I would like to say here that I watched the situation on Palm Island deteriorate and I can sympathise completely with those members who were caught up in this melee. I understand their fear and dwindling plight completely.

I came to know these sections of Cape York quite intimately and was always called upon by either the drug squad or the BCIQ to accompany them on surveillance or raids. I grew to know all the inhabitants and their either good or seedy natures. However, on one occasion, I was completely stumped when I began to get disturbing information that there was an unknown male preying on the Station stores while the men were out mustering.

This individual would wait until the males had left the station and then brazenly walk into the residence and steal food, never uttering a word. If he was caught in the act, he would take flight on foot, back out into the surrounding bush. The women were getting frightened for good reason and wanted this individual caught.

Using Tracker George Musgrave, we tracked this individual for days on horseback, but never got close. It was though he was the Phantom! Eventually he broke into the ranger station located at New Laura, an outstation of Lakefield National Park, and frightened the hell out of the Ranger's young wife.

As luck turned out, I was nearby with Ranger Ron when I was flagged down by the New Laura Ranger who told of what had occurred. I thought if I moved quickly enough, knowing the surrounding area of New Laura had been recently burnt, perhaps I may be lucky enough to pick his tracks up in the freshly burnt area. My luck held and on sighting him, and him me, he took flight.

By God he could run, but fortunately for me, not as fast as my Toyota; and with him ducking and weaving through the timber, my only hope was to run him out till he was out of breath, and as he slowed, I got him with my door and knocked him flat and handcuffed him.

His reign of terror was now over! I had gathered quite a few complainants' statements in relation to his offending, but we later found that he was of unsound mind and never faced trial for his offences. This was some years after the legendary "Tarzan", Alf Flamenco.

This poor tormented young soul was later released from the Mental Facility and took up residence on North Shore across the Endeavour River from the township of Cooktown. He would brave the crocodiles and sharks and swim naked across the river, landing near the jetty/boat ramp, where he would retrieve his shorts from an onion bag tied to his head and walk into town. On his return he would undress, and swim back the way he came.

Life continued on with the usual fights and domestics and one individual, a Golden Gloves award winner, returned back to Laura and was the cause of great discord. He would cause fights, bash his young wife and daughter and generally cause chaos. He was always arrested after a violent tussle. I grew ever more fearful that one day he would finally get the better of me. I decided on a plan that was not part of the Queensland Police Rules and Regulations which resulted in him relocating from Laura.

I later learnt from Sergeant Ken Salmon that he had hitch hiked his way over to Cooktown, where he had established his residence, claiming to all who would listen that the "Camp Sergeant" at Laura was mad. I did little to refute his claims and life in Laura settled back to a quiet routine. With this man no longer residing in Laura, life was a lot quieter and certainly less violent! Tracker George and his extended family were forever grateful as this man was not of the same clan and was regarded as both a trouble maker and a blow in.

Tracker George Musgrave could neither read nor write and his surname came from the Station on which he was born (Musgrave Station). This was a common practice, as was the assumption of the surname of the property owner.

You could always tell where the eldest sibling was born and who they were related to. Tracker George was also a gifted tracker and assisted me in the arrest of offenders and the recovery of cattle that had been stolen from different properties and the successful prosecution of these offenders.

Unfortunately, the powers that be during this period were adamant that Tracker George from Laura and Tracker Barry from Coen would be the last of the native trackers employed by the Queensland Police Force, and nothing, and I mean nothing, I could say or do would convince them to give him any recognition for his services nor an increase in pay.

I have literally lost count of the number of drug plantations Tracker George helped us discover along with the offender/s. The same applied to the Tracker from Coen, Barry Port.

Tracker Barry, during the commencement of an early "wet season", assisted in the location of a pensioner who was reported missing from his Coen residence. Together with Tracker Barry and Sergeant Bill Gettoes from Coen, we followed vehicle tracks for over 48 hours before locating the "missing person" caring for over 10,000 marihuana plants.

The offender was heavily armed, with a large range of heavy calibre weaponry. We had walked into his camp from a considerable distance away and found the camp area deserted but recently occupied and intact. It was decided that I would climb into a nearby tree and wait for the offenders to return, while Bill and Tracker Barry would retire out of sight and wait also.

I was armed with my personal rifle, a .22-250. Later in the afternoon, I was alerted after I heard whistling and the noise was getting louder. Our man was returning to his camp. He had another rifle slung of his shoulder and was pushing a wheelbarrow. This was our elderly missing person.

I called upon him to stop and drop his rifle to the ground, indicating to him that I was the Police and hoping that Bill and Tracker Barry had not gone to sleep. The offender hesitated for a brief moment, obviously considering his chances. Not wanting to get into any fire-fight while hanging out of a tree, I placed a carefully aimed shot into the ground next to his wheelbarrow, yelling that the next would be his head.

The wheelbarrow was deposited that quickly onto the ground it fell over, and the offender just as quickly discarded his weapon, standing with his hands up. On firing the shot, Bill and Tracker Barry came bolting from the camp site, yelling their heads off that it was the Police.

On speaking with the offender, it quickly became obvious that he thought we were crop robbers and that his life may have been in danger. He was for the most part, initially anyway, glad we were the Police. Now came the part of documenting what was in the camp, photographing everything and taking samples of "his" crop. As there was no vehicle present, the offender was questioned quite closely as to the whereabouts of his co-offender/s and just how he came to be in this location.

He told us that this was his usual "wet season" occupation and that his co-offenders had driven him out to the location, a location which they had used many times before, and then departed.

He was to remain on site until the plants had matured after the wet, whereon he would be picked up and returned to Coen. His arrangement for undertaking this "work" was a lump sum of money together with a percentage of the proceeds from the sale of the crop.

Returning to Coen was going to prove problematic, as we had undertaken this task in my Toyota Shortie. We took as much evidence as we could and placed the offender in the rear of the vehicle together with his arsenal, after removing the bolts and storing them in the glove box. We managed to travel approximately 50 kilometres on the return journey before it became too dark to continue. We made camp and I hand cuffed the offender to my left wrist for the night.

After a fitful night's sleep, I was glad of the first rays of sunlight heralding the dawn. I also saw a ghastly sight — the offender had a huge erection and I was anxious that somehow in my fitful sleep he was not fantasying about me! A detective was flown into Coen after our return, and the offender was air lifted back to Cairns. As a result, several other persons were arrested and charged with varying offenses and all served time in prison.

A search of our offender's residence located nine brand new outboard motors but no boat, a further cache of high-powered weapons, as well as an assortment of brand-new refrigerators and freezers, furniture and etc. Requested to explain all this material wealth, the offender explained that he was not able to bank these illicit funds as he would lose his aged pension!

One of my favourite duties however, was to accompany Sergeant Ken from Cooktown on our regular uniformed patrols north to the unoccupied vastness of Bathurst Bay, located on the eastern side of Princess Charlotte Bay.

To undertake this task would require the both of us being away for up to 10-14 days, relying solely on ourselves, the food we had brought with us and the vehicle. My vehicle was piled high with stores and food stuffs and our fishing gear.

With Sergeant Ken, the days never seemed boring and I was grateful for not only his company but also his fishing expertise. Fishing for our supper, we were always rewarded with fresh barramundi, mud crabs or grunter brim. The beauty of the entire area and the availability of fresh running streams in which to bath and swim (crocodile free) were magic. Cape Melville was heralded with immense hills of black boulders, similar to "Black Mountain" heralding the entrance to Cooktown.

These hills dominated the skyline as you approached the Bay and was the sole home of the "Fox Tail Palm Tree". Part of our reason for being in the area was to ensure smugglers weren't raiding the seeds from these trees, as well as deterring and monitoring any illicit activities in this remote part of the state.

On being issued a long wheelbase Toyota Troop carrier, these journeys allowed us to take a much larger assortment of gear and equipment as well as taking Tracker George along, as he was keen to see for himself the area as he had never been there before. Our journey normally commenced at Cooktown, before heading to "Starkie Station" homestead and enjoying lunch with the caretaker, Bertie Ahgum. Bertie made the most delicious fruit cake and was a good source of information.

Back at Laura, life trundled on with the usual fights and domestics and the occasional road accident. On one occasion late at night, during a particularly hot night pre "wet season", I had reason to incarcerate three gentleman who were intoxicated and causing a nuisance of themselves.

I allowed these gentlemen to remove the mattresses from the inner cell and sleep on the much cooler and meshed in veranda. Next morning, I saw all three sitting patient on their mattresses and I took them a hearty breakfast as was the norm; after bailing them out, all three returned to their residences.

Not long after this, Tracker George approached me and advised that those three scallywags had broken out of the lockup and returned to partying before carefully returning to the cell prior to daylight. They had bent the veranda mesh with their feet, making a small gap through which they had escaped.

In the morning, they came to the opinion that I would be very upset that they had damaged my Lock-up and so had returned early that morning and bent the mesh back into place! Although I was cranky at having my Lockup damaged, I soon had it back to "almost" escape proof and with the three scallywags profusely apologising, I set them to work under Tracker George's supervision, picking up rubbish from around the town.

I had made it a habit that whenever incarcerating anyone, I always supplied them with a good hearty breakfast. Knowing that their diet left a lot to be desired, I gave them a balanced high protein breakfast. Once every two months was the Royal Flying Doctor Clinic day at the Hall, and apart from collecting the Doctor, Sister and Pilot, I was to ferry any of those wanting to seek attention down to the doctor or those who appeared to me to be in need of medical attention.

Keeping the population healthy worked in my favour, as you see, if one of the community passed away, it was part of my lot in life to perform the burial. A "bush burial" went something like this. The deceased was delivered from either Cooktown or Cairns back to Laura. The coffin would be placed on shop keepers' old Toyota utility, and a procession of mourners would line up behind the utility and wail and throw freshly picked bush flowers behind the vehicle as it proceeded to the cemetery.

On arriving at the cemetery, I would say a few words about the deceased life and their accomplishments before the coffin was removed from the utility. On removal, the coffin was then lowered into the prepared grave, and I would read a few suitable passages from the Bible. The grave site was then filled, and I would bang in a wooden cross I had made previously at the head of the grave. The wailing and crying would continue on into the night as the relatives and friends grieved.

There was still active mining going on in the river near Maytown and I would perform checks of these sites and all those that worked in them to see that all was orderly, and no wanted persons were hiding out there.

I would often take a passenger for company on such trips, and of an evening would camp on the Palmer River and fish for Black Brim which we would then be cooked and eaten. Such trips normally took three-four days and were in the main most enjoyable. The area is teeming in history with quite a lot of the old mining equipment discarded on site.

One such trip I undertook was in the company of Sergeant Ken, and we were specifically looking for a male person wanted on warrant for failing to appear for Breaking and Entering and car stealing offences. By the look of the accompanying paperwork, this warrant had certainly done the rounds of the State! Not thinking we would be successful due to the accompanying paperwork, we took our fishing gear and a carton of stubbies, which we used to cool in my car fridge in the back of the shorty.

Unfortunately for all concerned, we located the offender and duly arrested him, handcuffing him to the grill behind the seats in the shortie. The offender had unfretted access to our beer supply. Not expecting to make any such arrest, we then had to travel the four to five hours back to the Palmer River Roadhouse. As it was around 10 pm, the jovial proprietor, Louie Comsik, was most happy to see us. He provided us with meals and refreshments, including the prisoner who we had handcuffed to the tow bar.

Unknown to neither Ken nor I, Louie was quietly taking stubbies out to the prisoner! By standing at the exit, I could see the Toyota and the prisoner but had no idea that he was getting drunker and drunker. We were induced to stay the night at the roadhouse as Cairns was another six/seven hours distant. By the time we had finished socializing and returning to the vehicle to roll my swag, I saw that the prisoner was well and truly intoxicated!

Next morning bright and early, Louie invited us into the roadhouse for a hearty breakfast, including our prisoner. On our journey to Cairns, both Ken and I were regaled by the prisoner of what great blokes we were, and that the next time he was arrested he wanted both of us to arrest him. He claimed it was the best arrest he had ever endured and a great going-to-prison party!

It was at this stage of my tour of duty at Laura that my wife left town, taking our young son with her. Being single meant that I could no longer be attached to a one-man station, living in a Police residence.

With some reluctance, I contacted my District Officer and the Brisbane Transfer Section and advised them of my predicament. I asked that I return to the Brisbane Traffic Office, where my mate, Greg Stiles, was currently on Police bikes.

Prior to taking up duty in Brisbane, I was detailed to undertake a Detective training course at the Oxley Police Academy

During the course, I was somewhat fortunate in that I had some experience in investigating sometimes complex criminal matters. I found the course excellent along with our instructor, a former detective, who had served with distinction. I am proud to state that I passed each examination with flying colours. Suffice to say, I had a most pleasant, sojourn in Brisbane and thoroughly enjoyed the detective training after the course.

Brisbane Traffic Office. October, 1985

In my duties as a member of the Brisbane Traffic Branch, my first duties were to be the writer of tickets on radar. In those days, a radar-reader would call out the offenders and their speed for us to pull over the driver and issue them with a Traffic Offence Notice. In a matter of weeks, a Police motorcyclist was transferred, and I was issued with his motorcycle. This was the motorcycle of Peter Kidd, who was to be shot and killed by a career criminal at Virginia some time later.

I enjoyed motorcycle duties, as I was able to ride with my good friend, Greg Stiles. We would sit off Stop Signs, Double Centre Lines and Red Lights and other traffic violations in a search for Traffic Offenders.

During this period whilst I was station in the Brisbane Traffic Office, I also arrested or detained a large number of drug offenders, stolen vehicles, break and enter criminals, and in one instance, two armed robbers who had just robbed an inner-city hotel. I even responded together with my good friend Greg Stiles to an urgent call to stop a "jumper" from jumping from the "Story Bridge".

We both rode our bikes along the pedestrian section of the eastern side of the Bridge where our "jumper", who had climbed down onto the under structure of the bridge, was sitting on a large girder, no doubt contemplating "to jump" or "not to jump". Greg Stiles went to the aid of this gentleman, who was later found to be of unsound mind.

Eventually, this individual was restrained and lifted back onto the roadway, where he was taken to the mental institution known as Lowson House, located at the Royal Brisbane Hospital. My friend, Greg Stiles, was to receive a well-earned Bravery Award for his efforts. Life was never boring in the Traffic Branch, and it was a section that I looked forward to working in whenever on shift.

Another duty that I found most rewarding was the "Special Duties", where we would be paid on our time off to escort wide loads to various destinations in North and Central Queensland. Being a motorcycle enthusiast, I enjoyed the ride both to and from our destination.

My favourite destination though was Blackwater, where my old boss from my Landsborough days was the Officer-in-Charge. On visiting both him and his wife, the old homemade bar-b-que would be fired up and a good time had, with many old stories reminisced.

Kingaroy Criminal Investigation Branch — Stock Squad May, 1987

Due to my country background and my experience with horses and cattle, I was asked if I would be interested in a position with Kingaroy Stock Investigation Squad, which was upgraded from two to three staff members. It was proposed that I make up the third man. With little thought, I agreed and was thus transferred to the Kingaroy Stock Squad in plain clothes.

I found I had quite some trouble in adjusting from the rigors and go, go, go of the Traffic Office to the laid-back atmosphere of a small-town Criminal Investigation Branch, Stock Investigation Unit. Our brief of duty centred on the investigation of all matters relating to livestock. This included, but was not limited to, stock stealing, butchering, unlawful use of stock and such.

Our area was from Landsborough in the east to Gin Gin in the North, Crow's Nest to the South and Chinchilla in the west. Quite a large area for a three-man squad. My boss was Detective Sergeant Keith Lipp.

My boss was a most learned man with a lengthy history in criminal and stock investigation. His knowledge of criminal law and procedure was almost unsurpassed. I found it difficult settling into this slow-moving way of life. I also found that although I had quite a history of criminal investigations under my belt from my times at Landsborough, Laura and the Brisbane Traffic Branch, I still had a lot to learn.

During this period attached to Kingaroy, I met and fell in love with a local girl, Tammy, who came from a well-known farming family and her heritage had deep roots in the District.

I was enjoying my time at Kingaroy and eventually I was seconded to the Kingaroy CI Branch, working with a Detective Sergeant, Tim Fenlon, who had a wealth of experience. Our stenographer was his charming wife, Kerry. She was proficient in short hand and this came to be a most useful tool, as working with Tim was full on and then Tim was selected from a list of Interstate Detectives to be the sole Australian representative at the United States Federal Bureau of Investigation, more commonly known as the FBI.

Tim was to undertake a six-month course at the premier law enforcement academy of the world. He excelled at the FBI Academy and he was asked to stay on there and gain valuable field experience in the United States, which of course he accepted.

Just prior to my boss's departure however, we received a complaint relating to the sexual assault of a 12-year-old girl. This complaint came via the victim's friend's parents, when the victim questioned why her friend's father only kissed her on the forehead when saying goodnight. It would seem that our victim received a good deal more. During every investigation, it came time to confront the offender, who in this instance didn't have a clue that we were onto him. On walking into the residence, I saw a .22 calibre semi-automatic rifle lying against the wall.

Before talking to the suspect further, I asked him if he had any further firearms in the house which he produced. We put the allegations to him which both he and his wife denied strenuously. I then interviewed the victim in the presence of a Department of Children's Services Office and the child's mother. The victim constantly looked terrified and glancing at her mother, denied any wrong-doing.

Separating mother and daughter produced the real story, which was confirmed through a medical examination at the local hospital. With the strange actions of the suspect and the amount of firearms in the house, I felt uneasy and knew that I would have to return to the residence some time later to question the suspect further and/or arrest him.

I therefore seized the firearms and took them to the Police Station for safe keeping for the moment. The suspect could have them back if he behaved himself. This was in the period before firearm owner/weapons licensing. Sure enough, with the child in custody of Children's Services, together we returned to the residence to speak further with the suspect. The residence in this instance was a high set wooden structure with a set of stairs leading to a small veranda on which only two people could fit.

I had seen an elderly lady next door gardening near the boundary fence in her front yard when reaching the veranda but paid little attention to her. On knocking on the front door, this door was flung violently open and the offender rushed forward, brandishing a large kitchen knife.

I saw all this in a split second and stepped backwards, with the suspect hitting the railing of the veranda and falling over, landing almost at our elderly gardener's feet. Needless to say, our suspect had all the fight knocked out of him as a result and he accompanied us quietly back to the Station. I was most pleased, as was Tim, that I had taken the precaution of seizing the firearms on our first visit, as I firmly believe that they would have been used against us and the situation would turn very nasty.

It was during this period that The Royal Commission of Inquiry into Police Corruption was being held in Brisbane. It was mind boggling the names of the people involved.

Detective Tim was eventually summonsed to return to Queensland and life returned to normal. He had such a wealth of knowledge prior to his departure and was extremely experienced in the techniques of criminal investigation.

Others further up the chain of command quite clearly saw this as well, and he was destined to bigger and better things. He gained rapid promotion and was put in charge of the security at the Commonwealth Leaders Summit held at Coolum.

He was lauded for the manner in which the security of World Leaders was undertaken, gaining many favourable comments from these leaders. Tim was eventually transferred to uniform duties and put in charge of the Drug and Alcohol Abuse Unit, where Tim remained for a period of time before resigning from the Police Service, when he gained employment with UNICEF, investigating atrocities against children.

MAREEBA CRIMINAL INVESTIGATION BRANCH-STOCK SQUAD — NOVEMBER 1989

Late in the year of 1989, I accepted a transfer to the Mareeba Criminal Investigation Branch, Stock Investigation Squad. One of my first tasks at Mareeba was to be summonsed to Cairns, where I spoke at length with the Regional Crime Coordinator Detective Inspector, Sid Churchill, who briefed me on my duties and what he expected of me.

Inspector Frank Wagner, the District Officer at Mareeba, was a man who I knew and respected. One of my first investigations was to travel to Brisbane with the Detective Sergeant from the Mareeba Stock Squad, and there interview a barrister concerning a large cattle stealing operation on one of the larger Gulf properties. The barrister in question specialised in criminal law, and it was essential due to the serious nature of the allegations that he was interviewed competently.

Unfortunately, the senior officer who accompanied me to Brisbane to conduct the interview abandoned me and undertook the interview alone without me being included. This resulted in serious consequences upon our arrival back at Cairns. The barrister was never charged and unfortunately this particular investigation did not reach a satisfactory conclusion.

During a visit to the Mareeba Primac Office in the course of investigating an unrelated stock stealing complaint, I found it necessary to seize a large number of documents including "Waybills" and sale yard sheets. (A waybill is a document that outlines the number, type, brands, and earmarks of cattle being moved, along with the address of the source of the journey and where such cattle will be taken.)

It is a formal document and is signed by the owner of the cattle or his agent. Going through these waybills, I saw one that I had completed when

I attended the cattle muster at Lakefield. It related to the movement of some 10 Kalpowar Station bullocks that we had mustered from Lakefield. These cattle had come across into the park as the boundary was unfenced, which was a common enough occurrence. I had personally mustered such cattle and therefore I had personally written out this document on behalf of the owner and had the cattle transported to Mareeba as per the cattle owner's request. I recall one such beast was a large Brahman cross type with huge horns.

The horns were so big the beast had to turn its head sideways to go through the race and up the ramp and onto the truck. Being curious, I wanted to know what this particular beast sold for, so I looked up the saleyards, paperwork and also the Primac paperwork and found that although this beast sold for a sizeable sum, it was marked down on the Primac paperwork as having died on arrival at the saleyard. The proceeds of the sale of this "dead" beast were then marked down to be paid to a "B.ENZO".

The owner of the cattle Kalpower Station was to be credited with an insurance payout for the "dead" beast being the average the entire pen of bullocks sold for. I did not know, nor had I heard of "B.ENZO", and strongly suspected that mischief was a foot. I then looked up further waybills and saleyard and Primac paperwork relating to the sale of cattle recorded on the 'Waybill" and found that it was a common practice. Cattle would normally be drafted off into lines and then pens and sold at auction accordingly.

I saw that the proceeds of quite a few of these cattle were directed to 'B.ENZO" with the owner being credited with an insurance payout for a beast that arrived at the saleyard "dead". Again this "B.ENZO" was mentioned. I looked for cheques being issued through Primac for "B.ENZO" but found none. I was becoming even more suspicious and at first thought the saleyard superintendent may have a hand in this. I seized the saleyard document book outlining records of cattle that had arrived at the saleyard prior to sale.

In every instance where the proceeds from the cattle had gone to "B.Enzo" and the owner of the stock being credited with a "D.O.A", there was no corresponding record listed in the Cattle Disposal Register. This would indicate that the beast did not die but was auctioned off together with his pen of mates and the proceeds of the beast diverted in "B.ENZO" account. There was however no corresponding cheque to "B.Enzo" for me to track.

It would seem that the agents may have some knowledge of this, but I was not sure.

D.O.A: Dead on arrival.

Digging deeper and going back five to six years, I saw that this practice continued right up to the last sale date in 1989. I had to find out who this 'B.ENZO" was, as all my lines of inquiry proved fruitless. I approached the saleyard superintendent and his wife, who operated the scales at the saleyard and was where the saleyard paperwork originated from. Neither person, who were locals and firmly entrenched in the Northern cattle industry, knew or had heard of "B. ENZO". As the payments were made through the Mareeba Primac agency, I realised that further investigations were necessary.

I had inquired of other agents operating at the Mareeba saleyards if they had ever heard of, or did they know, a "B.ENZO". All such inquiries were negative. My queries with the Telstra, the Electoral Roll and the Departments of Main Roads, Transport and Primary Industries indicated that "B.ENZO" did not exist. I told my immediate supervisor Detective Inspector Churchill of my suspicions and what I had gleaned so far.

I was instructed to bring all the relevant documentation down to him in Cairns. "B.ENZO" had to be someone from within the Primac Office in Mareeba. I was advised to travel to Brisbane and there meet up with the CEO of Primac. I was to be accompanied by a senior investigator fluent in the intricacies of a Fraud Investigation. His name was Detective Ken. I found him to be an all-round good guy and a highly experienced detective.

We arranged a meeting with the hierarchy of Brisbane Primac and laid out the documentation and our suspicions. To say they were completely and totally shocked would be an understatement. Not only were the two agents in Mareeba one of their best sales teams, but they quickly understood not only what had been happening but also the ramifications. We returned to Detective Ken's office in Police Headquarters and formulated a plan of where to proceed from here and how.

On returning to Cairns, I was summonsed to the Assistant Commissioner's Office, where in the presence of Detective Churchill, I was directed not to discuss anything relating to this Primac investigation with my immediate superior.

I returned to Mareeba and within days a team from Brisbane had arrived, and together we all went through a mountain of paperwork. There were literally hundreds of thousands of documents, all had to be scrutinized and married up to the relevant "waybills", saleyard documents and Primac Documents, as well as the Disposal Registered. This was proving to be a mammoth task, especially as there were no computers to assist in the compilation of all these documents.

Every dodgy piece of documentation, the owners, transport operators and the personal that received the cattle had to be listed with their full names and addresses and phone contact, if any recorded. Added to this was the fact that the large number of the complainants (although they at this stage did not know they were going to be complainants) were scattered between Normanton, Brisbane and Thursday Island. Each and every one of these witnesses had to be contacted and statements obtained.

Early one evening, I had a telephone conversation with the Officer in Charge of the uniform section at Cairns, Senior Sergeant Ken Cant, who informed me that I was required to help out at Mt Emerald, as it was believed that an aircraft carrying approximately 10 people had crash-landed in the area.

The exact whereabouts was at this stage unknown, as was the condition of the occupants of the aircraft. I knew that one of the helicopters that we had used when mustering was parked on the strip nearby, as I had seen the helicopter there when driving past that afternoon. I knew the owner/pilot and immediately contacted him to see if he could use his helicopter radios to tri-angulate the now functioning distress beacon of the missing aircraft. Together with this helicopter, we were able to more or less pinpoint the location given to us from the Canberra based search and rescue.

As with all such emergent incidents, our luck, or should I say the occupants' luck, was not with them, as the weather was squalling with high winds and heavy to light rain. In such conditions, it was pointless attempting to organize a ground search for the missing aircraft that night. All that night, I maintained a watch on the distress beacon and the channel on the radio that the aircraft had last been on.

If anything, the weather deteriorated in the early hours of the morning and this didn't bode well for the ground search to be conducted at first light.

Around midnight, I was greeted by a male person who told me that he was the husband of one of the two women on board the aircraft at the time it went missing. The other woman was a catholic nun. The aircraft, apart from the Pilot and the Nun, was carrying shire councillors and was expected to land in Mareeba.

Prior to daylight, two "Black Hawk" helicopters landed on our strip in anticipation of the pending daylight.

Just before dawn, one of these helicopters took off for the general search area. It was just after first light that the helicopter returned to our location, with the sad news that the Cessna Citation had collided with the top of Mount Emerald and that there did not appear to be any survivors. It was later confirmed that the aircraft was in fact carrying 10 passengers.

I was tasked with taking a recovery party to the sight and after a number of hours of walking came upon the scene. The majority of the wreckage was down in a gully, not far from the summit. Parts of the wreckage and the majority of the human remains were located over the top of the summit in the direction in which the plane had been flying.

On examining the site and reporting back to the airstrip which had now been organised as a base, I advised control that there were in fact no survivors and that the human remains would be difficult to identify.

I was instructed to assist in the recovery of the aircraft's two jet-turbine engines, which were airlifted from the site, under the direction of the Australian Bureau of Air Safety and Investigation.

Incidentally, this aircraft crash occurred on the same night in the month of May, 1990 that a send-off took place in Cairns for the recently promoted Assistant Commissioner, Laurie Pointing. Laurie arrived at Cairns in the month of May, 1989 as the District Officer.

One incident that took me away was the "Murder-Suicide of Julie-Anne Leahy and Vicki Arnold". Both women had been reported missing by Leahy's husband some days before, as a result, all personal were required to stop what they were doing and help in the search of these two presumed missing women. I was given the task of searching on horseback around the perimeter of Tinaroo Dam. After a number of days searching in this fashion for either the women or their short wheelbase Nissan Patrol, I was instructed to conduct a search of all nearby bushland on the Police Yamaha TT350 motorcycle.

I spent almost 10 days of the search for these two women, and it was only after the official search had wound down that they were discovered outside of Atherton deceased in the bushland, by two young men hunting wild pigs.

The circumstances of the deaths of these two women created controversy to this very day. In my opinion, both women met with foul play at the hands of a third party. It was very poorly investigated right from the outset, and there were a number of things that should have been done a lot better.

Another duty, which required me to be away for periods at a time and absent from the "Primac" investigation and also away from Mareeba, was the necessity of a detective to attend such events as the Einasleigh Rodeo. As I was the only one available at the time, the other detectives being engaged in the Leahy-Arnold investigation, I attended this event. Einasleigh is situated south west of Georgetown in the Gulf country.

These interludes were mostly quite pleasant, in that one got to walk around and talk to various people and watch the entertainment. The only time any Police work was called upon was when the uniformed staff needed assistance in drunken arguments or when any criminal matters needed attending to. On this occasion, I had to undertake one of the most unpleasant duties that befall a policeman and that is to deliver a sudden death message of a loved one.

On finding the poor man, I saw that it was the same gentleman who had sat all those lonely hours waiting to hear from his wife, who was on board the ill-fated Cessna Citation which crashed into Mt. Emerald some months earlier. He was residing with his two beautiful young girls and was attempting to move on after his tragic loss. It was extremely difficult advising him that his father had passed away earlier that day in Cairns.

Part of my duties when in these remote areas was the investigation of serious and sometimes fatal traffic accidents. Almost immediately after the Einasleigh Rodeo came to a close, I was advised that I was required to attend a traffic accident between Mt. Surprise and Georgetown in which four people had been killed.

The dead included two young teenage children. It took nearly two hours to get to the actual scene and on arrival, I saw that two four-wheel drives had collided head on.

I assisted the uniformed officer in photographing the scene and taking the necessary measurements. As this officer was even further south of Einasleigh and it would take at least three to four hours for him to travel home, I volunteered to accompany the bodies back to the morgue located in

Georgetown. By the time I got back to Georgetown, it was very late into the night and the kind matron of the facility provided outstanding assistance.

I knew exactly what it was like for that young, uniformed officer at the scene to investigate a multiple fatality accident, and I gave all the assistance and advice I could.

Prior to my arrival in Mareeba, police had taken possession of roughly 300-400 head of cattle from a Gulf Station and had them de-pastured on a nearby station located near Dimbulah. It was necessary for these cattle to be photographed accurately and described, and I was instructed to conduct a muster of the stock in question. As some time had passed since they were seized, a large number of these cattle had had calves, which also needed to be recorded.

Adding to the complexity of this task was the fact these particular cattle had a number of different owners, who naturally wanted their stock returned. The cattle once mustered were branded, photographed and an accurate description of them recorded. The photographs of the individual cattle were then pasted on a manila folder and later presented to court during the trial proceedings.

Since the seizure of these cattle, the female animals had produced some 75 to 90 calves. The beasts were also branded with the Police brand, indicating that it was in possession of the Police and was an exhibit. The beast was also given a numbered ear tag which was also photographed.

On the Court trial being successfully finalised, a direction was given to dispose of the cattle by the court. The cattle once again had to be mustered and drafted into their owner lots before being branded underneath the Police Brand with an inverted arrow, signifying that there was no longer any Court interest in that particular beast.

At this stage I travelled to Kingaroy, where Tammy and I were married, and travelled to the Snowy Mountains for our honeymoon. Returning to Tammy's family property at Kingaroy, I was subsequently informed that my leave had been cancelled and I was instructed to return to Mareeba to finalise the Primac investigation. On my arrival at Mareeba, I learnt that this investigation had now been politicised.

To compound the situation, I discovered paperwork involving our suspects and a consignment of cattle had been stolen. I saw that the proceeds of the sale of these cattle had been split three ways, a third to both agents and a third to a police officer.

As it was way above my pay scale to investigate fellow Police Officers, I advised Inspector Frank, who advised me to gather all the documentary evidence and travel to Cairns and place it before the Assistant Commissioner. He also told me I had done a thorough job, and that the investigation would now be investigated by an experienced commissioned officer owing to the fact that a police officer may be involved in unethical conduct. However, I was to continue with the obtaining of statements from numerous witnesses.

I was given a uniformed Senior Constable, Geoff F, who I had worked with at Kingaroy. When the majority of the witness statements had been gathered locally, it was then necessary to travel to isolated areas to obtain statements from remaining witnesses.

I was left to finalise the Primac investigation with the bulk of the witness statements having been taken, and I explained to Inspector Frank that I was close to finishing the investigation. It was a most satisfying day when the two Primac agents were arrested and charged.

Not long after finalising the Primac Brief, I was called out to a Eureka Creek property where my good friends, Darryl and Iris, formerly from Welcome Station just outside Laura, had discovered a freshly butchered steer. I attended the scene and took a series of photographs of the scene and of the vehicle tracks, which were unusual in that they were a motor car track and not a four-wheel drive, which was very unusual for this area.

Returning via Dimbulah, I stopped in at the BP agent to get fuel and while refueling, I looked across the roadway and there was a blue Mazda 808 sedan covered in dust. I asked the BP gentleman who was known to me, if he knew who in fact inhabited that house.

His reply was that they were renters from down south. I walked across the road and inspected the tyres of this vehicle and lo and behold, the tread patters matched. There was also blood on the driver's door and around the boot. Knocking on the door, I was approached by a male person with blood on his hands and arms and over his legs.

I told him I was investigating an unlawful bush kill out at Eureka Creek and that his vehicle tracks matched those which were found at the scene. After a little prompting, he confessed and showed me the remains of the cuts he had removed from the steer and also the rifle he used to dispatch the beast.

I seized all these items, including his vehicle and knives, and arrested the offender and transported him to Mareeba where he was charged. That evening, I rang my good friends who only made the comment "You do work fast"! I was pleased that I could give these lovely people closure and get compensation for them for their slaughtered steer.

Early one morning, I found the suspect Police Officer who may have been involved in receiving the funds from the sale of stolen cattle, on my own doorstep. Bullying me, he wanted to know what I had found and would I supply him with all the relevant incriminating documents. I advised him that I had forwarded them on to my Assistant Commissioner and that the matter was well and truly out of my hands.

This officer subsequently resigned from the Police Service without being charged with any criminal offence.

Unfortunately, trouble was brewing at the Gulf community of Croydon. A cattle stealing was that blatant from the larger company stations that T-Shirts were available in the town, depicting cows protecting their calves from the thieves. Something had to be done, and quickly, as the situation was totally out of control and growing worse.

The main victim being the Stanbroke companies "Strathmore Station". As the thieves were removing calves from this station's branded cows, I found it was almost impossible to prove that these calves belonged to the branded cows of Strathmore Station. (DNA was only a pipe dream at this stage.)

The thieves knew this of course, especially after the calves had been weaned from the mothers. I needed a way of proving these calves came from off of the Strathmore cows, and I came up with the idea of mothering these calves with their Strathmore Station mothers prior to their theft.

I could achieve this by documenting, that is photographing the pair and showing the brand of the cow and a photo of her calf suckling. I then injected a small steel bone pin with a jeweller inscribed code on the stainless-steel pin into a position of the calf's body known only to me, and let the calves go. Sure enough, they were soon stolen and weaned and later branded with the thieves' brand.

I could then conclusively prove that this calf had been stolen, and as there was quite a number of these "calves" located with the thief's brand, they, the thieves, could not claim it was mistakenly branded. The thieves were later sentenced to terms of imprisonment for their actions.

My old offsider, Kerry, was now relieving at Croydon and had relayed information to me relating to these thefts. Taking two motorcycles out to the area covertly, Kerry and I commenced to search and inspect cattle in the area.

Striking while the iron was hot for want of a better term, I then organized through the Strathmore manager for all the neighbouring stations to attend a joint muster involving Strathmore Station and all its smaller neighbours. A helicopter would be used, and I would attend.

All calves running with branded cattle were returned to the rightful owners and all clean skin (unbranded) cattle would be sold, with the proceeds going to pay for the helicopter and the remainder being split equally between all the participants.

Once the issues surrounding Croydon came to pass, my attention was drawn to issues at Normanton, involving the unlawful butchering of stock on Delta Downs Station. Person or persons unknown would go out of an evening and shoot a fat cow, steer or heifer and then butcher the beast up and steal the meat. After some careful sleuthing, I was able to determine exactly who the culprits were and on executing search warrants on these individuals' homes, located the weapons, knives and stolen meat.

Similar offences were a problem on the Peninsular Development Road around Mt Carbine and the property located north of this small community on a Station known as Curramough. Things were getting out of hand in this regard and the property owner, Dave Thornton, was getting most upset, as he was entitled to.

I made a decision, and we parked on a wide shoulder of the Desaileys Range and stopped vehicles as they travelled south and conducted searches of their fridges and eskies. When time would permit, we undertook this occupation and soon the word got out that there was some real chance that you would be caught if you plundered Dave's cattle.

On one such stop and search operation, my partner Sean and I had the occasion to stop a 16-tonne truck travelling south. As it was Sean's turn to make the interdiction and conduct the search, I walked to the back of the tarp covered truck and peaked inside. On seeing what was underneath this tarp, Sean called out to me to come and have a look at what he had found, holding a Tobacco tin up for me to examine. I saw that it had about enough green material inside to roll up two cigarettes. I advised him not to worry about that but to come and look under this tarp.

It was completely full, to a height of about six feet and the length and width of the truck, with cannabis plants that had been freshly harvested! I estimated a total haul of perhaps two to three tonnes of fresh cannabis.

It never ceased to amaze me what arrests could be undertaken when conducting these operations, as every time we set up in this location, we were only there two to three hours before we had to make an arrest and return to Mareeba with the prisoner/s.

This site proved to be a gold mine, as on another occasion when stopping a Land cruiser station wagon and searching this vehicle, we found brand-new camping equipment that had had little use and $150,000 in Australian bank notes. The male driver of this vehicle was unemployed and would not give any account as to how he had come by this money. Further inquiry found that the vehicle had been hired out of Cairns about one month previous, with the current mileage indicating that he had been well north of Coen.

Vegetation found in the vehicle and camping equipment indicated that he had been in the Peachy River and Iron Range areas. These areas were renowned for drug cultivation and smuggling. The suspect refused to answer any questions, apart from claiming that the money was his. The vehicle and the suspect's driver's license were in false names and it was only after taking the suspect's fingerprints that his true identity was known. Further investigations indicted that he had some very serious drug connections, and the suspect was charged with a number of criminal offences for which he was found guilty and subsequently served a lengthy period of imprisonment.

On another occasion while relieving as the Officer in Charge of the Mareeba CI.Branch, I was informed by two members of my unit of a shooting involving a husband and wife at Malanda earlier the night before.

Apparently, the husband had been shot multiple times and was in a dangerous condition in the Townsville base Hospital where he had been flown.

I instructed my staff to obtain the necessary search warrant and I then organised a raid on the occupants of the premises at five am the next morning.

Next morning with Search Warrant in hand, we raided the residence and seized the firearm used in the commission of the offence. It would seem that the wife and daughter were claiming that a dingo had momentarily appeared and that the mother/wife had fired seven to nine shots at the dingo, missing the dog, which ran off into the bush.

The problem I had with this was there were at least seven bullet holes through the driver's side door of a patrol four-wheel drive and a pool of blood immediately beyond the door. This was the same position that the husband was found and treated the night before by the Ambulance.

Taking possession of the rifle and spent cases, I had the entire scene photographed, including the eight/nine cannabis plants growing immediately beside the back steps. Taking the "wife" and the daughter back to the Atherton Police station, it was decided we would interview the teenage daughter first, thinking that she would be the first to divulge the full story.

How wrong we were, this young girl refused to deviate from the original "dingo" version of events. Bringing the mother/wife into the interview room and speaking with her, she readily confessed to shooting her husband and that during the course of shooting at the husband, he had taken shelter behind the driver's door of the four-wheel drive. I believe she was remorseful for her actions.

Early one morning, whilst still in charge of the Criminal Investigation Branch, I was summonsed to an avocado farm outside the township of Malanda. There the young son of the owners had become high on cannabis and later delusional, claiming that his parents were the devil and therefore had to be killed. This young man had held his parents hostage for most of the night, armed with a 12-gauge shotgun.

As the sun raised on a new day, the father managed to convince the son to come up to the packing shed with him, thus allowing the mother to escape to the neighbours and raise the alarm. The father meanwhile made a dash for his brand-new Nissan Patrol Utility. On gaining access to the vehicle, the father attempted to start the vehicle, whereon the deranged son placed two shoots in quick succession into his father's head through the window at point blank range. The father died instantly.

The son then went in search of his mother and eventually located her at the neighbour's residence where he laid siege, firing several more shots into this residence, before he was bravely overpowered and restrained by the neighbour until Police arrived on the scene.

Things were never dull in this unit, as the size of our operational area was huge and the issues many and varying. I received a complaint from a property owner near Cooktown that about 300 breeders had been missing over a number of years and that they, the owners, were of the belief that a neighbour was secreting them and taking the calves from them.

As these cows were all commercial stud quality cows, the calves were all quite valuable. How could an owner misplace 300 breeders, I hear someone ask; well, if you have a herd of 20,000 head, 300 is not a lot and could be believed to be missing in the vast paddocks and missed on mustering.

On this occasion, the owner had conducted a comprehensive muster utilizing helicopters and men on bikes and horseback and found he was short of approximately 300 to 400 head of cattle. He estimated that at least 300 head had been missing, after conducting his own research for some four to five years. Prior to this time period, he had been getting 95% total musters and it was only in recent years that the tally was down.

Conducting my own research prior to even going near the suspect, it was: (1) how was I to prove that he had possession of these breeders for an extended period, and (2) how could I prove his intent to deprive his neighbour of the cattle in that they had not merely wandered onto his holding.

After speaking with the complainant in this instance, it was agreed that I do some research into the issue of Botulism in cattle. I found that all cattle in the region were subject to the botulism toxin, which if not inoculated against, could cause death. I found that like a cold virus, cattle, depending on where they had been de-pastured, had their own anti-bodies to this toxin. This is similar to how humans who are exposed to a flu virus on a regular basis have more "Flu" anti-bodies in their blood than those people who aren't exposed so much.

This can be used in areas, such as people who live in crowded sections of Brisbane would have a high anti-body count than those at say Kingaroy. By taking a sample of blood from cattle de-pastured in a paddock where they have access to a water through a trough and comparing the average anti-body count of cattle that water in a lagoon, I could tell through laboratory analysis where they had been de-pastured and more importantly, how long how these cattle had been there.

Armed with information, I took blood from cattle depastured on the complainant's property and got the average anti-body count from these cattle. I then mustered the suspect's property and found the 300 or so missing breeders, with the suspect stating that such breeders had just wandered onto his property and the next time he mustered he would be handing them back — yeah right. I took blood samples from these "lost" cattle and also the suspect's breeders and got an average anti-body count from the "lost" cattle and the suspect's own breeders and found them to be identical.

The difference between the complainant's cattle anti-body count and the suspect's cattle and the lost cattle was enormous. By calculating the difference and dividing by a time period, I could accurately tell just how long these lost cattle had been depastured on the suspect's holding, and it had been years.

I could also tell what inoculant the complainant's cattle had been administered, and what the suspect's cattle and "lost" cattle had been administered, and the inoculant was different as well. Exit one cattle thief for a lengthy period of incarceration in the iron bar motel.

This technique was the first time it had been presented and accepted by a State Court and the first time it had been done in the world, let alone Australia. I had valuable assistance in perfecting this technique by a very knowledgeable Veterinary Surgeon at the James Cook University and I would not have been able to have succeeded without him and his team.

Strangely, as word got out about the technique, Law Enforcement agencies throughout Australia became interested, and even the United States of America's Department of Agriculture and the Indonesian Ministry for Agriculture all were interested to know the technique.

Part of my duties also involved surveillance of the coastline when time permitted. I knew that the trawlers operating on the east coast congregated around Bathurst Bay, especially in the harsher weather, as the anchorage was protected from the outside heavy conditions.

During one such mission, I also knew that my good friend, Tony M, was up at the head of the bay doing helicopter fishing. He had offered to take me between the headland east and then return from Cape Melville. Basically, this would mean I could traverse this entire area in one afternoon and just see who was about, an ideal opportunity for surveillance and Intelligence gathering.

Taking off, we flew along the coastline and saw the usual number of trawlers sheltering from the outside weather. Landing on the beach at Cape Melville, we found and interviewed a number of land-based interstate fishermen and searched their fridges and eskies. On our return journey, we flew further inland when we spotted a camouflaged camp.

Now, camouflaged camps mean only one thing, in that bad guys are usually growing illicit substances or bad guys are up to no good.

Returning to our destination at the head of Bathurst Bay, and together with one of my permanent men, Gil, we travelled overland in our Toyota for the rest of the day and stopped some distance away from this camp. On resuming our compass bearing next morning, we found a well-used track heading in the general direction of the camouflaged camp. Some hours later on, walking into this well-established camp, we found it was the camp of Fox Tail Palm seed smugglers.

On searching the camp thoroughly, we found the identities of the persons responsible. One of these persons was an assistant to a high-ranking Political figure, and the other was his brother.

They must had taken off when they heard the chopper and headed south, leaving behind approximately one and a quarter tonne of seeds, all stashed in corn bags and similar. Loading our Toyota Troop carrier to the roof from the seats back, we managed to cart the majority of the harvest away from the scene. The rest we burnt so as to deprive these villains of their bounty. Attempting to advise VKR Cairns of our find, we found our long range Codan SSB radio unserviceable. Here we were, in one of the most isolated places in the state, without communications.

We drove back towards Cooktown, camping overnight and arriving the next evening. On unloading these bags into one of the cells at Cooktown, it revealed just how much we had seized. Our haul filled the single cell almost to the roof!

When you stop to think that each seed back then was worth $50-$80, that was a hell of a lot of money we had taken from the smugglers' pockets.

Putting the evidence together and compiling a comprehensive report, I forwarded this information down to Brisbane to have the two men of the National Parks Squad interview the two main and named villains. I heard nothing further and knew that no charges had been brought against these two individuals.

A similar tale occurred, this time with a National Parks Ranger and the same two villains, with the result that the Parks Ranger was dismissed after he refused to back down. I was sort of glad that I didn't follow up my initial report as the same fate may have befallen me.

The workload was steadily getting greater, as with the pressure from above now that Inspector Frank Wagner had been promoted and transferred and another first time Inspector posted in his place.

History has shown that I was not compatible with the incoming Inspector in charge.

I demanded high standards from my men, and some had complained that I was pushing them too hard and at least two departed because of long periods of time away from home and the high standards which were expected of them.

Our arrest rate for criminal drug offences was extremely high as was our convictions for criminal stock offences, and I wanted this to stay this way. To compound this, I was also required to assist the CI.Branch whenever called upon and there were times I was conflicted between my own work and theirs. One such immediate call for assistance involved a mechanic who had gone to a remote residence on a mechanical call out and had not returned home.

The wife of this mechanic was not alarmed, as it was well known he enjoyed an ale or two. She contacted her neighbour to go and fetch him and the neighbour went to the address and he failed to return. It was well known that he enjoyed a drink or three also. The wife then sent her son to tell the two scallywags to come home at once, knowing her teenage son didn't drink. You guessed it — he to failed to return back to mum. Mum then called the CI.Branch. Venturing out to the address the situation at four am one morning, we stopped to regroup and check our weapons prior to entering the property.

Daylight was now starting to show, and on walking into the property we saw that it had been sprinkled with tyre deflation and horse crippling devices throughout its length. On walking in unannounced, I stopped a man squatting down in the front wheel well of an elderly Toyota Station Wagon, which had been placed on blocks and its wheel removed. I told him to stop where he was and not to move, but he kept inching his hand towards the front driver's chassis rail.

There were two infant children locked within the vehicle that were now crying and creating a distraction, when I observed this male quickly move his hand towards the chassis rail, saying he was getting his smokes. I placed my foot on his arm, pinning it to the mudguard of the vehicle. Looking in the direction of his arm, I saw not a packet of smokes but a cut down 12-gauge double barrel shotgun nestling on the chassis rail. Pushing him backwards, he was soon restrained by handcuffs.

The resultant noise had roused the "prisoners" who were located in a large tandem trailer just behind the Toyota station wagon. This trailer was covered on a large thick black plastic sheet over which was placed reo mesh and pinned down by about 20 besser blocks.

The only way into and out of this trailer without removing the "top" was through the locked tail gate. My attention was then drawn to one of my men calling out, "Sergeant, Sergeant, one has run away!" On this officer shouting out, I heard a number of rapid gunshots and screaming.

I saw the offender take careful aim again at my colleague and before he could fire, I yelled out to the offender to put it down, whereon he turned his weapon on me and started firing. A small iron bark tree off to my left side exploded to the impact of the projectile. The offender was using solid one oz lead shot and not the ball shot normally used in shotguns. Had he used a normal number four shot or SG rounds, I would not be here telling you this story.

He had stopped firing at my colleague and had now turned his weapon onto me. The ground in front of me exploded with his second shot and I dived behind a tree, took careful aim with my weapon and fired two carefully placed shots at the offended, both of which missed.

The offender then threw away his weapon and lay prostrate on the ground in the long grass. I retrieved his weapon and cleared it, after restraining the offender in handcuffs.

On thoroughly searching this offender, we found in excess of $50,000 taped to his legs underneath his jeans, all in large denomination bank notes. He had a number of festering injection marks up his arms. Both offenders were detained, and the property searched.

Our initial search located further sums of money and a large number of motorcycles and chainsaws and other motorised equipment, as well as more evidence of money.

I have had previous experience of drug smugglers and traffickers having the same type of cash for their only means of living, as they were often too scared to bank the large sums available to them for fear of being singled out and investigated.

The offenders were duly arrested and charged with quite a number of serious offences and both were later sentenced to lengthy periods of imprisonment.

On a personal note, it was around this time that I began to become quite short tempered and was experiencing heart palpitations. I kept this issue to myself, however, I could not keep my temper under control.

I found that when I was at home sitting quietly, I thought my heart was racing and about to pounce through my chest. I would start sweating even though I was in the air conditioning. Clearly something was wrong with me. Visiting my private doctor and swearing him to secrecy, I underwent ECG and heart scanning but they could find nothing out of the ordinary apart from high blood pressure, which I was advised was normal for the position I held within the department. Over time these symptoms did not disappear, and a sense of foreboding pervaded in my general living standard.

These conditions manifested themselves early one evening and I thought I was about to have a heart attack, so I had my dear wife take me to the ambulance, who referred me straight to Casualty of the Mareeba Hospital.

There I undertook a vast amount of tests, before the doctor approached me and advised that I was perfectly healthy apart from high blood pressure, but it was his opinion that I had hit a stress wall and my body was telling me that I had had enough. He advised me to take immediate leave over an extended period and to seek further professional advice.

I thought I could handle my health problems and so I attempted to push through, which only made the condition worse. I dare not tell my superiors, fearing that it would stifle my chances of promotion and hence my career. I had seen others fall into this trap and lose their careers and I thought I would ignore the symptoms in the hope that they went away. Secretly I was seeing my private doctor, who had referred me to a Physiatrist in Townville.

I was given drugs to help my blood pressure and I just boxed on. Things came to a head after I had received information relating to two suspicious males driving about the Windsor Tableland area in a four-wheel drive.

Now, Windsor Tableland at that stage was closed off, and a World Heritage listed area and very few people were allowed access to it. Departing Mareeba, I followed the vehicle tracks for two days, but I seemed to be not getting any closer to the offenders.

As luck would have it, Dave Thornton from Curramore Station, a neighbouring property, was utilizing a helicopter for his mustering and I managed to borrow the machine for an hour or so. Using this machine, I soon caught up to our two offenders in their Hi Lux utility. They had managed to travel into quite a remote part of the World Heritage Listed site.

Using the helicopter, I was able to direct my men into an intercept of the men and their vehicle. Liaising with the intercept crew, I found that one of the offenders was wanted in South Africa for murder, while the other offender was wanted in the same country for Military Desertion. A search of the vehicle located a number of firearms, personal equipment and camping equipment. No drug-related property was located.

On the return of the offender's vehicle, back at the Mareeba Station, I went through the vehicle again and discovered approx. 40,000 cannabis seeds that had been overlooked in the initial search.

Around this time, I received a complaint from some overseas business men who were the owners of two separate properties. Neither owner was connected nor was the properties connected. The connection in each instance was the property manager; he was the overall manager of each property.

It seemed that he was helping himself to the imported stud cattle from one property and the imported horses from the second such property. Each complaint came in separately with neither property owner knowing that the other had made a complaint. Inquiries established that the suspect lived a lavish lifestyle in the Mareeba area in a luxurious home and that he had a modest background.

A search of his bank records revealed that over the last couple of years, his wealth had increased enormously and hence the lavish house and land. He also had a large collection of rare exotic Australian parrots which he did not seem to have any permit for. Further inquiries were made, and it was revealed that this suspect had a brother who had convictions for rare and exotic bird smuggling. Things were starting to come together and a pattern was emerging.

There was one hitch apparently, not that this issue bothered me at all, because it didn't. The issue being that this person was also a serving politician.

During this period, I received word that my father was extremely ill with an inoperable brain tumor. I returned to mum and dads' home on the

Sunshine Coast, where he was admitted to the Buderim Private Hospital where he died some days later.

He was 77 year of age on his passing. It was a most sad period, but I was glad that he had not lingered incapacitated for to too long a period, as he would have not liked that at all, being quite an active man almost up until his death. My father was not an overly religious man, although he did believe in God, but I was taken aback late one afternoon when we were sitting together out the front of their house having a cuppa. He knew he was dying and he wanted to know if God would accept him in heaven.

I told him, course he would, why on earth wouldn't he? My father then for the first and only time related how he had machine gunned numerous Japanese soldiers whilst he was fighting during World War Two.

He believed that God may not accept him for that reason. I assured him that he was a good honest man and that he would make heaven a better place when he arrived. I hope this settled his troubled mind.

After my dad's funeral, I drove straight back to Mareeba and was again investigating my Station Manager. Not long into the investigation, I received a telephone call from a man who told me that I should proceed most carefully, as the suspect had been informed by someone in Mareeba that I was investigating him and that I should proceed with caution and watch my back.

He went on to say that members of the hierarchy were aware that I was conducting this investigation, and they were not happy that I or anybody else for that matter was undertaking it at all.

Not long after this, I was summonsed to my then Inspectors office and told to hand over everything that I had done and was proposing to do in relation to this investigation and that the investigation would now be taken out of my hands completely. To add further insult, the investigation into the Fox Tail Palm seed smugglers was to be dropped as others would be undertaking this investigation also.

I was fine with this development as long as something further was done and the suspects brought to justice. To this day the investigation was never investigated further and the offenders never brought to justice.

My superior at the time went onto bigger and better things and retired with a very senior rank within the Queensland Police Service.

My health deteriorated and I was discharged from the police service in the month of May, 1994, with my papers marked — 'Medical Retirement.'

The Police service had been my life for over 20 years; I had lived and breathed it for over 20 years. I was leaving a job I loved, where I was able to help people in need, and I loved the thrill of the investigation bringing villains to justice and allowing the Courts to do their job. As we left Mareeba for the last time, we said goodbye to some very close and wonderful friends and travelled back to my wife's parents' property at Kingaroy.

I was diagnosed with acute terminal kidney failure which required me to undertake dialysis every second day. To complicate this issue even further, I had a very real fear of needles! It was the Psychologist Jane, at the Bourke Street, Annerley Home Training unit, that finally diagnosed what my issues were and set not only me, but my immediate family, on the very slow road to recovery. I have been under treatment for P.T.S.D now for the many years; consulting a Psychiatrist every two weeks in Brisbane and a Psychologist every month since that time.

I have slowly but surely managed to gain a slight foot hold on these issues. My wife and I have borne the full burden of the medical expenses since 2015. To say such costs are crippling is an understatement but together as a family I am determined to succeed in a complete recovery.

After retiring from the Police Force, I purchased a property beneath the shadow of the Bunya Mountains, where my wife and I grew wheat, corn and sorghum and fattened steers and bred and broke in and educated horses. My wife and I made a living off farming, contract fencing and yard building, as well as earthmoving.

Life goes on!

About The Author

Laurie Pointing is a retired senior Queensland police officer with a country background. He served in many locations throughout the State of Queensland, both as a uniformed officer, member of the criminal investigation branch, stock investigation squad, police prosecutor and administrator.

In retirement, Laurie spends time travelling through the outback, reading and writing bush poetry. He is a lover of county music and the sport of cricket. He is a proud Queenslander. This is his sixth book and the fourth in the series of — *Keeping the Peace. Volume I* in 2013, *Volume II* in 2014 and *Volume III* in 2019.

For the past 12 years, Laurie has been the President of the Gympie Branch of the Queensland Retired Police Association, and in the Queen's Birthday Honours List, 2017, was awarded the A.M. for services to the Queensland Police Service and the community in general.